STAY LONGER

LISTEN DEEPER

QUALITY IN ACTION LEADERSHIP

"For persons itching to change the world
without knowing how it can be done"

Live your best life

Be a great soul

Make a great impact

Learn to receive

ISBN#: 978-1-387-82090-0

Also by John Davidson

Finding Financial Freedom: The Day I Built my Barbecue

Stand in the Presence of All you Are

Finding Creative Value: The Unstoppable U

Choice Points

Whole Life Planning Workbook

The Catalyst

This Splendid Place

CONTENTS

"For my wife Claudia, the compassionate one that helps others appear - with legitimacy and acceptance - in their basic goodness as loving beings. Thank you, Papa Fernando and Mama Virginia, for bringing this gifted soul friend, teacher, and partner, my Anam Cara into the world. And for my three life teachers, my children Hannah, Michel, and Camila. You show me every day that life is in the business of creating life, and that miracles are an every day experience to help someone nearby."

PREFACE

The man who learns the art of sharing is the richest man in the world. Even if empty is his wallet, his inner being has a quality of richness that even emperors may feel jealous. This open-hearted consideration for all living creatures is the touchstone of being "inter-wise" in today's world.

A poor man, very poor, a woodcutter, lived in the forest in a small hut. The hut was so small that he and his wife could only sleep …only that much space was in the hut. In the middle of one dark night, it was raining hard, and somebody knocked on the door. The wife was sleeping close to the door. The husband said to the wife, "Open the door. The rain is too much, and the man must have lost his way. It is a dark night and the forest is dangerous and full of wild animals. Open the door immediately!" She said, "But there is no space." The man laughed and said, "This is not a palace of a king, where you will always find a shortage of space. It is a poor man's hut. Two can sleep well; three can sit. We will create space. Just open the door."

And the door was opened. The man came in, and he was very grateful, and they all sat and started talking and gossiping and telling stories to each other. The night had to be passed somehow because they could not sleep; there was no space. And just then, another knock.

The man, the new guest, was now sitting by the side of the door. The owner of the hut said, "Friend, open the door. Somebody else is lost."

And the man said, "You seem to be a very strange fellow. There is no space." He said, "This was my wife's argument too. If I had listened to her argument, you would have still been in the forest, to be eaten by the wild animals. And you seem to be a strange man that you cannot understand that we are sitting just because of you. We are tired after a long day. I am a woodcutter — the whole day I cut the wood and then sell it in the market and then we can hardly get food once a day. Open the door. It is not your hut. If three persons can sit comfortably, four persons can sit a little closer, with a little less comfort. But we will create the space."

He had to open the door, although reluctantly. And a man entered, and he was very grateful. Now they were sitting very close; there was not even a single inch of space left. And then suddenly, a strange knock, which did not seem to be a man's! There was silence from all three; the wife and the two guests were afraid that he would say open the door. And he said it. "Open the door. I know who is knocking. It is my donkey. In this wide world, he is my only friend. I carry my wood on that donkey. He remains outside, but it is raining too much. Open the door." And now it was the fourth guest to be allowed in, and everybody resisted, and they said, "This is too much. Where is the donkey going to stand?"

This man said, "You don't understand. It is a poor man's hut; it is always spacious. Right now, we are sitting; when the donkey comes in we will all be standing, so we will keep the donkey in the middle. This way he feels warm and cozy and loved."

7

They said, "It was better to get lost in the jungle, rather than caught in your hut." But nothing could be done. When the owner said to open the door, the door suddenly was opened. And the donkey came in. The water was dripping from all over his body. The owner took him into the middle and told all the others to stand around. He said, "You don't understand. My donkey is of a very philosophical mind. You can say anything, yet he is never disturbed. He always listens silently, like the sky, everything else is just the weather."

Written by Osho – "Bodhidharma : The Greatest Zen Master"

Einstein said:

"The most important question a person can ask is, "Is the Universe a friendly place?"

There is the story of a king who once built a special palace. He made it so impregnable that no enemy could enter it. We also in life make just such castles and take all precautions to keep the enemy away and be safe. What does man do all his life, after all? Why does he amass wealth? Why does he yearn for position and fame? So that he may feel safe and secure and life holds no terror for him. But the fun of the whole thing, and the secret is that the more measures he takes to safeguard himself, his fear increases in the same proportion. The king had also conquered all there was to conquer. Know the only fear was to guard himself against the enemy; for the enemy conquered is still the enemy.

He who tries to conquer the other makes enemies of all. Only he who is ready to accept defeat from another man alone be a friend in this world. The king wished to conquer the whole world so the whole world was his enemy, and his fear had increased a thousand-fold. When fear increased, it became necessary to make provisions for safety. He built a big palace with only one door. There were no other doors and no windows; not even a hole for the enemy to work through. Only one door — guarded by thousands of soldiers with naked swords.

The neighboring king came to see this much-talked-of palace. He was impressed and determined to make a similar palace for his safety. While taking leave, he praised the king for his foresight and wisdom and reiterated his desire to follow his example. An old beggar sitting by the roadside heard this talk. He laughed aloud. The owner of the palace chided him by saying: "What makes you laugh, fool?" "Since you ask, Sire, I shall take the opportunity of telling you," said the beggar. "There is only one flaw in this marvelous structure. It is impregnable except for the door. The enemy can come through the door. If you step in and have the door covered with brick and mortar, it will be completely secure. Then no enemy can ever enter it."

"If I do as you say, you fool, this palace will become my grave," said the king. "It already is," said the fakir, "except for the door. Through this door, the enemy can come, and if not the enemy, death is bound to come." "But I will be dead before that!" raved the king. "Then understand this well." Said the fakir. "As many doors as you had in your palace, so much of existence was with you. When you decrease the doors, then life is diminished within you. Now one door is left — one lone opening to life; close it and shut out life forever. Therefore, I say, there is only one flaw." And he broke into peals of laughter again. "I too had castles, your majesty, "the fakir continued. "Then I felt that they were no more than prison-houses. So, I began to widen the doors and separate the walls. But I found that no matter how much I widened the doors the walls remained, so I got out of the walls and came out in the open. Now I stay beneath the open skies and am alive in the perfect sense of the word."

But have we not all built as many walls around us as we possibly could? The walls made of brick and mortar are not that dangerous, for they can be seen. There are other walls — subtle, imperceptible walls... These are the hard screens — glass screens of concepts, of doctrines, of scriptures. Absolutely invisible!

These walls we have built around our souls for complete security. The thicker the walls, the farther it keeps us away from the open skies of Truth. Then the soul becomes restless and struggles, and the more agitated the soul is, the more we strive to strengthen the walls. Then a fear grips us — perhaps this struggle, this restlessness, is due to the walls? The answer is "Yes." If the soul is confined, it cannot attain bliss. There is no sorrow except in captivity.

Written by Osho – "The Beginning of the Beginning"

Greetings! Nice to meet you, I'm John Davidson, the person who wrote this book and living what is in these pages. After 26,000 coaching sessions one on one with business leaders, I invite you on a learning journey of self-knowledge and understanding life and business with a new lens.

Slow is the new fast. I learned that if you stay longer, and listen deeper, understanding increases, and so too does something new surface within you—INVOLVEMENT AND ENGAGEMENT. This goes for anything---stay long and listen to your kids, your spouse, your clients, yourself, life, the community---you can tap into your deeper wisdom and follow where goodness is ready to expand. Awareness is the only way to slow time down to comprehend what is really going on from this place. And yet, the currents are strong, life can be a level five rapid pace, while becoming aware is a choice. When I started my executive career thirty years ago, I came from a scarcity-based mindset that speed was in, quality time was out, time is the enemy, not the advocate. Basically, "access equals success." I was completely going in the wrong direction because I was so busy doing things—governed by the to-do list and life that I was a mouse in a maze, unable to do what could make me a lot less busy. I was hungering to be involved in life and enjoy life all at once while I was on the way to where I wanted to be. I discovered a quality of being in the world called "inTen" where the level of involvement and engagement bring pleasure and joy into the creative process of living and creating. This book was made to bring you, the leader into contact with InTen.

As I neared my 50th year, I challenged myself to live my best life, be a great soul, learn to receive, and make a big difference, and then offered myself a space outside a worldview. All my life, I carried a belief that if the universe is unfriendly, I must operate in defense of it, so I cut myself off from these four commitments. With a shift of mind

11

and heart, a deeper listening emerged that made what I cut myself from return little by little, to construct a universe that is made of love at the essence of it, and as I'm a loving being so too is the universe. This love is like weather, a region from which all I could be was love. I started on a path in life that restored my armored heart, and everything shifted. My deepest wish is to set a process in motion, light the match for you the reader to access the same or reinforce what has already begun for you in this direction toward InTen.

When leaders integrate enjoyment and involvement with life and those around them, they mine each experience as a powerful seed to their life building process. We call the infusion of these two qualities: inTen™. Look at the illustration above, notice the roots and branches are symbolic to the roots of soulful self-expression, and the flourishing of a healthy tree that is growing and evolving. The more you become yourself, the greater market value you open up.

With inTen™, the character of business leaders improves with well-balanced intelligence, and so too does everyone around them gain from their quality in action and comprehension, because it is business leaders who change organizations and people, and in turn they change societies who makeup entire populations.

I wrote this book to convey the message that as helpers, *you* are the medicine people; the carriers of big blessings for others, to bring them back into their true inheritance and wholeness. To see that in the spirit of just showing up is an amazing healing ability. To sense what others are feeling is an active ingredient in their emotional wellness, and to actively presence by listening widely and generously to what is wanting to emerge, is the essential quality to helping bring others back into the best of themselves. This way of being in the world is what I now call "inter-wise."

THE GREAT SHIFT

A thing is a thing because of another thing. A person is a person because of another person. A place is a place because of another place. Nothing exists by itself; we are all made by *relationships*. It is the primary organizing force of the universe. A place, a beach, a forest, a city made by the state of interdependence in which it exists. This is life in motion. An island is shaped by the waves, the weather and the inhabitants. The relationship between them is influencing each instant in a dance of constant change.

As persons, we come into being by relating with others, originating from the pattern of interactions we enact we find our true properties. To say I love you is to have them bring you into the love that you are.

Any attempt at one's niche is made by the other. The audience makes the singer, the employees make the boss, the children make the parents, the song makes the band, and the kitchen makes the chef, and so on. We are each brought into our manner of operation and daily living by interaction with life because we operate within a living system of language. And yet we strive for independence, individuality, competitiveness, and mastery in a world that by nature is interconnected. We attempt to escape the way our true properties appear when governed by fear, shame, and judgment. Perhaps this makes us deaf, dumb, and blind in ways that lower our capacity for comprehending ourselves, others, and the world.

We find ourselves balancing our creative acts (intentions), driving our lives from our sense of power over our domains, while we take life in with natural order like a wildcard that is unpredictable. We attempt to create paths while we walk to know the path. This is the paradox. Despite setting our aims, nothing desired is to go as expected. We learn by doing, seeing, as we set our compass into the mystery plan. When we plan, God laughs, and, when we don't plan, then God cries. We are doomed to make choices, as both chess-piece and chess-master of our lives.

So, I ask you this question: *If you couldn't guarantee that creating whatever matters to you would bear fruit, why would you do it?* What's the point? Here's the point: you would be dead if you didn't, spiritually dead. You are being evolved, moved, changed, by the anatomy of a living system, an emerging society in which change remains in motion, and something stands in need of you.

In our society, we have a supernormal preoccupation with our identities. All too often we subscribe to the "me me me" orientation, so immersed that we are trapped individually, collectively, and universally from living well. This book is written to help you understand why getting you happy matters, in service to others, and what to do about it as a leader. It is not intended to fix something wrong with you.

Today, your success in business isn't based on what you sell; it's based on *how* you sell. More specific, it's based on the inner place from which you sell. This is rapidly becoming the new rule of selling. Character matters if you're going to reach a lot of people and help them, because without trust, nothing happens.

You enter the world daily with the opportunity to shift this orientation. You can attend and act from the place of "What am I doing?" or you can act from a place of "What are you doing?"

When you reassign your focus to the latter question, you place your attention on the "other" with an understanding that is more comprehensive than mere interpretations based on what you know already. Whatever that "other" is does not require you to signal how important you are, how special you are, how much better you are, how good you look, what you are getting attention for - all that is manipulation. Instead, life gets more interesting when you stop putting effort into being interesting and get *interested*. And you realize that the less you make it about you, the more you learn to be *you*. You realize how great it is with all your imperfections in a world with the same. Then life gets more interesting. It's about *helping others appear*. Success yields significance, ambitions turn to finding meaning. You confront your perceived immortality and give up power to the mystery every moment beholds like a pregnant seed. Mastery, competitiveness and individuation become love, service, and gratitude, as you play the second half of life after money.

When you're <u>not</u> preoccupied with *who you are or aren't, what you need to be or not be*, you're showing up to life on its terms, not yours. This is the great shift, and this is your first glimpse of *you*. For many of us, it is a return to the person we used to be. You come to terms with nothing you think about you is fixed. Everything is in constant flux, including you. And to show up to life on its terms is to unfix what you believe is certain and listen to what else is outside what you know. You pay attention like this to bring you back to yourself.

THE ESSENCE OF SELLING

Selling is a taboo subject. Most people I coach don't like to "sell" because it feels manipulative, and when it's not serving others, it is this way. However, the essence of selling is to stimulate the potential of another human being by consensual engagement. *Selling is help that is helpful.* This means helping people and organizations choose what is wanted, needed, and helpful. Confronting their freedom to choose is to engage them by consent with respect. A spouse invites their significant other to meet her emotional needs by meeting theirs. A mother creates an unforced space for her children to develop their authentic self. A leader engages others by seeing the nobility of a mission and cause. A teacher provides the context for a learning journey of discovery and intrigue. A coach builds the visibility to generate self-knowledge and apply it to performance situations when the player engages. The nature of the interactions is intended to be consensual in that they encourage authentic choice, not an obligation. Helping depends on the consensual engagement of one who has full freedom and control of personal motivation to make choices, based on what is important to them.

One quiet afternoon, my coaching client Gary and I had a chance to talk about the nature of the creative impetus in the sales domain and what's possible in the space of being together.

The focus remains directed into the experience of organic conversations where finding potential value creation for the joy of it shapes a dynamic urge to jump in. You setup a support structure around you to nourish the creative flow in all aspects of your life-building process. The information that is discovered, absorbed and transmuted into you during the creative process of value creation for another human being (serving), is revealed directly into the conversation. The best instrument to access this is cultivating a deeper, peripheral listening that is generative and ignites responsibility after new emergent, not yet embodied information is obtained. Listening from wisdom is like a key to a door to latent possibilities awaiting to come into visibility.

The impetus to create is internally motivated, so no, the creative impulse is not from a need to attain a goal or manipulate a decision. This outlaws trust when it's a preemptive agenda or pre-existing control lever. Instead it's about the atmosphere of engagement, and the depth of the conversation and commitment to the truth that brings something new into the space. This atmosphere like a flower in a garden is cultivated such that great ideas and possibilities come to the surface. One can create the spaces out of an internal motivation, desire, and the sensation one experiences in the circular currents that volley between buyer and seller. It is conversational, not a program with fixed ends or formal structures. You begin to feel a circle of connection made complete when a question or reflection is voiced, and then bounces back from the other such that meaning is made with trust, respect, and confidence.

The devotion to the art of living in the deep end of conversations and translating this as I do is what can be considered the genesis of a great path. The experience of naked conversations deliver an intimacy, which is the medicine, pure and simple. The conversation itself is more valuable than what you sell. The desire to experience "the heroic dose" is reached by engaging directly into the conversation for extended periods of creative time, day into night reflection afterwards, to marinate and see directionality in what is speaking itself from the space. This is the essence of listening deeper. Gary and I defined four qualities that bring forth "inter-wise selling."

Inter-wise is "wisdom-based help," which isn't fixing a world because we see it broken, or rescuing the world because it's weak, it is to *serve others with our souls*, like an eye looking through our eye. We hold life as a whole. It is the nature of help that is in fact helpful. This capacity for serving is latent, it hides within us, and emerges out of the horizon needing us to come together as citizens of a deeper conviction that we must find a way to work together. And it starts with love as the foundation. "Inter" from the Old Latin means "reciprocal", "among" or "carried on between" or "shared by two or more." Social intimacy is about connecting from a deeper place within us, one in which we cultivate a new awareness that is not concerned about projecting who we are on the world, instead, an atmosphere of trust is drawn from a collective connection. New possibilities then arise from the larger scale of the whole, where intention and action align with our authentic sense of self and basic goodness to serve others. Respecting, connecting, and listening embolden the capacity of giving helpful help to others and the community.

First, Gary conveyed the point that selling actually means <u>*helping*</u>*, which is shaped by a confluence of being, creating, relating, and earning.* This four-fold way mirrors the metaphor of planting vigorous seeds of renewal in the soil; a life forming place from which your way of being and the setting of new intentions arise from your true nature. Form (creation) follows consciousness (soil, inner place from that you operate; source). The painting depends on the moment the painter stands before beginning to paint, coming from an inner love for the painting to come into existence. He creates from the heart, head, and hand as if to bring forth his full intelligence and perception. The fusion of this brings forth the full dimensionality of his capacity to see, sense, and intuit as a fully human being to begin the creative process. No better process fuses this balanced intelligence than the creative.

Second, when you approach *helping* with the full dimensionality of the human being you are, head-heart-hand, you bring forth a higher level of comprehension. Many leaders have only a partial view of

19

themselves, and for this reason, they're likely to act in ways that cause greater suffering for others, not enrichment. They block their capacity to tap into the balance of intelligence within them. Hence their personal wisdom is cut off from expressing itself, as well as their compassion and kindness.

Third, helpful help is grounded in your deepest source of humanity, grounded in love. How you increase the quality of basic goodness (being) in the domain of selling starts with enriching and influencing others in ways that bypass your need to control them. When you focus on others' best interests, you have bypassed manipulation and gone to respect. You cut the cord on two conversations inside you: shame and fear. Shame is your story about your level of adequacy and worth, and fear is a concept predicting something dangerous will happen. Both are potent in contaminating your capacity for creating--- creating what you want, and great value for others, seeing what is going on, taking informed action—all that. Fear and shame are the outlaws of creating. These motivations lead to help that isn't helpful. When an unwanted belief of yourself is that you're not adequate or fear others isolating you, altruism goes off the deep-end, and helpful help turns to harming yourself. We must find the edge between self-sacrifices and serve others to bring forth the highest future possibility for value creation.

Fourth, finding this edge begins with awakening each moment with the quality of awareness to pinpoint the place within you (your interior condition) from which your helping is arising: From manipulation (for me), From Care (for other), or from Wisdom (from emergence). We occupy various places from which our listening, attending, and relating animates our ways of being in the moment.

I'm fascinated with the why, how, and when people selling operates more beautifully despite invitations to the contrary, such as greed, self-interest, and manipulation. These dark operatives, when rooting the seller's effort, contaminate hope and deactivate buyer trust. These emanate from fear, cynicism, and judgment, cutting off possibilities, opportunities, and connections. I've witnessed in thousands of individuals how these destructive traits can subside, vaporize, and fall away as the seller connects with a larger heart, mind, and will from which he helps others. This shift toward purification emerging from good will and character imbues a greater concern for others. My conviction to spotlight this goodwill inspired me to write this book after witnessing it. This gave me hope that selling can be derived from our way of being and most genuine intent for the welfare of others.

Quality of being in action is the secret ingredient that is missing; it is hindered by commoditizing professional industries fighting for survival from the kiss of death of automation and repetition. If we recover this death spiral to becoming machines, we must help sellers restore their humanity in helping and learn to access a level of operating that is latent and waiting to animate itself in their capacity for creativity by listening in more dynamic ways. Gary calls the commitment to this cause *Quality in Action Leadership*. It is the organic aspect of relatedness and helping from which value creation emerges. As we operate from our optimal ways of being, we shift our relationship with the world. We transform information to create value as we become more of ourselves. We experience time as dimensional, not linear, with helping in the truest sense becoming the gateway for accessing one's highest future possibilities, for self, other, and community. And this capacity, if balanced and restored in the character of the helper to give real help, brings self "integral" or "whole."

Candor, disclosure, and vulnerability become the nutrients in the soil that grow a different quality of conversation for inter-wise to emerge. The reflective human conversation rises where honest, unarmored conversation can give rise to helpful help. The constituents mutually understand issues and grow mutual support. What motivates this is people see they are players in a larger system and become aware of seeing the manifestation of it in themselves.

Gary originally suggested I call this book "helpwise." I wanted to write about the helpful help that comes from wisdom, respect, and love, not power, domination, and control (manipulation). I wanted to go beneath the "helping" to what delivers it: staying longer and listening deeper. Real service is help that is helpful, and when wisdom is the source, *the service is expressed from the soul.*

To love another human being needs no theory. It is simply the implicit soul service dormant in each of us ready to amplify and awaken in a capitalism milieu coming into collective consciousness. A hidden whole can be accessed as a new and greater source of animation in each of us as we stay longer, and listen deeper.

FROM EGO TO ECO

Spiritual starvation is poverty, not materially, but rather poor *internally*, unhappy with a bankrupt heart. Time-money-relationship-values tell the tale. Here is the conundrum:

We're too busy being busy to do what could make us a lot less busy, because of spending money and time we don't have on things we don't need, trying to impress people we don't like, trying to be a somebody, instead of creating what matters most to us.

Modern life is burglarizing our natural way of being in tune with life in a creative flow, and the implications are deadening to our happiness. Unhappy on the inside, the discontentment breeds greed, power, and encourages us to look for Shangri la in all the wrong places except within us. Money, fame, power, we gain it, and what remains, we want more. It's the game of identity (ideals; shoulds) vs. values. And our ambitions to be special ambushes our capacity-building to create a fulfilling life and live near life in all its ups and downs. Our imperfections scare us to death.

And our shallow identity-based drives (worth, power, status) become like a runaway train on a continuous search for individuality, mastery, and competition, leading to isolation and disconnection. Here is why our insatiable consumerism masks our longing for connection and love.

In the arts, singers, and songwriters speak of immersive experiences when writing and singing so deeply, that they forget who was bringing it to happen. They love what they do and do what they love, as you hear them say, "It felt like I was having an out of body experience." When they recognize this, they often express a sense of feeling home in themselves. Their moments of being aware of what they were aware of brought them closer to life, and as such, they heard their true voice. In such a way, they were brought back into contact with "What is going on here?" implying something other than "me." They said they felt changed by what was happening. Something directly inbound was entering while something outbound emerged, like taking off a tight shoe.

Becoming aware is learning *how* to learn by seeing your own habituated biases. When you attend from "me", you aren't in touch with what is going on. Instead, you are only aware of yourself. This is because you have a past history, accumulation, memory, which through your lifetime embed biases, habituated thinking, concepts, world-views, fears, beliefs, notions, from which you react, relate, and respond to life. You organize yourself by habits. And when these mental models continue to be in use to make sense of things, add meaning to things, interpret what things mean, you leap in with these thoughts still unchecked. You use concepts to see instead of actually seeing new things concept-free. When you see outside your automatic mind stuff, your models take a backseat. You learn to see.

Seeing with fresh eyes requires catching old assumptions that have embedded within our sense-making. Curiosity rises to the surface. You *see how you see* and separate the terms with life from your old ones. New findings turn in motion like a spinning wheel through time. Nothing stays the same. Everything must change.

24

Emergence suggests that from nowhere something rises like a speck, watered to a seed stage and then to full branches to a tree and living forest within a network of life. What is unfolding is life itself in the business of creating life, from what is unexpected, invisible, not yet embodied in a continuous flow of life contacting us. We learn from the future as it emerges in the now. We come at helping from a variety of places, suggesting that our ego-based awareness is not suitable to the helping needed on behalf of sellers to survive and thrive today.

The universe is open and not mechanical. From nothing, something originates in a creative process, and your natural way of being is love. *Loving, helping, and selling are the same.* All three are imbued from your "true nature" from which you unfold as life emerges. It is a continuous unfoldment of creating a continuous flow of steady streaming. Everything is waiting for you, yes, anything, because you do not know how the story ends at any point in your life. You have no key to the door of the secrets that are ahead of you. Every decision is a living guess.

What could happen when selling does not come from a small sense of self, instead of from a loving being? Yes, you heard that----nowhere isn't empty, it is the place from which something comes! Anything which emanates from within is your deepest source connecting to your highest future possibilities. This wiser place suggests a larger sense of self. Its ethos seeks care for all things, wisdom, and relaxed attentiveness to whatever arises. And If you sell from nowhere, then what arises when helping others is a source of genuine goodness, service, and orientation to the "other," by accessing your highest quality of expression at that moment. Selling is the process of accessing your highest quality of expression to give helpful help.

Your greatest sources of expression arise from giving value to others just for the joy of it. The spiritual pay is far greater than any other. It is a millionaire's heart. I'd take an empty pocket over an empty heart any day.

Let's face it; *there's a lot of help claiming to help when in fact is not helpful.* Why is this true? Why so much insincerity? Why so much blind, untested overconfidence? I'll attempt to answer this as you read forward.

Distractions may be our downfall, with 80 visits a day to our smartphones, and email. Our society assaults our attention by over-saturation and over-sharing of information leading to the "clutter factor." It's when we sit around a campfire, tell jokes, hear compelling life journeys, and relate that we are at our happiest. Interestingly, despite all the hunger to create an impressive lifestyle, these simple, priceless connections are what define our sense of a fulfilling life. In our attempt at arriving at what appear to fill the holes, we have fillable holes now to live as contented creators.

Contented creators live and create. Living is learning to receive the inbound wildcards life presents us as we go along. Living is about trusting that the future is giving us what it needs each moment. We can take every experience in trusting that it is a teacher. It's like a love affair with life itself to be involved and engaged in whatever arises for you. Happiness is a choice. This is InTen.

"Creating" is organizing our manner of living by an intention from which we orient ourselves to bring into being. These two, living and creating bring attention and intention into one place from which our terms with life position our involvement and engagement. Half of life is taking in what emerges, and the other part of the reality of our living is making what matters into life.

Being happy is a choice. It isn't something to pursue later; it is accessible despite the present conditions. Living and creating increase our capacity for being interested, fascinated and involved with life, which makes our life building and unfolding processes offer learning. Learning is living and creating. We unlearn as we go and learn by creating what matters. What matters is both discovered and conceived. We change our minds constantly.

Knowing what matters today may not have mattered beforehand because what we truly love is a generative source out of which we create. Knowing how others inspire, move, and change us by our compassion and understanding, gives rise to sources of creative urges. From discovering our relationship with what is wanting to emerge by staying present to what is unfolding as we walk. We learn the future by doing.

Martha Graham has a great quote that speaks to the artist in each of us:

> *"There is a vitality, a life force, an energy, a quickening that translates through you into action, and because there is only one of you in all of time, this expression is unique. And if you block it, it will never exist through any other medium, and it will*

fade away. The world will not have it. It is not your business to determine how good it is nor how valuable nor how it compares with other expressions. It is your business to keep it yours clearly and directly, to keep the channel open. You do not even have to believe in yourself or your work. You must keep yourself open and aware to the urges that motivate you. Keep the channel open. ... No artist is pleased. [There is] no satisfaction whatever at any time. There is only a queer divine dissatisfaction, a blessed unrest that keeps us marching and makes us more alive than the others."

"Never believe that a few caring people can't change the world. For, indeed, that's all who ever have." I love this quote by famous anthropologist Margaret Mead.

Selling is helping, which is the confluence of being, creating, relating, and earning. The conundrum is time, money, and relationship and values misaligned by being too busy to do what could make us a lot less busy, because of spending money we don't have on things we don't need, trying to impress people we don't like.

To summarize the key points here:
- Real help is grounded in our deepest source of humanity, grounded in love, and planting the seeds of renewal in the domains of being, relating, creating and earning. This is being "inter-wise."
- We must approach helping with the full dimensionality of the human being in coordination – past, present, and future. We integrate our experiences from the past and learn, we sense

what is emerging from the present moment and let it come into our way of being, and we long for future outcomes that matter to bring it into existence.

- We embody these dimensions human beings in the world, living, learning, and realizing a higher future possibility which is different, ongoing, and forever expanding as a journey with an unfolding narrative.
- Somewhere between our way of being in the world and our choices is a stream of wisdom waiting for each of us. Our outer lives are designers to our inner lives.
- Without a greater listening and understanding, we cannot access this infinite stream that is our perennial knowing, because too often leaders have a partial view of themselves, and for this, they're likely to act in ways that cause greater suffering for others instead of enrichment.
- We each can learn to increase the quality of basic goodness (being) in the domain of selling, enriching and influencing others in helpful ways.
- Great help always depends on the interior condition of the intervenor, and this interior shifting depends on self-knowledge.

We will take a deep dive into the nature of selling, and see how in its truest sense, selling must be done with a mind of wisdom and a heart of compassion. Underline these new terms from which you re-orient your work:

- Helping is the confluence of being, doing, relating, and earning in a web of interdependence.
- We can bring ourselves as leaders into the finest quality of expression which we can access at any moment---where meaning, service, and possibilities awaken us to our truest, most authentic selves, one that belongs to the world standing in need of it with great cause and purpose.
- Involvement and enjoyment in whatever arises in our life is InTen, where joy and pleasure arise from living whole.
- Serving and helping others depends on our capacity to operate with an open mind, open heart, and open will---our intellectual intelligence, emotional intelligence, and wisdom intelligence. Our capacity for collective intelligence arises from staying longer and listening deeper "inter-wise."

We will explore the micro and macro---from what the seller does, how she does it, and most of all, the source from which the heart of selling comes, being inter-wise. The World, the Next Generation, and Planet Earth depend on this generative source to continue flourishing, which on the one hand may or may not cause a global shift. That is not predictable, but the commitment and courage to connect and occupy the very best dimensions of a human being persevere anyway. It is in our deepest nature to make a positive difference in the lives of others we influence because it strengthens our own will to live. And with a greater abundance of open-hearted bravery in the world, spirituality and commerce can operate in confluence, to add value and helpful that is essential to humanity without manipulation or control. It starts with a love of life.

Just as I come up after a dive with sea turtles in Baja, all I want for my children is to see how beautiful the ocean is today; this is my life dream for Earth. None of us say we want to destroy it yet together we are killing the sea as we know it. The way you handle business will tell the tale.

For the world to come into reality according to this dream, we must co-commit to cultivate three capacities as human beings:

1) The capacity to see insights by opening our minds to see beyond what we already know and understand. We see with fresh eyes.
2) The capacity to honor differences by treating every other as a legitimate other with acceptance and respect, not control and manipulation. We can help others appear when we operate outside our fear and shame that blocks our open-hearted compassion and true service in making a difference and being where others are in their lives.
3) The capacity to integrate what we say with what we do, and to allow life in by welcoming what the future needs this moment, to come into being as it needs to be.

These capacities require greater awareness as human beings, deep listening to our hearts and generative listening by widening our perception to see things from a grander will, not our own will. We must take life in as well as bring forth our heart's intent, to merge outer design with inner design, in harmony before the self, other, and world. Each of us exists within a multi-verse of intention, action, and reception. We are both a human being and a human doing.

CHAPTER 1

A FORCE OF NATURE

"live my best life (create)
be a great soul (be)
make an impact (relate)
learn to receive (earn)"

These four modes of living are at the forefront of what my life building process entails and intended to focus your intent in a meaningful way. All four equal INTER-WISE in full operation:

Being	*Be a great soul*	Whole life integration	Whole
Creating	*Live your best life*	Personal Mastery	Self
Relating	*Make a big impact*	Social Development	Other
Earning	*Learn to receive*	Financial Freedom	Value

In this chart we see the four-fold modes of INTER-WISE, operating with balanced intelligence. We live in a multi-verse, a nexus of self, other, whole, and value to all life. Our quality of awareness shifts as we open these like access points of information. Operating from open mind, open heart, and open will, brings forth the highest quality human being we can be at any moment. If I define what a global citizen of value and contribution looks like, this is it. Moving toward our wholeness we shift our orientation to life, from reactive to receptive, to collective, and creative, embodying our highest quality of expression, espoused in love for self, other, whole, and gratefulness for the intrinsic and extrinsic rewards from enriching lives.

It appears something bigger is on the rise---the rise of a great warrior-ship, with great purpose to bring others closer to these live building elements. I think this is the fulcrum from which the art of living manifests.

The greatest trick of the mind is to give you the idea of that which you are not and to help you feel that you are already that. Gurdjieff used to tell a parable. There was a magician who was also a shepherd. He had thousands of sheep to look after, and he was a very miserly man, so he didn't want many servants, and he didn't want many guards. He did not want to pay anybody, and he did not want his sheep to be lost or taken by the wolves. But it was very difficult for him to take care of all the sheep alone. He was very rich, and he had many sheep.
So, he played a trick on the sheep. He hypnotized them — he was a magician. He hypnotized them and told every sheep, 'You are not a sheep. Don't be afraid.' To some, he said, 'You are a lion.' To some, he said, 'You are tigers.' To some, he even said, 'You are men. Nobody is going to kill you. Don't be afraid and don't try to escape from here.'

The sheep started believing in his hypnosis. Every day he would butcher a few sheep, but the others would think, 'We are not sheep. He is butchering only sheep. We are lions, we are tigers, we are wolves, we are this and that...' even that they were men. Some were even told that they were magicians — and they believed it. It was always some sheep which was butchered. They remained aloof, distant. They were not worried. And by and by they were all butchered.

As told by Osho in "Sufis the people of the path"

I have met many humans that were a magician and a shepherd. What a nice combination! I love them less when I see some of them had cheated and butchered the sheep; I started even to hate them. This hate was my self-aggression as if I was seeing others different than me, and yet I have those qualities in me too. My personal story is not about the magician, not about the shepherd. It is about the sheep. We allow our human friends to die of hunger, and in exploiting them we feel they are living in a faraway country, they are those sad souls who did not want to work, the lazy ones. We lull them into these beliefs that they are far from us, and it is not our responsibility to help. They are our brothers; our fellow sheep and we have all the responsibility to help them in every way we can. We must breathe this into our openness of the heart.

FEELING ALIVENESS

This day is the one day that is given to you as a gift. And it's the only gift that you have right now, which suggests the only appropriate response is gratefulness. If you do nothing else but to cultivate that response to the great gift on this unique day, it is to learn to respond as if the first day in your life and the very last day. This way you will have spent this day very well by opening your eyes and being surprised that you have eyes through which you notice incredible arrays of colors that are constantly offered to you. Your enjoyment of the sky and the weather, just think of all the many nuances of good weather and bad weather right now, notice the location of clouds in the sky, as they will never be the same. And right now, open your eyes and look at the faces of people you meet, as each one has an incredible story behind their face that you could never fully fathom. Not only their story but the story of the ancestors going back so far and this present moment on this day people you meet from generations and so many places all over the world. It's like life-giving water if you only open your heart to the gift of civilization given to us. You turn on the faucet with warm water and cold water that many millions and millions in the world will never experience. These are just a few of an enormous number of gifts to realize, so I'm wishing that you would open your heart and these blessings let them flow through you that everyone who you will meet on this day will be blessed by you by your smile, just by your presence let the gratefulness overflow into blessings all around you, and it will clearly become the best day of your life.

I get to be alive. My sweet, longtime friend Javier died recently. That is a unique day like no other to be grateful. On this day of death, the clouds are different, life is precarious, and as I look into the eyes of whoever I meet I am more present than ever before. Javier had a heart attack in his sleep during the night and went away quietly. At first much like you would do, it brought me to deep sorrow and grief. After several days of getting past this stage, my deepest appreciation and gratitude for what he was and the gift of his life in mine became clear. Javier was a sales shaman. It's simple. He wasn't a taker; he was a giver and contributor ready, willing, and able to add value to those he touched. His platform through his work was a taco business, and the most successful one in Baja California. What made him so special and noticeable was how he handled his customers. He'd seat you like you were royalty at a picnic table. He'd bring wet naps to cleanse your hands of any dirt or germs before eating tacos. And his ingredients were organic, and all materials involved were respectful of the environment.

As he took your order, the conversation was always about us, our kids, our lives, as he asked pertinent questions that only someone we mattered to would recall and ask. When we hadn't come around in a while, he'd give us a text or call and tell us how much he enjoyed seeing us. Javier was like a guardian angel. He loved selling tacos and seeing your face when you enjoyed great tastes. His process was simple and effective, and the results were astounding---more taco sales than anyone around. I couldn't believe the numbers he was doing, and the profits were twice as high as the average food venue. He always said, "It's not what we sell, it's the way we sell." A few years back we went to visit his daughter the day she gave birth to his beautiful grandson.

Every time we'd go to eat, Javier would share pictures as his grandson grew into a toddler. I realized that although I loved the tacos, I loved Javier, and that is why I continued to come around. Our exchanges brought me into a certain aliveness and nourishment through his diligence, dedication, and focus on value creation. After our table conversations, if he heard a need or opportunity we expressed, he connected us to someone and opened doors. I knew at that moment that Javier was an example of what each of us has in us, and he was sparkling in the form of greatness. We can see the light in the other, and when we do, we see ourselves anew. Javier gave me this gift, to help me become complete and trust the basic goodness in all human beings. He was an echo back to the best part of me, and Javier if you hear these words, *"Thank you for being who you are, and touching my life with your open heart. Being in your presence was magnificent. You are a blessing to the world, and I see that I can be too. When you're around me, I love everyone else a whole lot more."*

There are three qualities that I so much want to live from and incorporate from Javier. These are courage, compassion, and connection. All three aspects of my life speak loud and clear that the purpose of my life is to live it and live it. I dare to live from what my heart desires. Compassion is the part of me that knows deep down the intelligence of the heart to honor differences and maintain legitimacy regardless of who is in front of me. I want to lessen the suffering of others. This is collective awareness to draw forth empathy and respect.

We all live in a network of interconnected domains (a web of life) from which we integrate our experience of life at a deeper, more conscious level---1) to take in whatever challenges us beyond the familiar, 2) to be touched and moved in our hearts, and 3) to be inspired and astonished by what expresses itself in our lives. We let go of refusing influence of life living us in constant flux. Context is forever in motion

37

as if to be captured by defining features on the journey we live forward.

Javier's death was like an awakening to what could be considered a new manner of living. I ask myself: "what terms are you on with life?" Your terms, my terms, everyone's terms with life define the place from which you and I and all of us make decisions from moment to moment. When you sell from inner peace, a sense of joy for making a difference in others' lives, and from learning from what life presents now, a deeper sense of contentment and gratitude for life arises from the ethos of our being in the world. We each seek to buoy these qualities to the surface and access them as a higher quality of expression. I'm wondering what would be possible if together you and I come into ourselves the same way, as verified loving beings. I use the word *verify* here to suggest that to understand your true properties, you must be seen by another person as such. "I see you," is a strong statement because it verifies the "significant other" to exist. To take responsibility for seeing another is truly a remarkable responsibility.

Seeing is violated by memory. We can see from what we already anticipate, claim, and expect, or see things as if we see them freshly for the first time. To participate in validating what is great in something or someone, you convey which gifts are possible for the world by your seeing them. To see how others shine is naturally your shining too. What you see is what you get. When you see the gifts, they are made real by the process of perceiving them. Nothing is truly real or definable in the world without the act of being seen. Everything is in a state of flux, and interdependent by relating with everything else brought into its true properties. The patterns of interaction define our true selves. To love is to see this way. To see this way is the genius in you seeing a genius in the other. Neither goes unnoticed in the process of seeing.

This book is not full of research to prove a point or make a case. This book is an *invitation* to reclaim your life as a resource for the world. It is a call to action now. The question I'm wondering is, *"What is the source out of which value creation arises?"* I propose that all value creation arises from non-violated human beings. Four potential violations must be lifted to liberate contributing human beings in any society. These are first, lifting the violation of the self. I'm referring to self as a creative human being who organizes their life by what they intend. Second is lifting the violation of the other.

To be a loving human being is to accept those different from you as legitimate beings. Third, is lifting the violation of the world connecting to itself through us, our true nature. The world is the whole, the eco-system of life; it is our access point to our own wisdom and most basic goodness. I propose that there are properties within the whole cosmos of life that connect us to our highest future possibilities and helps us discover our place within this larger system. Much like a musician knows their place within the whole, so too does our ability to connect with the basic need to do good in the world as we begin to sense what calls us. The fourth violation to lift is to prosperity. Lifting the fourth violation to prosperity is about accessing the quality of life that we want if we create value for others in ways they want and need it and serve others with our basic goodness to help. When you bring fierce attention to the present moment, you witness a web of life altogether interconnected with three quelling currents. First is the process of initiation and beginning, the second is the process of ending and dying, and the third is the process of conserving what remains forward. As we integrate these to where we go, what we care for, and what stands in need of us, our highest quality of expression rises to the surface in service to something larger that beckons us to follow. Life is in constant flux, presenting service, meaning and revelation as we remain open and receptive for inspiration.

Here is the essence of *value creation*: to give value from our best self just for the joy of it. It is given via the vehicle of a business, a career, a job, a vehicle that helps the world get better at removing the first three violations and meet a liberated sense of what they can do in the world, in living their lives in meaningful and engaging ways. Pleasure is different than joy. Joy is what we receive from being ourselves in ways which enrich others' lives. George Lucas drew great pleasure from making films from powerful stories, and yet his joy was reached when his films would bring a remarkable difference to touching the lives of others.

To look further into this joy, you hear it like a dog whistle. Not everyone will pick it up, but you will if you're ready. A change in understanding offers something new to appear. When you see anew, what you see then changes

Consider for a moment how you integrate your experiences. The manner in which you use your experiences is key to constructing your sense of direction. How you experience others and reality directly influences the conditions in which learning becomes possible. You learn by experiencing life at many levels---from what you do or create, how you go about creating it, and what emerges from current reality. I tried to explain consciousness for years, and it is the *way you relate with your experiences.*

Energy follows attention. If you relate with experiences habitually, your behavior is born from the past (what you know; memory). When you relate with your experiences directly, you see what reality is without a lens. When you relate with your experience from a place of understanding, humility, and acceptance, your experiences move you and touch you internally and deeply. You can encounter the creative order of the cosmos revealing and unraveling itself if you pay attention from the living web of life that connects us to deeper sources of emergence, inner knowing, and purpose. We can move from our hunger for mastery to mystery. We can find the calmness in the center of our psyche and recapture ourselves to conserving this place as a core operative. The word psyche is "soul" or resident spirit living within us. And when we attend from this inner place, our relationship to what emerges shifts.

Each of us can live by a life plan or go with the flow of things. We can shift our orientation to life and when we do this our manner of living shifts. I've looked at how this fundamental shift gives rise to how entrepreneurs and selling shifts with it. When your experience is pointing toward what the emerging future is presenting, you use reflection in action to coordinate movement and conserve what matters. Someone creating uses one's own experiences far differently than someone who is reacting and responding to circumstances.

Without the truth, selling becomes manipulation, not helping. Helping is about honoring and respecting *what is* without attempting to place your conditions on it. You treat everything as a legitimate other in its unique way and manner of living. This quality of "letting" is letting things be just as they are in their perfection. Perfection means "genuine" or "purely true." And to help, a commitment to report the truth to yourself is required. Truth is about a connection to what is real for you, what is real for the other and is becoming real. Getting real is the fundamental choice to clarify what is going on, with courage. It is not about products or services, nor features, nor benefits; it is a relationship from which all of these become possible. Connection first, material second. Connection and community first, consumerism second.

Jeff, an amazing graphic designer in Seattle lets go of being the expert with answers and enters the design process with curiosity. Rather than beginning with a consumer and seller of service, Jeff's learned how to let go of his experience and start freshly. As he shows up and attends this way, the client begins to feel legitimized to discuss their emerging creation. They "tinker," "fiddle" together as the logo/design comes into life.

Jeff says when he starts, he let's go of the old self, which is his past tendency to predict a result. To get out of his way, he begins with action, not knowledge. He learns the creation by doing. He starts separate from what he knows. No creation for a client is ever the same. Power is transferred to the creation, not himself. The other (the client; buyer) seves as the co-creator, who is also dominated by the reference to the creation (logo, design, web page). The way forward becomes obvious as Jeff notices selling them on anything is unnecessary. His client responds with, "You get us." Jeff calls this "finding the game and trusting your instincts to follow where it wants to be." He said mindful action comes forth and a path crystallizes itself. Jeff calls this process of coming to understand something new, "social design sourcing."

How do we shift the interior condition from which the seller is coming to attend, listen, act, and behave in their work? Value creation can be a genuine effort to have the highest hopes for another human being or organization. Wishing them well ascends from a genuine place of interpersonal care and love for life and others.

Where the seller's listening originates is perhaps the biggest question this book is presenting. What about the inner place from which listening and attending come forth? You can remember moments when you jumped to prescribe a solution for your client's problem. How did you get there? Instead of inquiring into what is going on, you leap into getting paid. You probably toggled between the outcome, the process, and then the place from where your listening was happening.

If you've sold Business to Business, you know when your expertise gets the best of you. You probably experienced moments when you met the situation your client has and started to see what's different about it even if it's not within what you've encountered before. You don't reduce it by your knowledge, but instead seek to understand what is going on, how it got to be that way, and discover with the client's participation what is going on, even if that means you may not be able to help. The attempt to understand outside what you already know is called *factual listening*.

Factual listening is a nice position to start the helping process. Space allows for discovery and possibilities to arise. At certain moments in the conversation, you probably feel the client's angst, pain, experience, and how they are suffering. You hear the words they say, and the person saying them. Offering your listening to the other person's world is called *empathic listening*. Your listening originates from completely going outside your bubble into their experience. Then perhaps in some moments, an involuntary sense of something emerging surfaces from something underground, invisible into visible. An emerging future possibility presents itself to your listening completely from outside your factual and empathic listening levels. You *listen generatively* as if something larger in creative order and grandiosity is wanting to emerge.

I just spent three days present and free from distractions to enjoy my young daughters. We created cakes and cupcakes together. We began with a desired creation we envisioned. We learned by making mistakes together, and when we finalized our frostings, we enjoyed what we created. Most of all was the entrancing joy of making something we love. Each time we do things like this I see qualities in them that blow my mind and make me so happy. My heart is in being there and focused on them, nothing more. They are my teachers.

Going back to work the next day, I sat down with a sales producer and underneath his activity were the seeds of fear and manipulation. He couldn't see what he was doing. He felt like living a double life pretending to be there, but not present at all to what he was doing. I mentioned it was like walking the procession of the living dead. He didn't buy himself nor what he was helping people do. And this transmitted like white noise distorting a clear signal to the buyer. All I could think of was creating value for my daughters and what we could do together.

As we went back and forth in our discussion, he knew I wasn't there to motivate him or turn him around, but instead make him as honest as possible to himself. Once he found a bottom, he was in tears and wondering whether he had it in him to rise. He had never felt other people were there for him truly in his life. After the divorce, the kids leaving, and feeling lonely; his only assumption was nobody cared, so why should he care? He gave up on himself because he gave up on people as loving beings with goodness and consideration in them. As we looked at this belief system and what played out, he began to question the validity of his thinking. His generalization that other people don't care had no basis in truth. And he saw that if he didn't believe that thought, something could happen, a new dimension of himself could come forth because it was safe. And that if he decoupled from the belief, he could come out to the world a more loving and whole person, not a scared and frightened one held back by projecting his mistrust on others.

THE RESET BUTTON

The focus of redefining what sellers and buyers can do together starts with shifting the focus to a *social body* instead of the individual body. This requires a different type of attention, one that is self and other, not just from oneself, one's past, and one's own way of seeing things. This is important to clarify because we move from a fixed process, to an organic one that lives and breathes directionality at the level of the whole system. What sellers usually do is in thousands of books, and how buyers should buy, consume, and take control of their lives is equally in the thousands of books. But what about shifting the focus to creating a single social body or container called "the helping relationship?"

The role of the helper as seller and the role of needing help is the buyer. Together they collaborate such that that buyer continually is helped, and the helper also is continually adapting her process around the evolving desires and needs to be learned. Nothing is fixed, rather, it is an evolving relationship that is like an object they both work on together. It is beyond transaction into something more fundamental where the seller's authentic self translates into helping the buyer define needs together and come up with solutions that matter. I call this the "fundamental relationship" when this kind of impact for building value and innovating new solutions together in naturally collaborative ways becomes possible.

Out of *a fundamental relationship*, the atmosphere of trust gives rise to great deliveries, innovations, and powerful social change. Both buyer and seller are participants in the relationship with equal stature. It is not parenting-oriented, but instead partnering-oriented. Deficiency doesn't define the helping process, rather opportunity or deepening trust, reflection, and discoveries that provide a shared stream of information that reinforces trust. Much like teacher/student patriarchal structures can convert to learning allies, buyer and sellers come together much the same. No one is relegated to live imprisoned in their categories—sellers or buyers.

THE INNATE SACRED PROJECT HIDDEN WITHIN YOU

One component that brings forth the possibility of the fundamental relationship is your having a unique gift inside which belongs to the world (others) to make the creation of your life dreams possible. If you deny this force of nature within you, you deprive yourself of the aliveness that pre-exists in your expression. *Selling*, in a nutshell, boils down to: "Helping people access their dreams." And in doing so, you learn how to be truly you. Your authentic self comes alive when meaning and service rise and when you listen deeply to where another person is in life.

You didn't come to Earth a blank; you came with a sacred assignment to contribute and help others. I know this is true because it is what brings you into feeling alive. You are an extension of divine expression looking to become useful through your gifts and talents. Holding this back is the obstacle you must overcome and give it to the world is our primary purpose while here on Earth. God blesses those who find loving kindness and generosity in their heart.

Creating dreams is the hidden work in all you do, and more than ever it is the time to bring this outward. Could there be a better profession than to create your life dream by way of helping people create their own? You must tap into your places of most potential, listen, and bring forth help to buyers who depend on you for this, to create what matters most to them in their lives. You need to be there for yourself and be there for them in ways you may not have been there before now. And I'll be helping you see where and how to open these doors.

"The way you see people is the way you treat them, and the way you treat them is what they become."

Johann Wolfgang von Goethe

The more you become yourself, the more helpful you become as the world awaits you and depends on you. The longer you stay present and listen deeper, your understanding leads to something new. When something desirable is made from what emerges, your genius and purpose come to the surface. There's potential in you that can take hold in the world, be there for yourself, and be there for others. In fact, you have no idea yet how big the genius nature in you is, and you must turn toward your capacity to understand the terror and tragedy in the world today in order to connect with why I'm pulling this out of you. The genius in you already knows why you're here; you just need to awaken to it.

What you love is what your DNA is signaling to you what you must do. Strength is resonance. What you love is where you're gifted. And to love is to see. The way you see something---the game, the customer, your capabilities, what people are going through---this place from which you see initiates your genius to come forth. It's where your talent is ready to play. The purpose of education----is to know your genius and carry it through to where it's trying to go. The word "educate" originally meant to "lead or bring it out." Emerson said, *"When nature has work to be done, she creates a genius to do it."* Genius is secretly connecting you to the world. Culture and nature reconnect via the genius awakening in you. And when you find yours, you help others you serve to find theirs, like a chain reaction that expands and multiplies itself. This genius is necessary for having a fulfilled life. Without it, we turn to addictions that destroy it. We each can occupy our place in the ecosystem of our social domains.

Your genius must be called and triggered by a challenge. This challenge is not a problem you're to fix, but rather the desired outcome you seek to bring into reality. But when you lounge on your success, your genius is concealed. You drink your own Kool-Aid, smoke your own exhaust and delude yourself in over-confidence thinking you can out-last the hangover of opportunity cost when you're too comfortable. You can fall into despair when you're not creating. Success leaves bad lessons.

Creating is the one activity that brings your genius to the surface. To aim with your gifts, you consider what aims matter most to you. You bring something into being that didn't exist prior. You live into what you're creating separate from what you know; to learn, unlearn, until your desired creations come to fruition. Your genius is the apprentice appointed by your creations to come to life. It is the instrument through which something awesome is waiting to be born. I want you to learn how to establish a connection with your highest future possibility within your helping others, and act from this place. The quality of attention holds space for a pathway for reality to unfold what you came here to do.

I want buyers to know *the genius* behind the mask of a salesperson and see you anew because of all the good you have in you to bring to the world. The day you put your "salesperson" mask on you lost your true identity---your humanity. You succumbed to a method as if you're a programmed piece of software with an exiled soul, not a human being who carries a unique gift for others. I seek to restore humanity in selling by shifting your inner life as it pertains to the work you do in the world. And I'm interested in how you position selling as a key instrument for this to come about. You can find your place in the eco-system. But you must become more aware and listen carefully in order to tap into it via self-knowledge.

You have a job, a career, and a calling. Your job is how you support your needs. The job is what you do daily to fulfill your obligations. Your career is a skill-set that over time other people justify paying a premium for because you're superior at what you do. But your calling is the thread moving through your whole life (so far) that intends to move you forward, fused into your decisions, actions, and communications. Your calling is *a sacred project* pregnant within you to be expressed through all you do and toward everyone you contact. Take a moment and reflect on defining your own ideas on each: your job, your career, and your calling.

Your well-being depends on the impact you have on the well-being of others. Think of a doctor. The condition of the doctor is just as important in the healing process as the condition of the patient. As the doctor heals others, he heals himself. Like the doctor example, this source of well-being and generosity within you houses the prenatal seeds of your finest way of being and your finest quality of intention. You've probably selected your doctor not only because they're great technically at what they do, but more importantly the atmosphere of trust and confidence you feel when you're together. Healing starts by conserving the humanity in their approach to helping you. You've probably noticed after talking with them about your predicament helps restore you. Their loving presence can transform how you feel.

You will be invisible as a commodity from this day forward. And I will help you see why your buyers are latently yearning and longing for a different type of connection with you, and how you can bring it to the surface in your helping them. As you the salesperson receives rewards, you pay it forward by helping and contributing with your gifts. *You have something in you to bring to the world that no one else made with your DNA has.* And in this way, you find ways to grow your soul through the work of selling. You make yourself capable of the divine in the selling realm.

SELF-ISH TO SELF-LESS SPACE

Looking at today's economic model, we all tend to build our actions upon the notion that humans are about self-interest first. But what if we invert this belief to: *"what if everyone is self-less?"* What if we propose that each of us has this innate capacity within us to come forward and some are higher on it than others. Familiarity is the pathway to this. So, what if selling held this governing paradigm? What if people want to give value just for the joy of it? I'm pointing to a generous, voluntary energy. If this was among us in the world, what kind of world could we become? Salespeople would unleash the power of *compassion capital*. Understanding and listening would replace presenting and showing value. Adding value would become more important. The whole could become greater than the sum of the parts. When put together, the bond of buyer and seller could flourish into a co-creative state. These are the ingredients of a gift economy where consumption moves to contribution. Instead of "what can I get?" turn to "what can I give?" We need to count on people to be generous, not self-interested.

All sales training appears to be more about the process, and the result, not about the source from which the salesperson's attention and action originate. Selling begins with the quality of action through which value enriches another human being. It is to hold ourselves to the standard of being more of ourselves.

The key is how to create a space for intimacy for individuals and within organizations. The foundation for intimacy is in learning how to forgive, and treat others as legitimate others, even when you have different viewpoints. With respect, it is safe to be true. And when this dynamic is accessed, deeper connections lead to innovation, creativity, responsibility, and organization. The conversations become the pathway to seeing possibilities that before weren't witnessed. Breakthroughs and insights appear when certainty is suspended, but the courage and commitment to stay open and flexible is key to increasing learning and leading change.

Companies today are creating far too many takers and achievers with materialistic ambitions rooting their efforts rather than givers and helpers who provide value in ways that go beyond their puny will. Re-rooting from taker to giver involves character-building with the highest essential quality of action that is authentic. We haven't come at selling from the standpoint of the source out of which a sale occurs.

Ninety percent of value creation ignites from latent, hidden, and non-existent and can become real after a conversation between buyer and seller. Latency suggests that sellers don't have answers, but suggests buyers don't have needs, they have predispositions to be re-arranged and re-constructed to create value. The seller is positioned with the task of innovation by way of relating with and listening to the buyer in new and authentic ways. Dynamics like acceptance, trust, courage, compassion, and connection all play a major role in the reformation of a relationship between buyer and seller. What is the interior condition from which the seller is coming to attend, listen, act, and behave in their work? Value creation can be a genuine effort to have the highest hopes for another human being or organization. Wishing them well ascends from a genuine place of interpersonal care and love for life and others.

Commerce is becoming fundamentally more spiritual. The shift doesn't mean more religious; rather it means more focusing effort on what matters to and excites the constituents leading and driving the business *organization* at all levels. People on Earth are keeping death close at hand---the planet, their race, and their own lives. Our apocalyptic sense of the future has moved our attention to making key decisions today about how to use our lives more than ever before. We are participating consciously in our evolution as a species. Scarcity and brevity are shifting our relationship with work to be meaningful. Work is a place to merge our fundaments values. Anything else is not working it's a waste of precious time. You cannot make more time, but you can make more value from the time available.

Companies today like Twitter, Facebook, and others don't sell products and services; they connect people. Products and services emerge out of conversations. A network of conversations is a culture. Moreover, as a leader in business, we exist within many domains of these networks and combinations. Context is always in motion as if life is always breathing new conversations into our domain and flushing old ones out.

The speed of change is so much faster than before that developing a learning mentality with an open, flexible mindedness is key to staying relevant in the marketplace. You're going to grieve old ways and ideas far faster than ever before with your commitment never to stop learning.

So, to recap, the quality of your influence and impact on your own life, on others, and the world depends on cultivating an inner state such that your quality of intention, connection, and attention arise from the highest quality of expression you can bring forth. These three elements: intention, connection, and attention can integrate all at once such that your sense of what to do merges three— self/other/wholeness.

And the emergent properties hidden within the present moment can offer a sea of open possibilities from which a dormant, most essential self is pregnant with a sacred project, can come forth, as your place within the ecosystem comes into life. You relate with the present moment not from your personality (habitual self, patterns, and past-driven fear, judgment, and cynicism), but instead, occupy a way of being in the world that is truly *in* the world. The trip itinerary of your life unfolds by the journey of what life is seeking of you.

CHAPTER 2

CONFLUENCE

Ambition, if taken too far, can be very dangerous. It can cause you to impress others in a way and manipulate them according to how you want them to see you or react toward you. As you grow, this is probably something that will change in your behavior. As you grow and mature, people will object to you, not like you, say bad things, or misunderstand your motives. But as you grow, you will probably be less and less preoccupied with calling peoples' attention to you, and instead, you put attention on the world. When you're preoccupied with your inadequacies, you use others as a fix to feel you're up to par. When you do this, they become an object in your game to participate in putting you together in a way you want to appear in the world. It is called composing a "false self-system." At some point in your life, something, a situation or person will wake you up to living out of this. You'll shatter it to pieces and find that what lies beneath is something else to help organize your behavior toward others as well as your terms with life.

THE WATER OF MADNESS

Once upon a time, there lived a mysterious prophet and saint called Khidr. He rescued many from danger. He performed many miracles. They say the sea and sky obeyed his will and that he could appear anywhere and everywhere at the same time. His immortality came from the Water of Life. He used the shining jewel brought to Earth from paradise to find this water. When he found it, he dived in, and his body and clothing turned green. After this, wherever his feet touched, the Earth turned green.

Khidr offered guidance to many of the prophets of this Earth, among them Moses. One day when Moses was preaching, someone asked him who was the wisest man of all. When Moses answered that he was the wisest one, God revealed to him that there was someone wiser. This was Khidr. But long before the day Khidr met Moses, he came to his people with a warning.

He explained that soon all the water in the world would disappear and would be renewed with different water. "The new water will drive you mad," Khidr told the people. "To save yourselves, you must hoard all the water here on Earth. Save it, and you will be saved."

But only one man listened to Khidr's advice. This man began right away to collect all the water he could. He went to rivers and streams, lakes and waterfalls, and ponds and pools. Using jars and bottles, barrels and buckets, and pots and pans, he collected water. He stored the water in a secret cave. He told no one about his cave, and no one ever knew where it was.

And then one day, just as Khidr had warned, the streams stopped flowing. The lakes and wells and waterfalls dried up. Soon every riverbed was dust, and no matter where people turned, there was no water.

The man who had listened to Khidr secretly crept off to his hiding place. He was careful to make sure no one saw him, and then he sat inside and drank his hoarded water. From his dark, quiet cave he watched the sky, waiting for the new water to fall.

Sure enough, before long the new water came, and the lakes and rivers and wells were once again flowing. Waterfalls tumbled riotously over the rocks. Everywhere there once had been water, there was water again. The people were overjoyed, and they began to drink and drink.

The man in the cave, confident that everything was fine again, walked outside to return to his people. When he saw them drinking heartily from great buckets drawn from their wells, he approached and called, "Hello." But no one responded.

Very soon the man discovered that his people had gone mad. They spoke an entirely different language from the language they had once spoken. They had no memory of the time before. No one knew anything of the way the world had been before the new water. They seemed to recall no warning from Khidr, to know nothing of the days of the past. The man tried to tell them, but when he talked, no one could understand him.

And there was something worse he saw: They thought that he was the one who had gone mad!

He tried to argue with them. "You see that lake there? It was a desert. And that riverbed was only rocks and dust. Your well was dry."

They only stared. "What is he saying?" they asked, but they asked this in a language he did not understand, and so he had no idea what they were saying.

But he did understand their faces. They looked at him as if he were the one who was mad. They shook their fists. They shouted. Before long he was afraid. He could see they would never understand what he was trying to say. They would never remember the world as it had once been. And so he ran away, back to the safety of his cave and back to his secret water. He refused to drink this new water that drove everyone mad. No, he would stay in the safety of his world, with his own water.

But as time passed, he became more and more lonely. He had no family. He had no friends. He had no one to talk to. Sometimes, late at night, he crept out of his cave and stole to the village and wandered the streets; when he heard people talking together and laughing, his heart ached. He wished he could join them in their madness.

At last, he made a decision. He would drink this new water and become like all the others. He too would be mad.

That very day, he walked to the well that had once been his, and he drew up a bucket of water. Thirsty for friendship, he drank. In just one moment he understood the language the others were speaking, and when his old friends passed by, he joined them, and he forgot all about the past. He forgot his cave and his water.

His friends embraced him and cried, "You were mad, but you have been restored to sanity!"

And because he no longer remembered, he did not argue.

OVERSHARING

As you get older, you begin to awaken to letting go of moving other people along or changing their opinions of you. Approval seeking can be like an addiction. Getting others to like you, although an interesting idea, you cannot control other people's perceptions because you don't own the contents of their mind or past from which they label, categorize, and look at you. This responsibility you have to hand back to them. Trying to please everyone or make everyone happy and look at you favorably is an act of violence to yourself. Nothing is more self-mutilating than being different selves to different people. Approval seeking is a stressful way to live when one overshares based on a need to affirm one's value or sense of importance. This leads to harmful help, martyrdom, and burnout.

The hero role is one face of positioning your power over others. The hero is the caretaker, the one who makes others ok. But the underlying drive here isn't to save others from anything; rather it's performed to offset one's shame. It's a phony form of generosity and being there to assure oneself that their negative beliefs of themselves aren't going to be found out. The hero buries and smoke screens these secrets by appearing caring, kind, and so supportive of others, and yet it's all just a costume to lubricate shame. The motivator is NOT for love for the other, or in the spirit of true service, rather it is the egos way of getting affirmation, admiration, and adulation by calling attention to himself. I've met many phony holies in my life, who hide their self interest.

The selling journey starts from the quality of connection through the quality of attention, and hence the quality of receptivity that one has. Selling invokes both outgoing and incoming aspects to raise the comprehension at the level of intellectual, emotional, and ontological intelligence humans are invoking in everything they do. The basic building block is the ground of being from which the seller helps the buyer. The quality of this expression is either forced, superficial, or real and of one's deeper nature. The "come from" is a blind spot in sales performance today, and yet it is the most powerful form of leveraging value creation for another human being or organization. Four elements short-circuit the quality of one's come from 1) ignorance, 2) greed, 3) fear, and 4) shame

Ignorance is not seeing what is going on. Greed is manipulating another to serve one's desires or seek an advantage. Fear is predicting what could be ahead, and shame is reducing one's value or worth to less than normal levels. If the sales leader hasn't been in good company with these inner enemies, most likely he is acting from them because they are embedded in their behavior. All four are like four corners of ego-based behavior to put oneself at the center of everything. Preoccupation with looking stupid leads to misappropriated expertise and over-confidence.

Preoccupation with material gains leads to acting from greed and manipulation. Preoccupation with fear short circuits intimacy, honesty, and acceptance. And shame motivates outward misrepresentation to offset negative beliefs about oneself. When operating from the throw of these motivational forces, we negate our capacity to be available, open, and receptive to others. We reduce others to objects to serve our preoccupations to survive, control, and hoard power. We construct a world with others that is too dangerous to place our trust.

Deep generative listening is vital, and yet most people in sales use listening as a gimmick, not a sincerely interested-based activity. Active listening is a technique to probe and playback what the other is saying to you. But ask yourself if you're truly there, present behind the technique? Here is an important challenge to influencing your motivation. I cannot motivate you to care. But I can help you connect with the context in your life that brings you into a more caring position.

Having a method is to suggest you come into every situation with a pre-conceived, conventional approach. All performances tap into this memory system from which you do things the same way every single time. If McDonald's made a different burger every time, we probably wouldn't come back. To expect every production, every outcome to occur according to our model of success would be folly. Habits are repeatable when they become automatically inclined.

ATMOSPHERE

There is a significant release of energy that happens when people come together in an atmosphere of trust. The flow pattern of this energy is toward a new direction which is different than the past.

By learning from experience, what new is ready to arise will present itself. Making new things new and possible doesn't come from experience, it comes from the quality of trust between the buyer and seller. And when understanding is opened of another as another is, something new becomes possible. Content is bypassed by creating this atmosphere of trust such that a buyer curiously asks, "How do I do that?"

Egoic selling is to push a feature or benefit. "Ecoic Selling" is to make new needs clear and create a context in which the buyer wants to engage in change by disposing of old thinking in participation in discovering what could become possible through the seller's help in collaboration.

Any change of understanding is a change of world. Something new appears. Selling is unity where something more happens from a new understanding that both buyer and selling experience. The seller and buyer must release what they know to enter this field of potentiality.

Sellers create liberating conversations by conserving legitimacy and acceptance, out of which discernment, reflection, and interest come to the surface. Helping is possible through liberating conversations that help the buyer understand themselves and their reality in new and interesting ways.

Remember that you have the freedom of heart and mind to bring your spirit to anything you see, say or do. Through your helping process an authentic resident self in you appears that by its absolute nature knows to be kind, generous, loving, and compassionate. And you do not know the expansiveness or magnitude this profound way of being in the world can have on your walk of life and those of others. It is boundless.

So, the question I ask you to ask yourself is, "Why not?" You're not going to live forever. You've probably awakened to the fact that you are not immortal, your death is around the corner at some unknowable distance, so live into moments today and live them a little more dangerously than the past. And if there's one goal of spending good time on Earth, you may as well live fully, and make a difference, in fact, it is in your DNA to do so. My message to you here is a reminder and an invitation.

I'm proposing that self-knowledge is a primary influencer of how value creation comes forth. The highest possible output a seller can bring forth is honest help. This is help that is helpful. When helpful help occurs, the confluence of being, relating, creating, and earning come into play as a single intelligence.

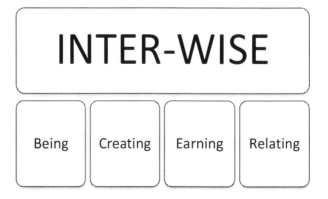

Helpful help originates like this: If I know myself to be a good person with a loving heart, others will sense this and circularity of the same is likely with the other, the buyer. Reproducing and maintaining a coordinated atmosphere of safety generates the exchange of expression for entering more into a conversation.

How do I know myself to be good? Your basic sense of goodness exists within a network of conversations. By asking others and acknowledging others for their help in our lives. Why did people in our lifetime come to know us, love us, and influence us? These sentient beings were part of a genesis process to help you come fully aware and alive with your gifts. And your presence in their life was probably helping the same process. Right now, if you remember the faces of those souls that initiated you, they came just at the perfect time to ready you for what life was about to bring in the door. They were echoes to show you the gifts you possessed to follow the thread running through your life. You could not know the full properties of your true self until they touched your life and revealed a quality of admiration and respect for what you are for them. No properties of you are definable in fullness without this true dependence. If you wrote down each of these people throughout your life, you could immediately gather what they put into you.

BRINGING FORTH BASIC GOODNESS AND CONCERN

You the seller conduct a transformative conversation by invoking the spirit of concern for the other in providing value just for the joy of it. You might call this 'clean energy' when life within is maintained better living in the other. A productive interaction is a system in which the components, buyer, and seller are naturally inclined toward value creation if the interior condition of the seller is the highest quality of expression he can occupy in the moment of being together.

If the seller can comprehend what is going on using different organs of perception and see from an open mind as an observer, her curiosity will alter what is being examined and listened to. And if the seller is listening generously to how the conversation is shifting intrinsically, such that what has potential value for the buyer is possible, this sudden urge can translate into generating significant impact.

What level of comprehension becomes available in our seeing, sensing, and generating change from standing ready, at hand with that which goodness presents itself, animates us to follow its expansiveness into where honest help is waiting. When a new initiative is invoked by caring, something magical becomes available for oneself and the world.

Start with being. Why? Because to invoke the highest quality of spirit at the start of any initiative, a genuine sense of concern is necessary. Mobilizing any change effort starts with the inner place from which the person and the group or organization operate. It starts with understanding the full dimensionality of a human being. Once you come toward this, you begin to gain a fuller comprehension of things. This comprehension integrates our innate desire to merge our true self, our truest connection to others emotionally, and our truest connection to what life is unfolding for us every moment. These aspects are learned and developed by living, not studying. Our experiences can be conserved to arouse our respect and admiration of others.

I'm saying the quality of being—the part of you that by nature is good and virtuous. To bring these aspects into the light of self-knowledge implies we come to know ourselves as compassionate, loving beings that can expand the basic goodness in each one of us. That means you are compassionate, loving, understanding, empathetic, wise, considerate, thoughtful and at the very roots of your character, a loving being. That also suggests the same lives in everyone, and given this, an amazing level of coordination naturally originates in a creative order from the relationship. Would you trust you or anyone holding steady to living from these qualities? If sincere, yes. If you trust you, so too will others. It is when you don't buy you that you create a reason for others to do the same. Write down why you do or do not trust you, then re-assign your focus to what your nature is composed of, do you trust you? You probably won't trust all of you because you can't, but you can take an objective inventory of you and remember what you do house inside of use. From this self-allocation is at your fingertips to know where to place yourself or not. Self-confidence is in self-honesty, which implies that you show up as a whole person with all your qualities, good, bad, and ugly---including your imperfections. Giving others the space to be true and human, makes it safe for genuine intimacy, relatedness, and connection to occur.

I don't have to tell you that to define this in yourself, you know it already. I know it in me already. And if we both remember our basic goodness and to root ourselves in it, that fundamental choice affects how we influence the world. Far too often, the doing is disattached action from the being, and the quality in action reduces to less third-person care. Let's be clear that your being is not your personality. It is a backdrop behind all things you experience and do.

Quality of Being is about range and fluency. When you see what is going on, you articulate it just as it is, and when you listen to another human being, you hear them in their voice and hear the person behind the words. Being is the place where something begins. It is nothingness, not the opposite of something, but the place where beginnings happen. The outcome of this is intelligence. We gain intelligence by knowing first the full dimensionality of a human being for new content to show itself. This place within each of us reveals a quality of self, relationship, and emergence. The quality of being we occupy is commensurate with the quality of intention, connection, and attention we draw forth to meet life. All three of these can bring us whole. We must seat ourselves in our ground of being and operate from this, not just our personality.

Our being brings us into contact with contradictions as we move forward through life. These contradictions are predictably inconsistent and yet can have coherence. Nothing guarantees that tomorrow will rise the way we might expect. What we see can be adjacent or non-adjacent to what we know. Stepping outside of time, one sees there is no now, it is a non-conceptual experience. All mental concepts are relative and given up. What lies beyond this is insight when we rest in non-conceptual attention. What becomes observable is richer and more interesting when insights arise. Releasing makes possibilities available.

What we sense in others may not calculate or reference the love we understand or invoke. The emerging possibilities that unfold from what appears from the mystery begin without expectations or anticipation.

Train your organs of perception, and you will lead with balanced intelligence, beginning with "learning to see," a key capacity to build upon seeing what is going on, concept-free. It is a prerequisite for helping because without this capacity you cannot access your wisdom.

Releasing is the activator for seeing new things. You let go and let come. A metaphor is taken from the camping world, "Pack less, and you'll encounter much more." As assumptions and generalizations you hold onto stay in check, the light enters, and insights enter. In fact, your way of being shapes reality ---the nature of the self; and the nature of the world shifts with it. The inner place from which you perceive things changes what you see in that it emerges according to the inner place from which you attend.

It is the ignorance of our own ignorance that reduces the world only to what we know. We fail to be comfortable with our ignorance and allow our wisdom to enter. We constantly start with what we already know, and this limits our capacity to gather greater comprehension levels of intelligence.

What we already know, expect, and anticipate is the basis of the ego, to make sense of a world that is predictable. To resist the corrupting influence of what we know (personality, pre-existing knowledge), we learn to see concept-free. We train our listening to receive by considering all others as a fully legitimate other. The more we know, the less we love. The less we are certain, the more we depend on our organs of perception to learn as we go along. We take everything out of the bag we drag behind us to get free for what is new.

Think of what I'm describing like an enlightened pilgrim in the ruins. Love is like a burnt match in a urinal. The secret of your life and mine is that we are responsible for the way the world is and the way it ought to be. Knowing the ruins for what they are among family and friends as well as in the wider communities of our lives, locally and globally, we decide that we are responsible for history – for love's sake.

Creating is both about the end-goal and the journey getting there. But all of this starts by seeing from what is upstream before a creation comes forth. As the leader deepens her understanding and sees the playing field with full comprehension, she finds herself by bending the beam from the subject matter back to herself. As this connection arises, a future self is awakened to perform works not by decision, but by what cannot not become itself. It must be because it's what one is born to do, like shining in the fullness of their potential.

Creating something that's loved first involves sustaining the contradiction of getting to the end goal and experiencing the quality of what appears now to ignite the creative habit. Starting separate from what you know, natural bravery and courage to learn and adapt come online by gathering "how" by "doing." The only way to how is through YES. You start with the "what," act from that place of not knowing, and as you go the capacity-building arises from figuring out how to create outcomes through reflection and strategic adjustments.

When we focus on just getting to the goal, we diminish the quality of being in the doing (getting the job done). What it is to be with the body, and with the social body, and to get underneath it all---not conceptual frameworks, but available wisdom ready to enter.

We're "feeling under the surface" as we experience reflection in conversation, the water is still despite the turbulence on the top. There is a bigger canvassing space of enormous energy and creativity like a system we hold within and around all things. What it means to be whole it is how all of us experience ourselves and the other in a social body. Creating and relating are essential to this by syncing the open mind and open heart. In other words — to pay attention while deepening connection stages the origins of quality of intention from a greater field of movement. The skill base is to feel the body (I, me) in conjunction with the greater social body (I and them = we).

Our faithfulness is obeying the design elements of this field of space and holding it for emerging information. Ambiguity teaches us the integrity to sustain it long enough to reveal what's there. We feel it without a label or a name. Then surrendering to what is moving there and vocalizing its formative influence. You let your attention rest on the body moving, then get still to connect the body-mind in unison. Sense the parts moving and the part that is still as these points of reference harmonize. You notice the moment to moment to moment unfolding of the feeling. It is not the same this moment to the next. If you get distracted by thinking, return your attention to the feeling of the social body ---both stillness and moving dynamics.

We relate as we are relatable. We create as we are creatable. We enter the world just as the world changes us. Feelings of reverence, respect, deep intention and service arise naturally from deep immersion into what is going on. Remembering that the universe is a helpful, friendly place can make life your teacher. And when you take life itself in this way, your collaboration with life is to integrate everything with welcome arms. All is good and essential, significant, and what is needed right now. We tap into this collaborative relationship by unlearning and releasing what we know. We are tapped by what's there and experience the rapture of the soul's nature to legitimize what would normally be hidden by habituated thought.

An active inner life orients us to respond to life's impressions. Our experience depends on the inner lives we have developed. We can sense the eternal language of world spirit as the means to inspiring our work into creating. We learn to not give ourselves up to our concerns. We should allow what the outer world has told us to linger on in quiet stillness. Stillness is the altar of the spirit. New mysteries disclosed combined with fresh eyes make the world different than before. Every decision is only a guess with faith to learn by action. Then we allow the experience to reveal something to us by letting it linger on within us. We must dwell on impressions and let the feeling quietly echo within us. No perceptions, expectations, interpretation is necessary. What is arising is given in the place between things.

Seeing is formed out of unanimated content. It is like the sense we feel when watching the sunrise.

In the back of this book, please see an InTen checklist of practices you can do to enhance your quality of being.

CHAPTER 3

RELATING

"Love is the Fundamental Organizing Principle of Selling"

There can be true collaboration in an atmosphere of competition where constituents share information with immutable dependence. Everyone becomes bigger better faster stronger instead of turf wars for market leadership. It is the age of competitive collaborators, not rugged individualism.

There is a higher necessity for self-care—energy, health, sleep, needs that must be met, and yet the "we" part is in combination with the "I" part. Our world of selling is moving from an "ego-system" to an "ecosystem." Essentially, we are becoming "Mwe's" Me + We = whole. One eye is on us, and one eye is on the other. Together we balance an inbound and outbound flow of energy and information that makes us better people. We realize that none of our true properties are actualized unless we relate in geniune ways with others. Relationship is the organizing force of bringing you fully into a greater sense of participation in the world. A small sense of self would be ME.

A greater sense of self with a "Capital S" is the one that is emerging. The communing between the current and future self is the path of leadership because the future self is a leaders' biggest weapon to create change. What one knows about the world helps him see where to participate in it with a sense of service and a cause for involvement through his capacity to connect with defining features existing in his periphery. This way the leader can expand sources where greater goodness is ready to prevail, from collective to individual energy integrating inward and outward aspects as design elements for directionality. Again, your true properties (beauty, strengths, genius, and authenticity) originate within the creative order brought forth by the fundamental patterns of relating with others. The world brings you fully into being when you stand in it with an open mind and heart that is available, with courage and willingness.

You look at where you are and then open up to the experience fully. It sounds so simple, and yet it isn't. Looking at where you may require you staying long enough to see the playing field; and second, opening to the experience is a process of personal cultivation to push away nothing, and welcome anything. One teacher Ward Mailliard calls it, "harnessing surprise." You bring curiosity and open-heartedness by leaning into the moment as if everything is significant, unreduced, and free to be as it is. You learn how to "meet" what's there even if it's unlikable, uncomfortable; you still get up-close and intimate even beyond what you can tolerate. What you begin to see is an amazing power, you evoke a certain spirit within you to remain present with courage in showing up.

The intelligence level at this level of engagement supports Einstein's claim that love is the greatest source of intelligence in the universe. Turning in the direction to meet wisdom ready to be expressed is inheriting the invisible wholeness ready to find you in the mystery of the moment. The mystery is the true gift of hope that mystery holds. If we accept what the universe must teach us, we open ourselves to transcending our history.

CHASING TO CREATING

Too often our primary motivation is chasing something because of our sense of being chased. We run from the boogeyman, our self-critic, our need to exercise power in some way, our fear of failure, humiliation, and death. Whatever we attempt to get rid of, we run and run but later find that we're running in place, and fail to reach anywhere significant. We work so hard to prove something to ourselves that we aren't inadequate or hide from our shame by jumping out of life, pumping ourselves with substance to pretend, but again, tread water. We chase happiness and the more we do, the less happy we are. Monitoring how unhappy we are and comparing ourselves to a happiness ideal reinforces our depression and despair. Who but a person who pursues happiness, is not? Instead, we can expand happiness instead of look into the future for it. We predict futures with optimism to survive, and yet we create a future. Predictions aren't real, they are fictitious, virtual realities that help us remain sane.

Then one day, you stop. You look around at the intersection you find yourself in. You look back at where you've been. You see the era of chasing as an era, like waking up from a trance or dream, or sleep-walking. You see what you had been chased by. Most likely these were active agents in thoughts that drove you to getting here, at the intersection. Are you thinking of the ending of the film Cast Away with Tom Hanks? Remember he brings the experience to this point. All the pieces are ready to self-organize. His direction wasn't a decision; life pointed him there, it was obvious. He couldn't NOT follow that impulse and timing to have the opportunity to be at that nexus in that moment. The web of life somehow moved the pieces in place (with a FedEx package) to follow its flow toward his new love.

Suddenly there's a gateway in front of you---choice! You gather yourself with other material that organizes your way forward. You consider what matters most from what you have and what you want most. You originate from a new place – from inside and outside. You consider what the world is presenting to you right now, like fresh air, then reel in what your community was wanting for you most, then imbue experiences that arouse your heart and ignite your creative fire. These are design elements from which you compose a sense of direction and "can't not do" spirit from something to come into existence, from the generative love you feel for it. Then a collective dream starts to burn bright from inside your heart. You sense something that deeply matters that you must do, it's been obvious and needs you turning in the direction of its invitation. You heed the call and surrender to what life is asking you to do from here, like animating from an electric field of power flowing to and from inner and outer domains.

Reflecting on these defining features lights the flame for a new path to take and investing your life spirit without compromise. You find a new spiritual law of economics---that creating what matters to you is a choice. And to be the predominant creative force in your life begins with what you want to create. Your hope depends on the expansion of bringing yourself closer to life and using it in combination with your intention. Your connections with others and the world bring the inner and outer world into one integrated design – Your path!

MARKET LEADERS

Market leadership is gained by who's *giving* the most, not by who's *taking* the most. Market leadership is gained by who cares the most, who listens the most, who understand the most and therefore can become the most essential. These qualities make you naturally remarkable, and this gives you reach that a commodity could not. The true work of a business is to love their clients, love their employees, and love their partners. This implies to exclude nothing and welcome every part of what is there. This approach makes the total sum of all behavior during the value chain define "marketing." *A brand is all behavior that a business does, and driven by the reasons for doing it.*

Competitive collaboration gains market leadership. Sharing information across lines is about everyone getting better in a market place. Sharing mistakes, experiences, and journeys bring everyone to a level of greater ability. "Green" has invited a biased buyer to corporate social citizenship. The reason for this is the business's green practice paints a compelling reason and story for buyers to favor givers who are socially responsible and considerate. Buyers are flocking to companies who're giving back. By supporting this aim, consumers become creators, and sellers become citizens of serving others with capabilities that enhance others, not interfere with their creative process.

There is hidden, untapped potential that is far greater and far bigger than you've probably yet experienced. The implication is not that you are larger, better, dominant, more masterful, but it is saying that you can personally master the creative process of real value created for others and the world. You are sitting on a potential that begins right here and now with your levels of awareness. And the more quality that awareness becomes, the greater capacity you possess to helping others in meaningful and rewarding ways intrinsically and extrinsically. It is an invitation to be great and to do something bigger than yourself that I hunger to arouse inside you. I want to awaken a creative bonfire in you that raises the standard of what you can do in the world by participating in your profession in ways that make differences you cannot yet fathom. Every conversation you have is one that can and will liberate people and will not violate their humanity.

CONNECTION OVER CONTENT

This restoring of our humanity is about connecting with the other person, in their conversation with life, with their best future, and to the whole, and it inspires a natural pattern of creative order from which a sale is made. No helping process - at least not yet - has called forth the balance of intelligence you're about to encounter in your work. This balance of head, heart, and hand is where your best self and truest work comes into play. You can transform the suffering of others by having a larger role than ever in the past. I call this "being a force of nature." The depth of understanding and listening involved is where this shift of mind begins. I am called upon to bring you close to this. It is in me to make this invitation as it is in you to support this approach.

Your biggest question is "*How can I create an atmosphere of intimacy and trust with others from which intelligence, discernment, and the capacity to see new things can become possible through cooperation and connection?*" The conversation and the quality of it is itself the goal. The product, the service, the buyer's need, the seller's offering is just a masquerade for conversation, yet being together is the key to descending into conversation is tantamount. Conversations are living, breathing frontiers of possibilities awaiting to emerge. When courage and vulnerability build trust, you notice that the atmosphere is something unifying, cross-cultural, and social much like a field of great potential. Unblocking reception together leads to a change of world. Responsibility and new desire emerge from reflection and collective inquiry, to inform decisions.

You can be an active agent in creating this field of potential by taking steps that cultivate trust. And within the building of this collective intelligence is meeting the future by faith. Your faith is in the connection that fosters trust, legitimacy, and acceptance of the other. This is the foundation for creating any content. Content is the product, service, or help that brings real value. You learn to please the customer by understanding them, before taking the approach. You sculpt the customer experience by innovating at the speed from which the collective is brewing content. The automobile maker "Local Motors" designs their vehicles in collaboration with the maker instinct of the customer as creator. They are experiment-centric, instead of factory-centric, which means they build markets as the means to take a prototype to full bloom. The best focus group is the fundamental relationship with the actual buyer.

In a fundamental relationship, the social field becomes the place which organizes action. First, you enter someone's world by leaning into and listening wide open, you enter a matrix of relationships in which the buyer exists. You suspend your certainty and move to curiosity as if you're maintaining your inexperience bringing a fresh mind to the forefront. Everything around you and the other brings you both into the way they do things. Each of us exists within a network of relationships that define our current properties. Our history is etched by our desires. Whatever you desired before is mirrored by the past. When you change desire to create something that matters now, you change your history. What matters to you is the most important thing to reflect upon. When others you influence have a shift of heart like this, and change their desires, their way of experiencing things forward shifts. It is the new patterns of desire and behavior that ensue and arise in these relationships that give rise to how we co-exist and come to understanding something new. As you encounter another human being's state, a movement of flow imbues basic goodness from interactions within this network, like a ping-pong effect. Flow patterns of energy and information come into a certain pattern of creative order from which you embody. You toggle back and forth from your intent to sensing the social field as it desires something within you to come forth. Gathering and giving volley as the field changes you to come into a higher quality of expression in service.

There is a story in motion; a context in motion as defining features that bring the individual into a current world in which they exist and attend. Their human process of development is never independent of this level of relating. Independence would negate the full picture. Each of us is interdependent; but our lives are independent in designing our niche. Our niches are defining features of ourselves that come to light through the interactions with others. If someone has a unique ability or personal gift it is not definable without the participation of other human beings in witnessing it and catching it. No one is independent of this web of influence. Each of us is born of the eco-system from which we exist like a constant narrative. You must see other's current reality structurally, not situationally.

When I first got on the phone with Jerry, he asked me to explain how my service works. I told him I was prepared to answer that, however first, I wanted to know what he wanted to create most in his life and business. I looked at my timer on my computer screen, and twenty-nine minutes past, and he was still talking about his aspirations and dream. At minute thirty he stopped, and told me that my coaching program sounded great, and asked if he could get started right away. I told him nothing about what I offer, yet all Jerry wanted to know was that it was about him. And that made all the difference. He signed up. When he told me he was a recovering addict after 7 years of hell, his vision was a key piece for him to create an alternative future. He broke down and became emotional as I sound-boarded what I was beginning to picture when he expressed his future self.

When you see others (like Jerry) structurally, you see patterns, shapes, geometry, and the story that they're coming from and living towards. You place yourself in a moment in time in which the living being is living as an open circuit. The medium of this ecosystem realizes life. It is a fact that people are governed primarily by the existing structures and patterns between things that give rise to how they behave. Newton's third law is "pairs create form." The cause and effect which comes forth depends on the interplay between the parts. If you miss this, you will not have an intelligent picture of what is going on, and what can become possible for them, with your help. The social field is a living breathing frontier of not-yet embodied information informing your listening with quality in action, attention, and communication.

Operating from the integrated state of the social field and contouring with emergence is a skill. Sales becomes *social meditation*, with the capacity to turn disruptive changes and new information into constructive elements. Your diligence seeking helpful questions for more information, clarity, and implications help you to form a picture that captures the underlying structures giving rise to the current state the person is in. This way of seeing things is far more oriental than occidental as a view of things. Most of the individuals you probably influence will not be familiar with this way of sense-making of things. I call this ability "symphony" to pull together the whole view, the story, and the narrative to discern the current reality. Picture a symphony conductor that operates as a vessel capturing and channeling the larger whole of the space, the orchestra, and the sound-current, as she brings forth a quality of expression as she's changed by the field opening itself through her conducting. A violinist once said, "often I play from the macro violin when I play from the entire space—the frequency in the room, the audience, and all that is quelling as if it is asking for something in my playing."

You create a space such that the other person can trust they're entering into liberating conversations that help see the larger systems in which they are enacting. The movements are invisible, much like an iceberg influenced from down below, all we see are surface issues and symptoms. If you are an honest, loving being who will not betray them, and who listens, it can cultivate the capacity to listen to you. People don't care what you know until they know you care. And if they feel listened to, they can participate in this discernment I'm describing.

Transparency is your most important way to visibility. Visibility is very powerful, and when you understand something on a new level, something different becomes possible. You shift the conversation to one of direction, especially when people you help see things they didn't see before. Their habitual thinking and modeling may have discerned cause and effort from their past frameworks instead of through you discerning what the current results they're experiencing are happening, and how they're an active agent in creating unwanted consequences.

Fundamental trust becomes the catalyst for moving toward positive change. Your role is one of confronting the other's freedom to engage by consent. Power is given to then choose an alternative future, alternative life, with legitimacy and acceptance, not manipulation and force. A butterfly transforms via an innate trust that metamorphosis is safe. A buyer you see as a loving, creative, good human being will emerge with greater engagement via your conserving acceptance and legitimacy. You're free from theories and categorizing, which have no you're your knowing of them living in this moment as a legitimate human being regardless of conditions gives rise to liberating conversation. It is not parenting; it is true partnering with respect, not control.

Your truest work is creating an atmosphere of trust. You trust others are intelligent, want to do things well, and want to succeed. They are doing their very very best despite at times falling short. Coming together in positive regard gives rise to a release of new energy that has the potential for enormous value and helping. Whatever the person is living in that moment is valid. You don't need a theory to express love by creating value for the other that you care about. Love doesn't arise from the theory; it arises from the present moment. You center yourself in the experience with the buyer that you're having together, explaining things together, and using your experience to discern needs..

You go out into the marketplace, and you develop new and current customers. But what do you bring with you? You don't bring a presentation, that's not a conversation! You don't bring the answers, because you haven't understood the buyer's situation. You don't bring your script because you wouldn't be able to listen. The seller goes out into the marketplace and courageously places himself into possibilities to be helpful and resourceful. His serving of the other is animated by what has heart and meaning for her.

This means giving buyers something they cannot do by themselves— access to new capabilities, opportunities, and new sources of confidence by being more of yourself. You might call it bringing your own original medicine to the assistance of the other. This presupposes that the seller leaves everything at home to give real help to the buyer. It makes you think how much unnecessary help happens without justification. Product knowledge is overrated. In fact, it just makes communication unilateral.

This "showing up" piece for the seller becomes a key piece to the conversation leading to value creation and innovation by humble inquiry. He shows up to a transformative conversation ready to unfold by following his curiosity and asking intuitive questions. And all he has before him is just this---a transformative conversation. All value creation, all business, all commerce is a series of transformative conversations that compose a living system called a business. What gives rise to a transformative conversation is what this book is about.

You might ask, "Can you give me practical steps, a template?" Remember that human connection isn't possible if we're machine-like. Automation is an emotional death sentence. The passage to liberate the buyer is born from the quality of connection you can establish. This isn't mechanical; it is born from your openness. It begins with your quality of action, and more specifically your way of being. There is no template or right answers, best practice, to mastery. If you're looking to compete, you've lost what I'm saying. This is about showing up—being there—listening---jumping into what is real for the other person, real for you emerging from within, and leaning into where goodness is ready to expand. Your quality of awareness is the single biggest leverage point for opening the aperture for this level of interaction.

My father taught me chess, and I learned that no chess game is the same. Likewise, no conversation is the same, it is a living breathing adapting frontier with a certain creative order that you learn and build upon by starting out.

Admiring your buyers is perhaps the greatest way for you to gain their trust. When you admire them, you see them as amazing beings, loaded with great potential, love, capability, much like a beautiful song that you are helping them to bring forth. You seeing the buyer as such is the key to shifting the atmosphere of trust which is fundamental to any change. You cannot make decisions for them, but given that you see their inner potential for doing great things, you invite them toward just that. Is there anything more amazingly rewarding than moving another person's life to be all they are, create all they have in them, and realize all their dreams and the dreams that depend on their creativity, and livelihood? Just pause for a moment and pinch yourself silly until you get just how many other lives you touch by treating others with this kind of loving respect.

A "Shaman" in the indigenous world is the one with big medicine. The shaman is the one who bridges the spirit world to the material world. They bring wisdom to the ordinary. A sales shaman is one who bridges the current situation to a new directional hope. A sales shaman is one who bridges challenges and worries to new levels of confidence. New frontiers in society become closely linked to the interior condition of the salesperson, such that every intervention, every conversation is a crucial unit for composing a new wholeness worldwide. This dynamic will be greater in proportion to human evolution as we know it than the World Wide Web thus far. A sales shaman is one who bridges opportunities and strengths to creativity and capability. Bridge-building is the work of the Sales Shaman. Perhaps the most important bridge of all is the one between the future possibilities awaiting who they help, and the unique talents and divine abilities activated by the call to help. Something stands in need of each of us, a purpose or destiny which is waiting to surface. To answer its call is to listen from such a place that your innermost knowing is whispering what wants to emerge, and you step into with great conviction, commitment, and open-hearted bravery.

According to Chinese wisdom 2500 years ago, the ancients who wished to illustrate illustrious virtue throughout the world:

1 First ordered well their own states.

2 Wishing to order well their States, they first harmonized their families.

3 Wishing to harmonize their families, they first cultivated their persons.

4 Wishing to cultivate their persons, they first rectified their hearts.

5 Wishing to rectify their hearts, they first sought to be sincere in their thoughts.

6 Wishing to be sincere in their thoughts, they first extended to the utmost their awareness.

7 Such extension of awareness lay in the investigation of the underlying matrix of mind and matter.

8 The underlying matrix of mind and matter being investigated, awareness becomes complete.

9 Awareness being complete, thoughts then become sincere.

10 Thoughts being sincere, hearts then become rectified.

11 Hearts being rectified, persons then become cultivated.

12 Persons being cultivated, families then become harmonized.

13 Families being harmonized, states then become rightly governed.

It starts with a shift of awareness, from which sincere thoughts and a rectified heart open a new path for systemic change. If you focus on making the buck, you may trick a few prospects into buying what you have, but it won't last. When you're mechanical and money-focused in your efforts, people can smell it a mile away. The suckers will fall for it, but not the majority. Conversely, when you come from the soulful desire to create value for another, your quality of expression is animated by sincere care and service. When you listen and discover where value can be created, you can let go of money worries, because it'll flow into you never like before. Peter Drucker said, *"The oxygen of business is profit, but if one thinks breathing is what winning the game is about, they're truly lost."* Profits, opportunities, positive word of mouth remarks are earned first by creating true value for someone else, without entitlements. Profit is a holistic figure measured over large swaths of time to measure how much value was perceived by the beholder, the customer. Value creation starts with *quality of being*. It is not a process; it is a place to enter from as all situations are approached like a lighthouse lookout that's always scanning for ways to engage.

In the Buddhist traditions, this quality of your being is called "Maitri" meaning "loving kindness." In the Hindu traditions, this quality is called "Seva" or "the genuine urge to serve." "Karuna" in Buddhism is compassion. It is the urge to make others suffer less. When you connect with these energies within you, something almost magical emerges. You awaken a light within you. The interior condition of you changes the quality of your interaction.

This light is seeing the divinity in oneself. "Namaste" means "I see the divinity in you." "Simran" means "here I am" in Hindu. The original meaning is a Punjabi word derived from the Sanskrit word *smarana*, "the act of remembrance, reminiscence, recollection," which leads to the realization of that which is of the highest aspect and purpose in one's life. It is the continuous remembrance of the finest aspect of the self or the continuous remembrance (or feeling) of God, thus used for introducing spirituality. This state is maintained continuously while carrying out the worldly works outside. *Simran* is commonly used to refer to the ultimate feeling of Ultimate. This place within you, within others, holds the gift that belongs to the world, and if trusted, learning to be more ourselves is how we relate with one another to grant allowance to this natural drift. Learning how to be you is a great curriculum.

How can sincere generosity and helpfulness exist without Simran? How can the community be without Simran? All serving energy begins with the recognition of what is in you to give. In Tibetan "Tashi Delek" is to wish another well. "May all auspicious signs come to this environment". This wish arises from your ground of being; your deepest source from which you seek the betterment of all things. It is love. It is a quality of desire which is "of the king" (de sire).

"Tat Tvam Asi" in Sanskrit means "I am that, too". That thou art, this means that you accept others as legitimate others. I see you, therefore you are seen, as you see me, I am brought into being seen. A tribe in Africa greets others saying "Sawa Bono" which is to say "I see you" and the response in return is to say, "Thank you, I am seen." When the factories in Lagos took in indigenous workers, walking through the hallways people would walk by without saying a word. To these people this is to say, "you do not exist, you are not seen." Being seen is a profound dynamic, because we each come into being by the orientation of other things around us. We are each made whole by the space in which we are brought whole.

You owe the world your happiness. When you are connected to what has heart and meaning, and to being in true service to another, and remaining comfortable with your own ignorance, you touch happiness. Once you get this is the game of life, you will never go backward; and never will you lower your standard to bring forth anything less than this. The other; the world; the environment; the world can change you. At times, there is a divide between your current self and future self that short-circuits this permeation of your being. Your voice of judgment neutralizes this bridge when you believe your certainties too much. You are overconfident in what you know. You don't maintain your inexperience enough. And you don't listen.

People buy people. Nothing moves on the planet until someone is emotional about something. When you connect with wiser care of yourself for all things, you are more mindful in your intention and attention. I came across this Thomas Merton poem. I love what it says about the source of your effort, and how if it's about value for others, the relationships become the most important thing:

> *"Do not depend on the hope of results. You may have to face the fact that your work will be worthless and even achieve no result at all, if not perhaps results opposite to what you expect. As you get used to this idea, you start more and more to*

concentrate not on the results, but on the value, the rightness, the truth of the work itself. You gradually struggle less and less for an idea and more and more for specific people. In the end, it is the reality of a personal relationship that saves everything."

As I see it, *Seva* is to serve the other in the natural way of offering one's best self. The energy (will to live) makes a difference when it matters most. According to a law of Spiritual Economics: E = Dm. Energy (the will to live) = that which makes a difference multiplied by what matters. Mahatma Gandhi said that "Service to Man is Service to God. (*Nar Seva, Narayan Seva*)." It is an inside-out approach to living. One definition of *Seva* is: "Service which is given without consideration of anything in return, at the right place and time to one that is qualified, with the feeling that it is one's duty, is regarded as the nature of goodness." — *Bhagavad Gita 17.20*

If you ask your clients why they buy from you, it is not because of your product or service. It is because you have a personal gift they see and remain loyal to you because of it. You trust this gift to *Simran* and *Seva* practices. *Simran* is the place within you that gives your life when illuminated, while *Seva* is to serve others for the joy of it. When these two come together, you align with soul service. You serve in honor of the *Simran*; the gift you see in each other.

The dynamic suggests that something you represent; something you bring forth connects them to you in ways that trust your basic goodness to help. This ability is factory-made, inherent with you, and is the service you have ready in your soul to give others. It is touched when you give value to others for the joy of it with mastery level skill.

The word "genius" means "genie in us" or "magic in us." First, you must see this life-giving ability in yourself and know it. It is the groundwater beneath all that you do, and the magnet from which all your relationships begin, build, flourish, and remain.

Many of us are trying to run away from ourselves, but each of us has a genius inside of us which is conserved, to win the game of life. If we come home to ourselves, we assume we will suffer. Our quest for mastery, competitiveness, and individuality (to be special) has moved us away from the quality of relationship that brings our best expression to the surface of who we are. We hide behind fears of humiliation; that we are not enough and keep our wounds and flaws from the world as if to impress others with a costume to manipulate them. Instead of these wounds being what makes us equal to others in vulnerable ways that foster connectedness, our artificial selves are worn by material things that we fear we'll lose credibility if absent. We seek to build impressive lifestyles instead of fulfilling lives.

You must know that you carry so much music in you to be played. And as your guide, author, and coach, I'll do anything to melt any barrier that does not liberate you, bring you alive, to live a life of difference and contribution. Matt, a sales producer, earning $250k per year said that of all the tasks in his life that gave him joy and the most satisfaction was his helping the athletes in the Special Olympics. After scanning every experience for meaning and energy, this one was tantamount. It pointed him to our law of spiritual economics $E = Dm$. Matt's energy is a function of what makes a difference times what matters to him. For Matt this model is fundamental to evoking his personal energy and enthusiasm for life. Cherishing moments like these for Matt remind him to keep death close at hand because life is precarious.

The brevity of life motivates you to a new level of seriousness about how you choose to spend the time that's life---on what, with who, and how? You're not immortal. Come to terms with this truth. The sense of urgency I intend to raise is to realize you can't get to everything, but you can organize your attention on the things that matter to you most. I'm asking you to consider the bigger questions you must ask yourself: What animates me or calls me right now? What do I seek to focus this precious of life toward accomplishing? The way you see the world around you, take it in, and influence from this will defines your place to take in the ecosystem of life (the whole). How you see, and what you see and notice houses your authentic self.

I look at selling as a *transformative conversation* from which something ready to begin is animating itself through the words. That's me relating to my own experience authentically. To this, I find my way into the process, and this is the narrative from which my coaching is revealed, learned, and delivered.

Reflection is to step into a moment and check something out---take it in, receive its significance---how it lines up with who you are, where you're going and what the true nature of your *work* entails? This work is a capital "W" Work because it is not a job or career, but a cause for greatness your self-knowledge uses to enlightens the path. "Follow your Dharma" as they say in the Buddhist tradition. Surrendering to this energy is to foster the way of what has heart and meaning for you and trust it with conviction. Author Peter Senge refers to it as "your domain of self-efficacy", analogous to a circle, and you operate within that space with your decisions, actions, and communications as the primary source from which you seed your life building process.

Consciousness is measured by how you use your experiences and more especially what is conserved. You identify with your experiences based on your level of awareness. If you attend from your heart, and love, from wisdom, and humanness, then you conserve legitimacy and acceptance, with respect for others' differences. If you conserve power and domination, then others are competitive sources of comparison to seek status or impunity.

How do you integrate your experiences? You can bring a higher quality of attention to this, yet too often clutter and distractions ambush your attention spans by puny stuff. Email, messaging, texting, social media all have us on the hook to devote our attention to this, rather than reflection and revelation. You must be your own bouncer; be the "stuff police" to enforce yourself to control these tendencies. Otherwise, your attention is so taken that you lose your full capacity to operate intelligently. Controlling your levels of reactionary tasks and to-dos are essential to taking inspiration with perspective and building towards a strategic direction. Thinking and operating strategic is knowing what matters most, having a clear sense of where you are in relationship to this, and having a next step to bring you toward the outcomes desired.

I heard a CEO recently state that "hard work cannot substitute intelligence." Interestingly, this remark was delivered after a heart attack that nearly took his life away. Finding your place of rest in the middle of chaos is a necessity; in fact, it is the way to change the way things to come play out. He also said that today, his creative process was "listening his way to creating the desired result." He was referring to using his attention control to learn as the future emerges. In other words, explore the future by acting on it in creative ways until the conceptual vision desiring itself to come to life becomes fully clear.

Ambiguity, volatility, uncertainty, and complexity are all fearless invitations into unfolding a future by experiencing it as we go. The future is happening every second we breathe into it. Context is always in motion. What we learn in flux is that we're making the future up as we go along, there are no experts. We can't predict a future; *we can only create one*. We make something real by describing what it is. In effect, we name the world we see into reality, just as the ancient ones would do around the campfire telling real stories becoming present. Changing language to describe what is going on makes for an alternative future possibility.

Defining context in the world today yields new aspiration that we use to harness and define features that motivate and imbue leadership. Today we're consuming 1.5 Earths. Three people are killing themselves to one dying at the hands of another. These defining features in our life building process shape our orientation, life spirit, and course of action, if we listen, and listen from the stillness. The still space in our life speaks through meaningful action, service, mystery, and context, the hurry in our life deafens these essential feeds, cutting the world off from the gift in each of us that belongs to the whole. When you're tired and overworked, the world cannot see you.

Let's boil all this down to the super simple lesson: it's about character, in that the way you sell is far more important than what you sell. Your manner of influencing others comes forth according to where you're coming from inside. Your way of being is a prequel to your setting a direction and creating the desired outcome. A priori knowledge, in Western philosophy, has been studied since the time of Immanuel Kant. A priori knowledge is independent of all particular experiences, as opposed to a posteriori knowledge, which derives from experience in itself. Posteriori is to essentially know by doing, show up, and know what to do. Trusting your own nature and seeing life as whole brings forth this stance in service to what is about to begin. All expectations are suspended as if any knowing is doing, and any doing is knowing.

If the spirit behind what you're selling is to win the sale, you'll position yourself to take the sale, a priori. If your heart is helping people with a sincere interest in adding value to them and their situation, you'll position it that way. The key here is that you have a way to compare what comes before selling. This is an intention you can conserve—to suspend all pre-existing knowledge and listen from the here and now. As you offer your attention this way you stay in tune with what is really going on, meeting the moment just it is now. Soul service is accessed naturally and effortless as you begin this way.

As you become aware of this aspect, you begin to see range and fluency in toggling between different levels of awareness, from yourself, to other, to the whole in a web of life that is not fixed, but rather, random and present, like a living breathing frontier of possibilities. Basic social goodness isn't an enemy to profit, even though the purpose of many businesses today is shareholder equity. Goodness is the means to great work with a sense of embodied purpose, with profits being the oxygen for a business to stay alive, paves the runway for this purpose to come to the fullest. Natural resources are human resources, and you can't measure spirit. *The business with the greatest spiritual punch behind their work is mostly built to outlast the alternative.*

REAL LOVE

Why do people believe doing what you love to do is a luxury? Tell this to George Lucas or Babe Ruth. Tell that to Steve Jobs or Juan Gabriel. Loving what they do is essential, not optional. They could not NOT do what they love to do because it was their DNA talking to them. A lot of things give you pleasure, but that type of passion is self-serving. Another character of passion is other-serving, as the joy of doing what others stand in need of you giving them.

George Lucas loved making movies and didn't know how to do anything but this. Juan Gabriel, the famous singer no longer living, wrote 1,800 Latin American music songs after his difficult backstory of loss and suffering all his adolescent life. He could not not sing what he was experiencing. Steve Jobs chose to put a dent in the universe by helping people take delivery of technology in their lives to depend on it for essential living requirements eventually.

Babe Ruth embodied baseball. When you watched the film "Field of Dreams" you knew what embodiment meant when Shoeless Joe Jackson said why they play---for the love of the game, the smell of the grass, and the fun of playing.

What you invest your life spirit in isn't anything out there. It is a future that is already there, you open your eyes to see, sense, and step into it willingly with courage. It is your place to take in the ecosystem of life. It is the pleasure you retrieve from a certain activity you do. And the joy hits you when others to whom you offer your work gain value and enrichment from it. When Lucas made his films, both pleasure and joy combined to define what made him happy. That which makes a difference multiplied by what matters most is equal to life-giving energy and happiness.

The Holy Grail doesn't deliver its sky-opening purpose to you through thunderbolts. If you look backward, you'll see themes that have canvassed your life building process and story all along. You'll see what had heart, meaning, energy, and inspiration. You'll see what astonished and fascinated you.

One activity probably had these qualities in common. And it is this one activity that motivates you for a life that could be the center of gravity from which you reach into investing your life spirit without compromise. The real love is the activity that brings you home to the love that made you.

Enthusiasm is a great work because it means "life activity principle within you." En-theo = God within. When you encounter this activity, you can choose what to do with it. You determine where to put it. If it is a current source for why others relate with you, then you're already operating within this domain. The key is not to fowl out of it. Don't take the invitation to leave the lanes of this pathway. Trust it like a pilot trust their instruments while flying in the night or bad weather. This authentic self is made of a larger, grander will than your puny will.

Your relationship with this will is your relationship with the whole. To claim it means to sense where goodness is ready to expand and stay in coordination with it by trusting it. Leadership is the process of trusting an uncertain future possibility that stands waiting for you to come into being. It is to take meaningful leaps into uncertainty with alacrity, courage, and openness.

I remember ten years ago my wife and I watching Prem Rawat in awe, the Indian inspirational speaker on finding peace in oneself. As he paused between sentences in front of a concert hall of 10,000 people, we both felt sucked into his presence. You could feel in the bottom of your being where he was operating. He wasn't attempting to tell us what to do, or have all the answers, or call importance to himself, or position his dominance and mastery. He was speaking from the entire space (the room, the crowd, the ambience, the grand array) around him as if the universe brought its creative surges into him as a channel to the people. He was surprised by the words that found him in the moment of speaking them as if revealed each word as a piece of the whole. His alacrity to dive into the subject was like adding water to expand a coil into a full length.

Prem's gift is obvious: *to have micro and macro conversations*. He could connect with one person like the entire room and connect with the entire room as if we're one person. The intimacy was fantastic. The word *intimacy* is "in to me see." To see into Prem's face is comforting, calming, and inspiring with a sense of high hopes for the gift of our very own life. He looks out at the people listening as if he was the student, sensing, and pre-sensing emerging teachings coming to him just at that moment. His light-hearted manner of poking fun at humanness makes you feel safe to let it all hang out, show up as a whole person without preoccupations, with flaws. He has nothing to hide, only openness and compassionate transparency through which the crowd is ready for something to be given. As I write these words to you, I'm aware of my own database, and yet able to trust these words are the right ones because I'm writing as I listen and draw them forth into my fingers and type them here to you.

TO LOVE IS TO SEE

Seeing is quite a phenomenon. What do you see? And what do you not see? These are fundamental questions. Competency is greater than any advertising. The inside reality is greater in capacity to attracting opportunities, compared to outside impressions. Buyers are aware of suspicious pushy interruptive ads they don't care about, nor find relevant to them. The key is in seeing what is going on in their world and creating a conversation relative to this. To do this, you must *see your own seeing.* Seeing your own seeing requires that you separate from the thoughts in your head. What you see is often what you habitually leap to assume, as if you were projecting slides on the wall believing it's all real. At best, we see the tips of our noses, not what is going on. We minimize, exaggerate and edit ourselves and life by seeing what is consistent with our lens. Listening from preconceptions and interpretations is called "downloading" as Otto Scharmer puts it.

When you see from a place beyond the past, by decoupling from what you expect to see, you see something different than what is familiar. You see new aspects of reality that your outdated thinking causes you

100

to miss. You'll find that in conversations you probably move from downloading to seeing instantly. You'll hear information that you'll suddenly convince yourself you understand because it seems consistent with what you expect to see. You've probably experienced this in informal conversations when you separate from your interpretations of things and take in the world directly. Then you find yourself not just listening to the words, but the person saying them, as you're behind their words experiencing what they see, hear, and feel outside the boundaries of the familiar. This place that you access is where you can accept the other as a legitimate other. It is accessing your open heart to let the other be just as they are without changing them to accommodate your ways. I call this capacity to "let."

Letting the other be the legitimate other nurtures an atmosphere of safety and trust, such that the conversation can deepen into what I call a living truth. A "living truth" is a container in which anything private is accessible as public. Whatever self-talk takes place inside is allowed to go live outside. You probably experienced this when you first fell in love---you loved how you were able to say anything you thought or felt as a form of intimacy with your partner. They could see into you just as you were seeing and feeling it. That made them feel ok to do the same with you. And this combination of feeling safe gave rise to such a connection that its influence entranced you. You might say this is the ultimate sense of feeling in love---to move fluently from the inside out, from outside in without blockages or restrictions. You shared unrestricted visibility, uncensored, and unblocked. What poured out of you was a circularity of love and acceptance. You probably accessed the highest of all qualities of expression that you or anyone could access in their lifetime.

101

You see the world as you perceive it, instead of perceiving the world as you see it. A woman sees reality different than a man, just as a doctor sees a situation differently than an attorney. We edit the world we see until our awareness sees our own seeing and limits of its contents.

When you tell another person what is real, it's making a demand for obedience instead of choice. You are asserting that you have a privileged view of reality and that you can correct the other person from their delusion. It could be either expressed or implicit.

But when you appreciate the real nature of human perception as a living system, it has huge implications for how we work together and get along. Essentially no one is an expert; we're all learning and building as we go along, despite people claiming he or she "know what they're doing." To help another human being, it starts with curiosity, not answers. It starts with questions, not statements. We can get interested, instead of being interesting, to help another.

When you become comfortable with not knowing what is going on, it generates a grounding spirit because not a single one of us sees reality as it is. We are not recording devices; we are living systems. We often reduce verbs to nouns. We define this or that, such as a "relationship" instead of "relating is." Verbs imply living systems.

When we become comfortable with our own ignorance, we begin to participate in the living system in which our certainty disclaims to notice. Within systems intelligence, we can learn what to change or where to change, to shift the underlying structures and systems that lead to lasting change efforts and new domains of collaboration. We brace interdependence at all levels, seeing the whole with the impact of our perceptions on it. When we change how we see; *what we see, changes.*

I take several trips a year to Latin America, and I love to visit historic churches. When I enter a church, it's as if I'm traveling back in time connecting with the voices, energies, and contents held by the field structure of the church itself. The space emits an energy that blends the past with the present moment. It as if I'm seeing the macro church in its entire time and space and it enters me such that I'm in awe, even to tears. The space is a safe refuge for people needing to address the individual and social shadows in their lives---negative emotions, temptation, all the above. The church is like a distillery to absorb all the pain and suffering.

TO LOVE IS TO LEARN

Learning to learn is how well you use your awareness to keep the past from creeping up on what you see, as well as learning by creating what matters to you moment by moment. The best conditions to produce for real learning are 1) to hold steady to a desired state or goal that matters to you, 2) have an accurate picture of current reality as you go along, and 3) having some tool or leverage to accelerate progress and build capacity with greater impact.

The leadership instrument to tune here is being able to suspend the voice of judgment. And your will to notice more in your world goes up, due to putting curiosity ahead of certainty. The process accelerates to becoming more fully human, without refusing confusion. By not refusing confusion, ambiguity, uncertainty, complexity, and volatility, all can lead to learning and understanding. The poet Izumi Shikubu wrote:

> *"Although the wind*
> *blows terribly here,*
> *the moonlight also leaks*
> *between the roof planks*
> *of this ruined house."*

When we bring fierce, welcoming attention to meet whatever arises, the light is there despite the roughness in the encounter. This is possible if we bear witness to the current reality that is present. When we see things as they are, we tap into our innate resourcefulness by understanding something new.

TO LOVE IS TO CONNECT

You are forever a dependent being on others to define your truth. Only through giving and receiving love can you see what you have in yourself. Seeing what you have in yourself requires you showing up to life as a whole person.

The leadership instrument to tune here is the capacity to suspend one's voice of cynicism, and redirect the attention back to the inner place, the source from which you're operating in serving and helping another human being from an open heart. All the understanding, generosity, and reverence you need is available for you. Equanimity is the capacity to work with strong emotions without being side-tracked by them. You are an emotional being; it's part of your makeup. Some of the most sterile and cold people that claim themselves as unemotional are in fact the most emotional people around. They focus on hiding it from the world because working with and dealing with emotions isn't something familiar they can register.

The word 'conversation' in Latin is to "turn together." By following our heart, developing leadership by doing what we love, and loving what we do, we must build supporting infrastructures that allow us to cultivate a deeper level of listening and coming into knowing what we're called to do in the world. This must be done on a community level for it to go live and become transformative on a larger scale in societies.

Does anyone come from a non-dysfunctional family? A family by nature of its groupness is full of complexity. No matter who has good intentions, it'll never sanitize bad impact. Like a microcosm of society, together we can tend to create results that nobody wants. Some people are rotting on the inside and yet looking like a rose on the outside. They hide their secret self from the world to deal with their shame. There are those who are happy inside yet outside their lives are crappy. But when inside and outside both are great, it's amazing.

At some level, we all go through a stage of preoccupation with our own inadequacy. It's called adolescence. We compose an identity by what we have, do, know, or by what others think of us. All this is so tempting to us to offset our preoccupation with power.

TO LOVE IS TO LIVE

You can learn to accept the present moment as if the future needed it. Everything is *unexpected perfection* when you pull back and quit editing life coming at you. Whatever is knocking on your door, trust it.

Connect with it. Ask it whether it is for or against where you want to be? Listen.

The listening I'm referring to is generative, not just receptive. What comes into you, touches you, moves you, amazes you is your soul talking. What you love is what your DNA has assigned you to follow and master. Life is in the business of creative life, and you are one granule, an actor in a larger whole. Your place in that ecosystem illuminates an awakening when you make contact with content in your life that you seek to create because you love it. Divine will is imbued in your loving will to bring something desired into being.

And life has all sorts of neat moments you bump into to see what has heart and meaning to you. To encounter life directly and meet it, you must be willing to show up. Showing up takes courage because you don't argue with life, you say it's like this. Saying it's like this is orienting yourself to the fact of what life is bringing in right now, without minimizing, denying, or exaggerating what it is. As you meet it like this, you offer your attention in such a way that life can change you. Like porousness, you are permeable to life. Permeability is the sensitivity to experiences entering you. Love is offering acceptance to whatever is trending right now. It is the only attention possible to soften your edges into whatever is now and meet it constructively.

TO LOVE IS TO CREATE

Creating starts with love. If you look at creations people create, they do it for one simple reason. They loved it before they brought it to life. The creative urge isn't the receptive side of love that we're all too familiar with, rather; it is generative. Loving the future possibility, idea, or aspiration beholds and drives forth this loving effort. The power to create isn't in you; it is in the love you have for this creation. Babies generate great power by bringing mothers into the generative love I'm describing. The mother decentralizes herself to the dominance of loving the baby into getting to the first breath of life.

Making love is to help the world such that it brings you home to the love that is inside you. Seeing others as loving beings, conserving acceptance, and serving for the joy of it, you will never be empty of great rewards throughout your lifetime. Making love is finding the expanding goodness in all things and expanding it, raising, liberating, and lifting it toward its highest future possibilities. You make others shine in the fullness of their potential; you will never live a life of emptiness or boredom.

JUST KEEP WALKING

As I attend from love as I see, learn, live, connect, and create, I keep walking upon territory where I have no certainty. After 25 years of marriage, my wife and I drifted apart into raising our three kids and found ourselves sleeping in separate bedrooms. At times, we would court each other like the early days by sneaking into each other's room and sleeping together. But overall, we fell off the bond and connection of sharing our bedroom together and leg-hugging during the night.

A new opportunity presented itself with a property developer to buy land and build a house on a bank loan. After months and months, our desperation grew as the banks couldn't meet the terms that the developer proposed to us. We were feeling so let down after cutting ties with the project, and yet open to what would come next to replace it. Driving by a street three blocks down we saw a house for sale that looked just perfect. We pulled over, knocked on the door and the owner warmly invited us inside. The house was spacious and suited my lifestyle and office needs perfectly. It was as if someone ordered it up on the menu for us. Who was listening? And the banks stepped right in, and we got into the house without any snags. You're probably saying it was meant to be.

As we began our plans on constructing and upgrading bathrooms and fixings, my wife came to me saying the third room would remain a pantry and laundry room. We would stay with two bedrooms only. She then said that this means sharing the same bed and sleeping together. This dream was speaking to the universe all along. The house we originally were to build had five bedrooms planned, which would have contradicted my deep longing to love my bedtime with my wife and reconnect with my marriage. But the house we were meant to live in will have two bedrooms. Is this unexpected perfection?

When we set intentions, we have to let go of our expectations. Intention and expectation are not the same. I loved the intention (vision; idea; goal) of building the house. It brought me to an aim and organized my decisions, yet down the road, something unexpected from the mystery was coming toward me. Quality of intention must be balanced with wise innocence. We must leave the part out for the universe to do its part.

The tension between the intention and the current reality as it emerges is where I must learn to learn as I go, accept what is going on as it comes, and truly embrace life on its own terms, not just mine.

With this, I tone down my level of arrogance, and pay attention, listen to what life is creating. Life itself is an unfolding creative process with its own expression. This is the path of the sales shaman. She is an enlightened doer marrying her commitment to her deepest intention with the presence of what begins. I call the process "awareness-based creating."

CHAPTER 4

A BIG QUESTION

What is the link between what vitality you experience from your work and what level of value is there for others to receive?

There is something essential between that which brings you into aliveness (real love) and enthusiasm in your work and how others become aware of what you do for them (joy). People love to watch people land in what they love. We as a culture pay big money to go see a singer or songwriter give their gift to the world. If you've ever seen Santana play live, what entrances you about his performance is how much he's moved by what he's doing.

When I ask salespeople what they love most about their work, almost everyone says when they're in a conversation with a potential or current client. During this conversation, they find themselves with a devoted listening, a sense of true service to another, and in a position of helping. For them, these activities bring them closer to what gives them the most amount of energy. It isn't pushing paperwork, answering emails, or any back-office work, rather, it is the opportunity to connect with others that can help them bring them into feeling alive. In fact, they get access to the joy all the time instead of some rarified moments of spiritual fulfillment. Their biggest discouragement is being cut off from this capacity to access this place.

For salespeople, their day-to-day conversations and connections bring them into a normal moment of energy and fullness like a spiritual punch or orgasm. Being able to access this as a normal course of life is extraordinary. I'd like to explore what tapping into this energy is about, and how to maximize the access to it, such that it becomes the most important source of creativity, capability, and leadership in the process of value creation for other human beings.

Let me introduce you to a concept I refer to as "The Reliance Matrix." A matrix according to the dictionary definition is:

: something (such as a situation or a set of conditions) in which something else develops or forms

: something shaped like a pattern of lines and spaces

: a container that can be filled with a material (such as very hot metal) to give the material a new shape

The big question is *what fills you to act, form, create, and attend from it?* What brings you into aliveness? What do you rely upon for movement? What is the source of your movement? What brings you to life? To rely on the *self* is to rely on a key part of you---either the current self that already has come to be as you know or the future self that has not become embodied yet. You can choose to rely on a higher place or higher self that organizes your attention and action today. But this alone denies you the materialization of other qualities that organize you in your life---such as the "other."

The "other" is that which is inside and around you in the community. When you cut the divide, and cut the cord to an internal voice of cynicism and return to whole-hearted connection, you bridge self to other. You are changed and permeated by your care and concern for other people. You find yourself understanding, caring, and compassionate about that which is in the third person---he, she, it, them, instead of orienting yourself in the first person. You listen to their listening, their conversation, and the person saying it, not just the words spoken. You might think of leaders like Martin Luther King who acted from the place of understanding the motivation of his followers as well as his oppressors. This understanding was an impetus for his call to lead and grow his message outward. This care and concern got him out of his way back to find his voice and stance in his charge. He transcended hate and anger toward his oppressors to understanding their pain and predicament. He relied on this aspect of his perception to mobilize himself to remain creative, tolerant, and strong with convictions.

More than this is the reliance on a larger will; the whole; the ecosystem that if you listen to what is needed, you can act from this place. You rely not on your puny will but a grander will, the one from which you're in service to something greater than just your wants and needs. As you incorporate all three of these organs of perception, you inherit a total reliance process from which you animate expression. The Reliance Matrix is the combination of all three of these into a state of moving creatively from these places of potentiality. It is the place from which you sell with balanced intelligence. This book is intended to help you,, the seller, focus all three as you pay attention and intend great things into the world.

Remember that you are highly aware of others (more than usual, you're like a radio tower), such that your sensing perceptions (heart-centered sensitivities to understand, empathize) are highly tuned where places of significance you can see. Seeing these, you move in the direction of personal wisdom.

If I'm given beauty even after I haven't been beautiful, I am honored and seen as beautiful anyway, to remind me of my true self. Why not join the seer in seeing me truly? I'm not always at my best, but the grace I'm given by the love around me is everlasting, and there because what I see isn't what he sees. I want to see as he sees. It begins with the most basic question.

IS THE UNIVERSE A FRIENDLY PLACE?

I had lived for 50 years of my own life under the assumption that the universe is a dangerous place. The pain I couldn't get away from as a teenager during my parents' divorce eroded my sense of trust for others and all things.

Now reflecting, I can see that when everything and everyone is made out to be dangerous, you cannot access yourself safely either. I wasn't at home in my being; my heart; my world. I couldn't relax, enjoy the moments, and give myself to others. I lost touch with my basic goodness and shut down and used my technologies and other defense mechanisms to keep out all that was unfriendly. I distracted myself in things as a form of protection. I couldn't surpass the grip of fear armoring my heart. I shunned any chance to receive love around me, to preemptively strike at incoming hurts I made up like phantoms. Making the world out to be this way, dangerously camouflaged my sense of feeling unlovable.

Later in life, I came to see everything and everyone as a friendly place instead of as phantoms, and when I saw it like this, I found myself seeking to reach out, understand better, and show up. I saw how I saw things as just a model of the world from which I was living.

Nature often plays the role of the significant other. I encountered this in a true story from New Zealand, about a native called the Kanuka tree. She is a nursing mother tree. She comes first into traumatized forests. Those that are razed to the ground or destroyed by falling. And she plants herself as a pioneer and a watcher. She waits for the seeds of the other natives to be dropped by birds flying over this barrenness and, as they germinate, she shelters them. One day they grow strong enough for her to yield and let them surpass her with their strength and longevity. In despair, a women with an intergenerational mother wound, without knowing she would answer, laid her head against her branches, and with such tender wisdom she took it all and showed me how to 'stand' it, and how to yield, and how to bear

the mother lode, and how we do so for one another —
wholeheartedly. "Such love in solid wood". The poet and the
mystic know with deep-rooted knowing that there is such wisdom
in tree and stone. The standing still and watching, tenderly
supporting the human who can continue to lean in and learn, not
leave but love, still now and still moving, walking with and forever
yielding and holding the tension between "given" and giving from
and to the carver's hands.

EXPLORING THE SOCIAL FIELD

Think of your connection between you and other as a "social
body" or field of power, where you get to experience the creative
process emerging from perceptions when your senses are highly
activated, and you're touched and changed by another human
being.

Transforming the social field is an amazing dynamic, especially
when you shift the source from which you act and pay attention
to another human being---by conserving acceptance, legitimacy,
and love. Examples:

1. Picking up on signals there is a danger (hunches), and moving
from this
2. Sensing they're not saying what they mean inside (outer/inner
misalignment) and making it safe to bring it forth
3. They're not seeing where potential exists (blind-spots), and
opening their eyes to hidden potential waiting

4. They're not seeing the whole picture---how dots connect (symphony), and helping complexity turn to simplicity.

"Seeing" and "Sensing" are accessing the organs of perceiving from the open mind, and the open heart. When you sense and act from an emerging future possibility, you learn from the future as it emerges. Leadership is stepping into this field of possibility where your authentic self (your original medicine) is accessed, in the highest level of expression you can access at any given moment. What shuts down these access points? Judgment, shame, and fear.

Judgment implies pre-meditated, pre-existing unchecked information used to construct what is going on. Ignorance is basing what we see on what we already know, which for the sake of defining a type of cognition, we download what we already know to interpret what is going on. We hold mental models that conclude who we are, the way the world is, and of whom others seem to be. Instead of learning to think, we categorize, name, and label the world we perceive much like projecting slides on a wall.

On the one hand, we look at things and say, "Wow look at that, I wonder how that got to be this or that?" But what we fail to recognize is how our habitual ways of thinking reinforce like a reflex what we're inclined to see. Downloading acts like a powerful cognitive reflex which inclines our attention to catch what is consistent with what we expect instead of what could be going on without editing it. All-or-nothing thinking is referencing reality as if it is a fact which it remains non-fact. None of us know how we know what we know. We cling to know things unchecked without any validation.

Healthy shame is knowing we make mistakes, yet an excessive level of shame is toxic. Instead of knowing we make mistakes (humility, imperfect), we think *we* are a mistake. We take winning or losing personally. We form an unwanted belief of ourselves and strike up an ideal to offset it. We compose a standard of ourselves that we should meet. We impersonate a false image to offset our secret unwanted opinion of ourselves to appear better than we think. Our ideal doesn't bring us closer or connected to others. Instead, it distances us from others and knowing what is real about us. The fear of humiliation points us to using cynicism to shut down the risks of vulnerability when we connect in our own truth.

The social body has a certain pattern or creative order and frequency where creations are ready to be expressed. When you cut the divide between you and other---you see the world through their eyes and listen to their listening. Perceiving from the heart is "sensing." What surfaces is a connection to your 'best self' and 'truest service' to the other human being. Love is the intentional act of accepting another as a legitimate other. When you act from this place, you transform the social field into one where it is safe to be real and make real contact in genuine and new ways that create change. This is the essence of collective intelligence, and how emotional intelligence plays a role in accessing it.

I think it's about remembering that you can bring a loving presence to whatever is showing up---*be ready for anything, expect nothing. The true threat is amnesia---forgetting that you are a loving being.* It's a firm stance in love---to conserve legitimacy because God gave you this poise in relating with a wild-card reality that is in constant flux, but you can meet it. Probably the way in is to create a space for intentional silence. This works is probably best when the brain is quiet and empty, so the "mind" can enter----the mind is the higher part of our self that by nature occupies love as a source of generous attention (no judgment, no cynicism, and no fear). Cutting the cord on these, you begin to relate with and make space for suffering--- (aging, dying, illness), and live with it and in spite of it.

As you're reading this, you probably recognize that there is no room for techniques into a great conversation until you pay attention in a way that you care, and you're interested. Remember that everyone knows something that you don't. When you suspend your voice of judgment, you set yourself aside and let the other person enter. As judgment comes in, you let it go. If you have a point to make, jot it down, then open back up to the other person. And remember that all experiences are individual; you don't need to say you experienced the same. You haven't in the way they did. Be careful not to follow your clever cue to yourself to find something in common. Looking for things in common is you caught in your fear of their feeling you don't like them or them not liking you is more like it. You listen with the intent to reply. Instead, listen with the intent to *understand*. Being interested is far greater than being interesting.

YOUR PRACTICE:

DON'T SUPPRESS THE COLLECTIVE SOURCES OF INFORMATION (INTEL) FROM THE SOCIAL BODY THAT IMBUE YOU. YOU NEED TO CONNECT WITH AND ACT FROM THIS PLACE WHEN BEING THERE FOR AND HELPING OTHERS. DO NOT HOLD ONTO THIS, MAKING SURE YOU CHANNEL IT TO WHERE IT BELONGS AT THE MOST OF RECEIPT. THE ONLY ENEMY IN BETWEEN IS CYNICISM, WHICH IS EASY TO LET GO, TO LET COME THIS RICH AND ENERGETIC INTEL FROM THE SOCIAL FIELD. LET THE OTHER CHANGE YOU.

THIS ALSO SUPPORTS WHY LISTENING IS SO KEY: TO LEAN INTO ANOTHER UNTIL YOU'RE CHANGED BY THEM, NOT JUST HEARING WORDS, BUT THE PERSON SAYING THEM.

My Heart Burns like Fire

Soyen Shaku, the first Zen teacher to come to America, said: "My heart burns like fire, but my eyes are as cold as dead ashes." He made the following rules which he practiced every day of his life.

* In the morning before dressing, light incense and meditate.

* Retire at a regular hour. Partake of food at regular intervals. Eat with moderation and never to the point of satisfaction.

* Receive a guest with the same attitude you have when alone. When alone, maintain the same attitude you have in receiving guests.

* Watch what you say, and whatever you say, practice it.

* When an opportunity comes do not let it pass you by, yet always think twice before acting.

* Do not regret the past. Look to the future.

* Have the fearless attitude of a hero and the loving heart of a child.

* Upon retiring, sleep as if you had entered your last sleep. Upon awakening, leave your bed behind you instantly as if you had cast away a pair of old shoes.

CHAPTER 5

I GOTTA BE SOMEBODY

Have you heard this before? *"Everything in your life reflects a choice you once made. If you want different results, make different choices."*

Everything? Really? You mean nothing new is allowed to be independent of my choices? Wow? I didn't understand that I'm ruler over everything that arises in my life. This points at a dynamic I call *reckless responsibility*. Somewhere along the way, our 20th century generation responded to how powerless we find we are by attempting to seem powerful. Taking responsibility for everything is a way of activating this attempt to control our own universe. This means that if things don't go our way, there's something wrong with us. If everything in my life now reflects choices I made I'd be pretty reluctant to make more of them. The fact is the universe is a wild-card, sometimes it cooperates, and other times it does not. YOU DON'T HAVE TO LOVE YOURSELF OR HOLD A HIGH OPINION OF YOURSELF TO CREATE WHAT YOU WANT. WHAT YOU THINK OF YOURSELF ISN'T RELEVANT TO CREATING WHAT MATTERS MOST TO YOU IN LIFE.

I think the notion of loving yourself is folly. It's a nice idea and often touted by new age proponents who tie everything to themselves instead of getting their attention away from this. They haven't come to terms with their sense of power yet and haven't learned to be where it is, instead of in themselves. "Loving oneself" is a nice way to protest losing control or having the less than preferred experiences we each endure.

New age proponents take life personal—what happens to me says whether I'm a good or bad person. They link their worth to their experiences and keep a tab on themselves, which draws them into who they are, instead of building the capacity and skillsets to bring into reality what they seek to create. They tie bad things that happen to them, or experiences are referenced such that they are responsible. But life is a wildcard, how could that be true?

Sometimes it cooperates, others times it doesn't. To learn from one's current reality, as an ally, it can't be made personal. Otherwise learning is stunted. The fact of the matter is, you cannot love what isn't lovable, and love isn't manufactured or superficial. And loving yourself isn't a prerequisite for creating what matters to you.

What you love about you, you love, and what you don't, you don't, keep it honest. That's a choice. You love some qualities and don't love others. Nothing in the rules says you can't not like yourself, or you must love yourself first to create what you want. Deserving and desiring are not linked, only if you make it up to be so.

The desire for the sake of creating a desired outcome or state is purely a generative love and concern for the outcome to exist. The power is in the outcome, and this is what pulls forward new responses, action, trials, experiments to build new capacity until a creation comes into being.

Knowing your quirks, your flaws, your concepts, skills - this is a vast inventory to know, because when you're creating something that matters, it gets you to make strategic decisions when you see current reality as it is.

You can learn a new skill, use teamwork, and navigate favorable situations that are favorable to you. Self-knowledge is not self-love. There will be moments you will not be lovable, you'll screw up, not meet your expectations, and other moments where you'll be at your very best.

Let go of the idea of trying to love yourself in an attempt to create what matters to you, and put your focus on discerning what you have in relation to what you want. Being true to yourself is observing what you have—skill levels, likes, dislikes, propensities, talents, soft-spots, vulnerabilities. And this brings you to be resourceful and to create what matters to you.

Why are people so preoccupied with fixing what is wrong with themselves? Self-improvement is a fetish that puts the self-help industry into a billion-dollar marketplace with only 20% of the audience getting actual help.

Our fallibility and imperfection are permanent, it's not great it's not what we ordered, but it sure helps knowing parts we like or don't like about ourselves and leave it at that. But hiding unwanted beliefs of ourselves in what we own, do, or have others think of us is in our ideal to be special. Yet when we construct experiences to hide our wholeness, we cut the intimacy we long to live meaningful lives.

Maybe it's far too grandiose to assume that we each can turn the world around. And instead show up as a whole person, with kryptonite, because we all have wounds, troubles, and challenges that warrant depending on each other. So how do each of us be in our life, our work, with full conviction that what we're doing is fun, makes a difference, and has lasting enthusiasm, without any guarantee of it bearing success? What if perfectionism and ideals of ourselves we rid, and legitimize our fallibility?

Can we let go of needing to be the ones solely responsible for changing the world? Controlling chaos is like watering weeds. Who but a person that would convince themselves and others they can change the world would be someone who doubts they can? Who but a person that needs to convey the grand hope of making everything better is someone who is concerned with power? It is dishonest the true vulnerability we all have that we are powerless when it comes to what happens to us. Life is a wildcard, and we're busy attempting to predict a future instead of creating one. Making less room for imperfections makes life less interesting. Controlling it all misses what the brevity of life teaches us: to live it! That is the purpose of life.

We're not as powerful as we would like to appear to be to offset our concerns about being insignificant. We would love to be master of our own universe to convince ourselves that life ahead is predictable. We're nervous not having answers. So, we turn to our human potential as if to conserve hidden, latent magic powers to unlock in our mind and when things aren't going our way, we look to ourselves to power up our avenging magic. We take life far too personally and turn to improve ourselves as if something were wrong with us, and it must be fixed first, like victim fighting for power. Yet we are not victims of the system, we are systems of the victim. Our notion of power is out of proportion with the capacity for nature to influence our lives. We operate within a living system, despite our obsession with being somebody special. We attempt to master nature instead of harmonizing within it.

For this, we obsess about working on ourselves, lifting our self-esteem, believing positive things will come, affirm what isn't true, pretend things are great---we try it all to get ahead of hard work. In fact, some of us have actually convinced ourselves that we can do nothing and just by the thoughts we can call into our lives like a magician all our pots of gold and fame. After all, if we had all that we might not depend on the world especially if we assume it is unfriendly in the first place. Our cynicism seeks entertainment to supplement our deep longing for connection. Then the emptiness of our acquisitions not quenching our thirst seeks to leave our body to fix the misery and discomfort. We use overwork, drugs, sex, addictions, lying, and other fixes to deal with our empty state of mind and isolation, only to perpetuate the same.

STRUCTURE

Perhaps another way of putting how things are now is based on the underlying structures that led to the path of least resistance to here. Like the way a building is shaped it determines the path to the door or the human body is shaped to direct blood-flow, our lives are coordinated by structures that we're in. And of these naturally determine where the energy is easiest to go. In spite of the choices I've made, many underlying structures in my life didn't support it, and the results created were ones in which I did not intend.

Many of us hold a model of achieving our dreams and aspirations that in order to have them, we must deserve them. We place ideals of ourselves to become someone fit and shoring up to what we expect or want to create. So much extra effort just to convince ourselves that we are a good enough person to deserve what we want. Question: Why do we have to marry our identity/worthiness to what we want to create?

Self-improvement may correct your quirks and imperfections, but it doesn't guarantee you anywhere nearer what you want to create. Working on being someone you should be is an attempt to deal with your self-doubts and the quirks you feel disqualify you. You're the only one keeping score! What if you realized that in the creative process whether you have doubts or not, whether you love yourself or not, isn't a prerequisite for creating what you want. In fact, the more you work on yourself and fix yourself, the lousier creator you will be.

126

I've coached thousands of leaders over 30,000+ coaching sessions to be precise on this, and all of them had doubts about themselves and whether things would work out. Just read a bio of a famous person in history, they all had inner conflicts and doubts that shook their confidence. But their causes and callings weren't about them. The power came from their creations, not themselves. Like Picasso said, "the Power originates from painting not me," implying that the vision of the creation did something to him that didn't require self-manipulation or will power, the will was a natural flow stemming from the love that motivated his creative process. Picasso and other creators found their flaws and brokenness part of the human experience. What's wrong with doubting something that hasn't been created yet?

They found that positive thinking wasn't useful, in fact, it was positive lying. The more truth telling about where the actual state of things was, the more resourceful they became as creators in knowing their next steps.

They didn't have to believe in what they were doing. Instead they are following their generous love for their desired creations and outcomes. Affirmations weren't important, because pretending something was going on and lying to themselves lessened respect for themselves. Instead, as they went along, they learned and unlearned, things worked and didn't work, trials and experimentation led to successes and failures. All of this indicated that 1) their focus wasn't on themselves, but instead their creations, and 2) their identities were left in the bleachers, so they could use failures as assets for learning and adjusting along the way.

Had they been hung up on deserving their desires they would have always been unhappy even had they created their desires, because their ideals were impossible to satisfy. But when they rid themselves of their ideals and just focus on creating what they valued, everything became simple. In fact, it's so simple, it's hard. We make creating a process of verifying who we are first. But when we take our identity out of the process, whether we succeed or fail becomes a useful point of reference, instead of defining whether we're a good or bad person.

The Take Away: Choose to separate deserve from desire. Just create what you love for its own sake. Those are the best kinds of creations to learn from as you go, and the best avenue to organize your life building process.

ENCOUNTERS WITH THE FIELD

Brian, a financial advisor of 30 years in New York, says there is no way he would be doing anything else than what he is doing right now. What he "gets" to do as Brian describes it is not what he "has" to do. He sees his work as a privilege to be able to help so many people create financial independence through planning and preparing for their retirement. Brian says he has a concept he calls the "thank you model to great work."

Essentially the thrust is to create value for his clients such that they are so thankful for his help that Brian is successful. Only one thing matters most---the client is receiving great value. This is important because Brian says being essential to his clients always starts with how they perceive good value and that if they're removing what they fear losing, reaching what they truly want, and reinforcing what is most exciting in their lives, their loyalty, referrals, and retention is for Brian.

Brian also brings his thank you system back to three key building blocks: seeing, helping, and loving. He says that to see what is there, he has to keep his experience from creeping up on him. Brian has thirty years to unlearn so that he can help someone. You might wonder why he unlearns. It is because he claims that maintaining his inexperience keeps him looking at clients with fresh eyes. He says that seeing the miraculous that astonishes him isn't seeing new things. Instead it involves seeing the miraculous in the ordinary. He cuts the cord to his certainties, and follows his curiosity when fact finding to help his new clients.

To help, Brian says it starts with empathy. He says it's like walking in the other's shoes as if he could shape shift into living inside them. Through their eyes, he can experience their way of interacting with the world. He sees their predicaments and vulnerabilities as wells as strengths and assets. And he stays in this place until it changes him. Brian knows that the quality of his interventions always starts with the interior condition of the helper.

What amazes Brian is that opening the heart this way always reveals something latent for the client to see suddenly. He calls this the "surprise accident." No client situation is ever quite the same, much like a game of Chess. He listens to their listening and stays in their conversation, not his database from the past. He says he becomes an agent of a future that is trying to emerge. By being aware, Brian says life at that moment with the client will take its course. Safety and trust-building start with Brian fostering legitimacy and acceptance. He taught me that you show up and meet the moment as if it was an invited guest. You hold the space for differences, such that whatever arises is acted towards with acceptance. He say's financial planning is about anything other than the quality of relationship with the advisor, nothing else. If that is established, something is produced in the way of value creation for the client. Brian told me that when he listens to their listening, they feel so respected that they want to be with him all the time. They can't wait to come back. And when he has a greater awareness of the other, Brian says he has greater access to reflect on himself.

As he enters the conversation as this agent of the future about to unfold, something comes into Brian as if a shipping messenger brought a golden package knocking at his door. When Brian opens the door, something ground swells like a wave emerging from his entire being that commits him to what words, questions, and service must be done. He calls this "listening from the field," and something emerges from the conversation that nobody thought about or knew of before. It is completely made of original sources.

At this point in the conversation, Brian has aligned with something quite vibrant, radiant, and ready to emerge, as if goodness was spotted and he super-sizes it. Brian says at that moment it's as if his entire being was transmitting a message like a channel, as if his presence was total, connected as if something magical surfaces from within that is wanting to get expressed. It is love, not the receptive aspect, but a more generative love that is beyond his own space, ready to come alive like the spirit behind the message. Something new is always trying to crawl out of the conversations he experiences.

These encounters with the space itself, Brian says, are like reclaiming or restoring a hidden wholeness to be blessed and usable, in the true service of another. He finds within him the highest hopes he has for another human being to wish them into being well.

When we session, Brian often describes the way he transforms a social body or field in between he and the other in which something is wanting expression and itching him to imbue it. He is invited to jump in, acting in an instant, leading with *what*, and letting *how* come after. He says that leaping into this space is a courageous commitment to compassionate action through connection. All three qualities he finds in himself at this moment, as he accesses the finest quality of being he can occupy.

Brian treats each conversation as if something not-yet-embodied and animates it. The way in requires a "pealing back the layers" to let the conversation find you. Brian has experienced the creative process in movement and natural order as if he danced with the tides of life in the business of creating life. The courage to let go and let come he says is the process of dying back into life, into a sort of meaning and service that is waiting to become alive from the mystery he walks gallantly into when helping clients. It is tapping this voluntary energy that Brian says brings him into so much aliveness that he has retired from the thought of ever retiring in his own work.

Is this self-actualization? Yes, it appears that way, but only complete via social actualization. Social intelligence positions self-intelligence, as if the future self is shaped and carved in properties by the transformation of the social field when the boundaries come down and connection happens. Brian often describes this experience like a time warp, where an hour goes by which seems like a minute.

One of the aspects Brian most emphasizes is that advisors today, based on the social and economic context in which they help others need a more balanced intelligence, intellectual, emotional, and spiritual. The level of complexity for humans in modern life has called up leadership that blends individual, social, and holistic sensibilities to generate real value. Building our capacity to listen, connect, and be together and legitimize differences, is a new manner of helping first, succeeding second. No opportunities are entitled without first connecting someone else to real value.

What always staggers me about Brian is he knows like a pro musician every technique in the book. His processes are so solid, and yet his conviction to start with a genuine connection is first, before getting mechanical. Brian balances humanity with being a performer. The ability to think together and be together is directly proportional to what we can produce together. The root of this is a conversation, meaning "conversary" which is "turning inward" and moving together by the quality of listening involved. As we move beyond the words and hear the person saying them, we are transforming the space. It is about much subtler qualities in listening that helping conversations lead to animation. Conversation animation is the ethos of changing the social field when our listening is at its best, without any agenda or hurry.

The conversation is possible when the other person (the one needing help) is talking about something they care deeply about. There are three areas that characterize content that matters. First are the difficulties. Buyers are wrestling with something in the way of creating what they really want, and they've struggled to get rid of it. These dangers are aspects people fear losing the most.

People care about losing their reputation, money, marriage, physical abilities, life-span, wellness, connection, and so many more. At our most basic level of motivation, we care a lot about losing something that matters to us. Second, we care a lot about opportunities. These are attractive sources of what we consider to be a success. We cherish job opportunities, client opportunities, dream opportunities, vacation opportunities, learning opportunities, and so many more. Our lives are organized around opportunities we love to reach. Third, we care a lot about aspects of our lives that are energizing and exciting. We love aspects that give us confidence, and motivate us to reinforce these to continue on and grow them.

When the conversation content is in the realm of any of or all of these three, the other person needing help will give you the helper the opening to listening, just like Brian does to transform lives. Today my admiration for Brian has continued to grow because his intellectual ideas (intellect) are deeply complemented by his actions behind the scenes (character development). He lives what he claims. The profound respect I feel for him comes from this *integration*. The words he says are in his blood and come full circle as I witness alignment between his words and his acts. The greater this *integration,* the greater others trust what Brian says. His interior condition between his words and his actions imbue the character needed to bring Brian into the helping leader he is today.

BEYOND ME

My son Michel knew at that one moment in time when his coaching client told their story about what was holding her back from her CrossFit goals. As he listened to her pain and discouragement, it was as if a voice from the future was calling him into what lies beyond his past. In the past, he was a person motivated to be an athlete, but now something or someone else was calling on his soul service, and he could hear it like a dog whistle.

That night he called me, it was his 29th birthday and said, "Dad for the first time I sensed in myself something beyond me that I must do now. I must help her and help others because it inspired and touched me like never before. My reply to him was, "Michel this is because you're not the same person relating to these moments like you were before, and your values are shifting. If you don't reply to these creative

134

energies installing into your software, you'll feel depressed, just follow what your heart is telling you." He knew I was right on the mark with this feedback, and from that day he never looked back, quit his day job and went into coaching and helping full time in the service to that sudden guiding idea that called, and he answered. When the epiphany hits you, respond the first time, or it'll hit harder and harder until you say, "I give." I told Michel that perhaps this is telling him what to do with this gift he has for helping, and to trust his gift with his life.

DOING THINGS THE RIGHT WAY

Throughout our journey, we're taught by our teachers, parents, and others to do things this way or that way. We take their input as an authority and insert what they ask, to be adequate. We begin to attach what we know to an identity. We wear our names on our educations and become attached to what we know. We then try to convince others that they're wrong. Curiosity goes out the door. Symbols of power and control become the most immediate need—to be significant and adequate.

We seek the perfect recipes to get things right the first time. We become performers instead of learners, inclined to find a recipe for success to apply. We become attached to our sense of competency, and guard threats of incompetence from others' opinions of us. All of this is what makes us lousy creators. The creative process requires stages of incompetency, looking like a fool, and successful failures to build capacity. The process involves generating something we want independent of what we know. It requires us to take a closer look at our current reality, which includes our current capacity.

135

There are no recipes for success. This notion is probably surprising to you because like most of us, you don't want to reinvent the wheel. What you miss is the engagement, involvement, and enjoyment of creating what you truly desire. To create, most of what you learn is from the future as it emerges, not from the past. Often the past is what prohibits the creative process because we revert to the familiar instead of experimentation and prototyping.

JUMP IN

You can jump into the present moment because it's a 50/50 deal. Half the time things will work, and the other half things won't. But decide to treat both of these outcomes with equal value.

Act in an instant. Hesitation inhibits the velocity of learning. The faster you begin a new business venture, the faster the mistakes you eat for breakfast afford you a real business education. The greatest risk is not taking them. If you want to learn how to create a business, start one.

If you desire something, decide to create or not create it. It's a choice you make. You don't predict a future; you create one. Action equals clarity. Clarity doesn't create action. Most resistance for you, for others, is due to lack of clarity. And yet to get it, action must be put first, while resistance is watching. A coaching client calls this "putting resistances in the bleachers and watching you do your thing, as a spectator, not a governor."

So, trust your decisions because they are guesses that, when acted upon, lead to learning and clarity; it is an iterative process of learning by deciding to act. Stop getting ready to get ready to get ready to get ready. You're not ready until you're ready to stop making things safe. Leveling up requires you to leave your security, status, and comfort behind.

Jump in. Preparation is never enough for what's coming next. Set an intention. Then be wisely innocent to learn as you go along. There are no experts. You don't know what you don't know until you try.

A SUFI STORY ABOUT CABBAGE

A story is told of an island and its inhabitants. The people longed to move to another land where they could have a healthier and better life. The problem was that the practical skills of swimming and sailing had never been developed – or may have been lost long before. For that reason, there were some people who simply refused to think of alternatives to life on the island, whereas others intended to seek a solution to problems locally, without any thought of crossing the waters. From time to time, some islanders reinvented the arts of swimming and sailing. Also from time to time a student would come up to them, and the following exchange would take place:
"I want to swim to another land." "For that you have to learn how to swim. Are you ready to learn?"
"Yes, but I want to take with me my ton of cabbages."
"What cabbages?"

"The food I'll need on the other side or wherever it is."

"But what if there's food on the other side?"

"I don't know what you mean. I'm not sure. I have to bring my cabbages with me."

"But you won't be able to swim with a ton of cabbages. It's too much weight."

"Then I can't learn how to swim. You call my cabbages weight. I call them my basic food."

"Suppose this were an allegory and, instead of talking about cabbages we talked about fixed ideas, presuppositions, or certainties?"

"Hummm... I'm going to bring my cabbages to someone who understands my needs."

Nan-in, a Japanese master during the Meiji era (1868-1912), received a university professor who came to inquire about Zen. Nan-in served tea. He poured his visitor's cup full and then kept on pouring.
The professor watched the overflow until he no longer could restrain himself. "It is overfull. No more will go in!" "Like this cup," Nan-in said, "you are full of your own opinions and speculations. How can I show you Zen unless you first empty your cup?"

SUSPENSION

Stepping ahead into the unknown is what creating is about. The boldness involved is one of suspension and redirection.
Suspension is the capacity to extricate your obedience to the past, to your assumptions and generalizations you hold of what exists. It is

what I call a state of "don't know mind." Don't know mind is having mindfulness of the content of your thoughts as just theory, but not fact. Suspending these certainties cultivates the openness to wonder, astonishment, and curiosity that inspires inquiry.

Redirection is the capacity to move from the mental models we have back to the current reality. We pay attention to our paying attention. This is the capacity to remain mindful of our own inner dialog and downloading, and also dialog with others as a means to bending the beam back to seeing our own seeing. With this shift in the source from which we perceive, we can access our sensing perceptions to see the positions and viewpoints of others around us empathically. Compassion arises when we foster this shift.

To see is to be in a direct and factual relationship with current reality, it's like an acquired taste. Honesty is scary because we may have to acknowledge what's not working and change something. Fear is a natural reaction to moving closer to the truth. Suspension is key because it separates our identity from what we're seeing. We tend to relate to life though we're preoccupied with not being. When we have the notion that we're not enough, reality becomes a threat rather than our teacher. But when we keep our opinions of ourselves from the creative process, our identity is a non-issue.

Backing up from what is going on helps see aspects of what is real as it relates to structure. Mom always said that love could blind you. She was right. When you step away, you see part of the other person, dynamics at play, and patterns that up close weren't in sight.

When you separate from what is going on, you get intimate in new ways. Watching a film from the back row isn't the same as the front of the cinema. Seeing a game from the field isn't the same as watching form the upper booth. If you back up far enough from what you see, what you see looks different. You see how the dots connect and patterns of behavior.

What is the cost of being right? Static. The word "ecstatic" means to leave the familiar. To be ecstatic is to move toward what matters to us by letting go of our need to make sense of everything. Letting go of being right means you let the mysteries be mysteries. You forget to chase the unknowable and place attention on the creative process. Rather than figuring out who you are, it unfolds and is shaped by that which you seek and create.

Questions to consider:
1. What am I holding onto that is keeping me from being creatively free?
2. What do I deeply desire to create, and to what will I choose to devote my life spirit and gifts?
3. What aspects of my life matter most to me now and what steps can I take to amplify and foster them?
4. Who are the people who matter most to me in my life story and what steps can I take to build upon these relationships?

DON'T KNOW MIND

My Mexican father in law Fernando always asked me, "Did you eat well today?" "Did you sleep well last night?" "Are you free of serious illness?" He implied the only thing then that worries you is you're thinking about something, but there isn't a need to worry, life is simply beautiful unless you struggle against yourself with worries that don't solve a thing. Ruminating and worrying is like shadow boxing hungry ghosts in the mind, not in reality. He went on to teach me that with a good night's sleep, letting problems go, a new day with a rested mind is one that can solve the problems far better than a worried, tired mind.

How do you stop thinking? Why would you do this? My experience has been that you don't stop thinking, it isn't possible, however becoming aware of when you are thinking suggests an observation that it is happening. There is a sense of becoming aware of your thinking. It's not that thinking is bad, it's when you forget you think that is concerning.

How you learn is correlated with how you learn to think. When you make a claim that you know what is going on, you are categorizing, not thinking. You're drawing from your existing database as a source of coming up with certainty, interpretation, and perception. Learning is seeing something new that didn't appear before.

Learning at a fundamental level is a mistake making process. When we learn to walk and speak we start a journey of experimentation, motivated by the aspiration compelling our movement. The traditional classroom model of today is out of touch with the needs we have in modern life, where learning is increasingly becoming a collective process, not the individual. Learning that matters is done in social systems---family, teams, and groups. It's about solving problems you haven't seen before, drawing upon a model of learning from the future as it emerges, rather than drawing upon the past.

Selling as it is done today is evolving with this industrial age shift of how learning carries the most important role in helping customers. To get at the essence of helping today, knowing the nature of learning is equally relevant.

True suspension is about holding a don't know mind at all times. While walking. While driving. While eating. This don't know mind is free from ideas, concepts and catastrophizing. It's free from the tyranny of the me-me-me mind that's caught up in worry, fear, and want. This don't know mind is wide open and vast.

> "Don't-know mind cuts through thinking. It is before thinking. Before thinking there is no doctor, no patient; also, no God, no Buddha, no "I" no words — nothing at all. Then you and the universe become one. We call this nothing-mind or primary point. Some people say this is God, or universal energy, or bliss, or extinction. But these are only teaching words. Nothing-mind is before words."

142

This not knowing or "Don't Know Mind" cracks us open from our shells and frees us so that we may flow with life again. The conceptual, every day, I-me-my mind is a hungry ghost, and no matter how much information we feed it, this me-me-me mind will never be satisfied. It always wants more. It wants something to grab hold of. Some new problem to solve. Some new worry to stew on. And if we're trying to find true authentic happiness via this mind, we'll be searching for countless lifetimes.

Thinking is the problem because thinking gives rise to the needy I and when we drop this type of mind state we enter into a responsive, compassionate, open, flowing, all embracing mind-state that seeks to help others because the lines between me over here and a you over there have been dissolved.

So even though it may seem like "Don't Know Mind" is a vacant wasteland of nothingness devoid of wisdom, we see that it gives rise to ultimate wisdom which leads to compassionate action. Knowing how you know is an interesting exploration. Consider that all knowing is doing, and all doing is knowing. You come to know by relating together with the level of love and respect to know. Anything you knew before if unaware or unchecked can reduce what is possible to know by the manner of relating in trust.

The mother comes to know how to mother by mothering. The restaurant business owner comes to know by taking care of and listening to his customers. The doctor comes to know how to heal

143

others by healing them. What we come into knowing is not yet embodied until we do something. The brain is the mechanism that stores memory as knowledge. Coming into knowing isn't learning when we claim certainties from the past. Our mind is the awareness that regulates these certainties by accessing continuously an open mind and heart from which we come to know. As Peter Block says, "the way to how is through yes" By acting instantly and learning by doing, without making predications prior to entry. This is done by making up our minds instead of "not having enough this or that." Courage and commitment lead to the mistake-making and learning such that capability grows, and knowing becomes trust, and confidence. Without courage and commitment, there is no breakthrough to access what is new to learn and know. All knowing is doing and doing is knowing. We make the world up as we go along learning from what emerges. To make sense of it and gain from it, we depend on reflection and relationship to bring it into possibilities.

This practice of dropping the thinking, calculating, conniving, me-me-me mind is like a fast track to peace. In this mind-state, there's wide-eyed wakefulness that sees all the universe, is connected to all of it freely and responds to everything spontaneously. We may have the pre-conceived notion that what we seek in the way of freedom and true authentic happiness will take years to cultivate, but this practice of "Don't Know Mind" is like a lightning bolt that cracks through our minds to illuminate clearly that we are what we're seeking. What is sought is seeking itself to coming into reality, so why not just drop it all and see it for yourself right now?

"Don't Know Mind" is beyond any clearly defined lines or rules. It is a wide open possibility. Don't Know Mind can be frustrating and paradoxical. In one moment it's utterly freeing and the next we feel tied up in knots. I know it has challenged me and my own insatiable need to know, to read, and to gather that next piece of information.

One of my teachers said to me,

> "We have to continue to put down our ideas, our concepts, and our beliefs. As soon as we think we know what enlightenment is – we are wrong."

Letting go of old certainties, beliefs, and ideas is a terrifying place. Why? Because we're left wide open, naked and vulnerable. We hide behind our concepts, calculations and hypothesizes. Information is a weapon. Data points collected – a badge of honor.

But here, with Don't-Know-Mind we're presented with something that shatters that way of thinking. It breaks apart our solidified idea of whom we think we are.

> "There's all of this bias toward knowing. But we don't really know. We have this radical teaching: How about admitting the truth that we don't know and go from there. If we really live that, it changes everything. Don't Know Mind doesn't mean stupid. It means What Is It? Suddenly our eyes are open; we're vibrating with energy because we wonder, 'What?'…rather than, 'Oh yeah, I know that!'"

145

"So, this Not-Knowing actually gives us life. It gives vibrancy and energy to the world we live in. This kind of I-Know shuts everything down, and we get stuck…

We fill our minds up with all this stuff, and it gets stale and repetitive. Not knowing is what opens us up and comes alive…

Clear it away. Return to zero. What do we see, what do we smell, what do we taste, and what do we touch? Everything is truth. What we know blocks the truth. Returning to not knowing opens us up."

Let the practice of Don't Know Mind open you up and clear away everything that you're clinging to. Come back to the freedom of not knowing.

There is a powerful concept I call THE AMNESIA EFFECT.

The AE is the falling asleep to what current position one is actually in. The tendency is to become so blind that one actually forgets, is handicapped from seeing how they're positioned at any time.

EXERCISE: LIST YOUR FORGET-ME-NOT'S

FMT'S are all the intentional remembrances that you get to experience every day

Pinch yourself to these FMT's you get to experience:

- The sky
- The color around you
- The water you have
- The touch you feel
- The smell
- The taste of the food
- The persons you meet
- The feelings they give you
- The presence you have to give
- The smile you can offer
- The learning from life's offerings hi and lo
- The element of surprise
- The relaxation obtained from breathing

These when not forgotten, you get to have, and for this, your only response is: GRATEFULNESS

You can enter from this sense of wonder for things you get to experience, that your AMNESIA EFFECT bypasses, and then you forget, like divorcing from life, not near it. Cultivating a don't know mind offers you the alternative. You are so available, not lost in your head, to see what life has to offer and what you have around you.

HUMILITY

Humility is realizing that you need to learn through yourself, through others, and through the web of life. Your notion of power shifts from

147

yourself to your environment. The will to learn means accessing the open mind, heart, and open will. As you become aware of these three, you begin to meet all the mental chatter that sounds off in your head. You don't attempt to do anything with it or aggress on it. You let it be there and run its course. You begin to feel the pain and injury of rejection, hurt feelings, anger, and a whole range of emotions that have armored your open heart. And when you feel in the depth of your entire being a knowing, where divine guidance has arises, yet you haven't acted on it or trusted it, all of this pops up. You make space for all of this. And what you make space for, can move, expand, and grow. Joy comes from humility when you're willing to open up to what life really is, not what you expect it to be.

When you don't have to act as if you know all the time, so much stress rolls off your back. Curiosity replaces stess like a revitalizing force re-entering you young again. No more proving that you are somebody. Instead, you can live with a nobody. Each of us is just a bozo on the same bus. We all are incomplete, broken, and flawed, and if we attempt to use pretense to offset it, we aren't true to ourselves. We keep something hidden and secret from the life that is here. When you live with a nobody, you have tracked your ideals that offset your shame and see how they trap you in perfectionism. You rid yourself of these ideals and replace what organizes your life with your true values and aspirations as your conscious compass.

ON TRUE SERVICE

I sold collection systems to business clients. One of the reps on my team we called "robo-rep." He was like the terminator who never stopped. Ed was all about the flare and mastery of the science of the sales system, and he was the ruthless salesperson who made every prospecting call, scripted his presentation, and enjoyed perfect demonstrations in sales meetings to show off his obedience. As I watched him create sales, he was able to make things happen, but he wasn't there. It was as if he wasn't allowed to be a human being. No one had a personal relationship with him because his warmth was gone. Ed lasted about a year and then left. He hid behind a sales system to help the world stay away from himself. He was greedy and very lonely all at once, and Ed's success didn't buy him out of his longing for connection. Last I heard about Ed, he was in drug rehab for cocaine abuse. My guess is he'd been medicating a deep longing and pain in his heart because he couldn't get fulfillment from his work. He was holding onto so much inside him that he couldn't unleash. What had made it harder for him was his promotion for being so faithful to the company system and institutionalized methods. He was the perfect rep in their eyes, and to Ed, he took this as a message from God.

Two years later I found Ed outside an apartment complex near me, and he took me in. After talking for three hours on a Sunday afternoon Ed said early in life he was betrayed, and it took all the goodness and trust in him to the underground to defend his own goodness. He buried his vulnerability of out shear fear that others would take advantage of him. After reflecting carefully, we could see how others who buy from him miss the fullness of Ed when he operates from the shadows with surface sales systems to sterilize his fears. A cold heart can't be hidden in a system, nor trained. Ed admitted he had a long way to get back home to himself and let go and forgive the pain and shame from being betrayed. He started to see that under the wound was a profound place of wonder and curiosity that was tender and soft. And beyond the social norms of being a man, he could see he still was a soulful person anyway. Thinking he was played the fool by everyone made him cynical, disconnected, and distant. He let the tears come to his eyes, and he broke down on his knees pleading for help. He wanted to "feel love" again instead of the self-aggression of his anger and revenge upon the views he held deeply embedded and conditioned in his thinking. It was like a gash releasing poison in his heart, giving way to another moisture-like elixir. I often looked at Ed's story like "the man of melting ice" because his transformation was one of thawing out a deep-frozen feeling state to keep himself safe from danger.

Rather than buyers being categorized as the carriers of betrayal, Ed let this hateful discrimination go to the rise of buyers as loving beings. Ed was on the path of a return to an unarmored heart. Three weeks later he phoned me to share that his most recent client meeting was a 180-degree shift to letting go of fear, control, and outcome, and conserving acceptance and loving his client with listening deeply. He said he could see his own humility in understanding his client Dave anew after a ten-year period. Dave told him that he felt different, connected, and saw Ed's gifts. Tears running down his eyes, Ed's renewal came like a release of imprisonment, and he began a new life. Undoing the past—the background of the betrayal became possible by coming to the truth of it—with such fluency, self-intimacy, and understanding that it transformed into a wise, liberating heart that could hold space without morphing into hate. The injustices don't require turning against it any more, rather, letting it be just as it is without manipulation or attempts to contradict the brokenness. Healing the underground is different from perpetuating it. Forgiveness is letting go of the tendency to perpetuate by dissolving the barriers that constrict access to a larger sense of self.

Stories like Ed's indicate how sometimes with the best of intentions and with a full heart, our professional training does cruel things to people. We become so mechanical as performers that we forget we're two humans having a conversation. Any time we begin working a system we lift our humanity out of our work. This isn't putting down having a system; there certainly is a place for routine, planning, and design. But when it edges out your soul, it affects what emerges in helping other people by blocking intimacy. We must remember that there is something larger than both of us at play that is relational, not transactional. In understanding their current reality---pain, opportunities, limitations, strengths, and positionality are all key ways they can begin to see, own, and start from through you being there.

We are starving for a living truth. When we are contained in the "buyer" and "seller", our intimacy is closed off to emerging and flowing potentiality. Anger, insecurity, fear, cynicism, and judgment scares our ability to be truthful. When we offer the irrelevance of our truth, we make space for what is true.

Not keeping it in is what gives rise to a living truth to realize real human contact. It takes longer; it is volatile to deal with truth. It isn't that you have to tell everybody everything, it is that you are able to tell everyone everything. You are willing to share it because it is a living, breathing relationship. You must train yourself in the capacity to be able to share. You are an open free environment for the other person to come and play and choose.

EMBRACING IRRELEVANCE

Many men go fishing all their lives without knowing that it is not fish they are after. -Henry David Thoreau

Real epiphanies are possible for any mind that embraces irrelevance. The way my trash goes out and left there to be picked up, and the way the pens in the coffee cup sit, these at first don't appear correlative to my comprehension of other matters. Is it my attention span that lacks the thickness to see connections between instances like these? Are these inclusive to my other experience as I make sense going along through time as if context is in motion? What is there to conserve?

You are on the road to somewhere, but you have no predictability of where that is going to be. You get to live into the mystery of what is unfolding. You begin talking with someone with no control of the outcome. As the conversation opens doors, you begin to open into what is next as if the words could sense where to take you. This is what is experienced when you aren't getting your knowledge in the way of your directness to your experience. Ego is trying to avoid this directness, while the alternative is making direct contact with no edits or filters in between.

The problem with a sales "method" or "technique" is one word: Repetition. Once you get habituated in it, you ignore inconsistencies with it and reconfirm what you know. The limits of this are endless disturbances of accessing a greater capacity for what is really going on.

Embracing irrelevance suggests that you give space to see current reality — you, them, the situation. When seeing your own seeing you recognize the method as a model or a lens, not fact. Self-deception believes what you think when it is non-fact, only unchecked fiction. Like shadow boxing, you operate from your voice of judgment with missing information. This creates less flexible attention to everything and blinds your ability to see and listen peripherally. It's like lifting an existing framework on to the situation, hampering possibilities.

Peripheral listening involves the practice of embracing irrelevance. I like to think of this as "don't fill the parenthesis," and instead see from outside what you already anticipate. To download what we know is like trusting a theory from our experience. Once aware we have a mental model in use, we can espouse different access to understanding what is going on, in fact, not fiction.

As we meet what is going on directly, we embrace irrelevance and see differences between what we know and what we see. This capacity evokes insight. When we courageously decouple from downloading life as we know it is just one part of a whole new world awakens our comprehension levels and animates our sense of wonder and curiosity by seeing with fresh eyes. As Alan Alda from

Mash once said, "Maybe if we suspend our assumptions more often the light can come in." Francisco Varela, a neurobiologist from Chile, passed away in 2001. Varela studied perception and the phenomenon of suspending our voice of judgment and redirecting our attention to the current reality outside.

To see from another source is to suspend, redirect our attention to understanding from sensing what is wanting to emerge, and then letting go of everything impeding the opening of the head, heart, and body to catch new comprehension levels that animate us from the whole. A peripheral listening arises as she uses her quality of awareness to access new levels of intelligence. Artists often describe this moment of awakening as the primary event when they were given inspiration directly from an experience that grabbed them with astonishment, meaning, and surprise. Or the entrepreneur describes a great moment of epiphany when the "eureka" idea comes to light. We are more inclined to receive breakthroughs in our thinking that come from the capacity to suspend, redirect, and let go. Something new presents itself that connects deeply to who we are and what we must do in a given situation. Our path emerges, and setting foot into it is the essence of leadership. Our inner knowing becomes the internal to external compass informing our next step, and with enough agility acting directly from our heart, we unfold as we go.

We must learn to hold ambiguity for significant periods of time. I call this *"hanging in the grey until something comes forth that is substantial."* We fiddle with what we have long enough with a quiet mind to see what is in need of it. This is our greatest source of

154

innovation. We tinker with something long enough and begin to see its directionality. I suppose famed inventors like Burton tinkered long enough with a flat board in the snow to find the runway for the snowboard we have today. Or the inventor of the razor skateboard fiddled with a prototype until it found a marketplace to create demand. The baby diaper came to life when playing around with a pin and a towel or two surfaced a clearer way forward to a creation. Interestingly, when we tinker, the subject matter begins to configure a pathway as if to write its own story, as our instinct is activated through fiddling and stillness. What this says is we are addicted to doing things and fearful of time passing without structure. Without liminal periods there are no breakthroughs. Ask any entrepreneur innovating and optimizing a product, and they'll tell you they get their best insights during downtime when they are relaxed, in the shower, going somewhere other than doing tasks. Stopping, backing up, just *being* is the best access point for taking inspiration and reifying it to a vision.

Try this: In your next conversation, track the number of questions you asked versus the number of statements. A good benchmark to compare to is ten to one. Keep a ratio of ten questions to one statement. Asking questions shows you how comfortable you are with suspending your certainty. This step may not come easy because you have a version of you as an expert to position credibility and gain a competitive advantage over another.

"MOVE AWAY FROM CERTAINTY AND BRING CURIOSITY!"

To be of service at a profound level is to be truly of service, and trust in the process of being there, as you are without pretense. You move from pretense to presence. It is a generous listening to be so open that you allow others to change you. Instead of operating from how they think of you, you release your preoccupation with that, and pay direct attention to them and what they're saying and experiencing. I've taught active listening for almost 20 years, and it's easy to act like you're listening, but ask yourself how truly sincere your interest level is. You find a trusting to rest and hold your being, listening at the moment that life is allowable just as it is. You are ready for anything, expecting nothing. In your walk in helping others, you meet people living agonizing stories as well as amazing moments. It's not about the system, it's about the truth. You create an atmosphere to tell the truth because you hold the acceptance of whatever is true.

You don't have it all together, nobody does. Yet society expects us to have it all together to win in life, according to some script defined by social expectations. We subscribe to looking good by pretending like we have it all together. Avoiding isolation drives us into unnecessary preoccupations with getting people to like us, admire us, respect us, and accept us.

At some level we all need approval. After all, we would damage the relationships we love if we disregard their reactions to us. Peoples' reactions to you are important, yet they don't define your identity. When you define yourself by what others think, you wear a disguise that pushes your secret self down, such that you don't have to risk being rejected or isolated.

There are several trends in the modern world that you must attend to and respond to with your gifts. First, that people feel tremendous isolation. Their attempts to reach mastery, compete and get ahead, and individuate their lives have them learning how to depend less on others around them.

To show up is to be with what is happening right now as a unique and perfect moment. It isn't significant why it's happened or why it shouldn't but that it is ok as "happening." What takes you away from being here and now? Maybe the fear of uncertainty fills you. Perhaps you attempt to trade mystery for mastery over life.

THE FRAGILITY OF LIFE

I coached an insurance agency leader in New York. When we began to define his brand, I'll never forget what he told me. "We're nice." "Nice?" I asked. Randy said that we're nice to talk to. I asked why people on his team are so nice. Every morning they conduct a 15-minute standing huddle to stand close to death. He reminds the team that death is close at hand every day. Randy's been bringing this message to the team for over three years and says it's the one thing that makes everyone so kind to each other. His team doesn't have time to waste on the pettiness of being cruel, mean, or inconsiderate. To confront death is to live it fully with conviction and aliveness.

This agency's retention levels are 36% higher than the average in their class. Why? Because being nice keeps their clients from behaving badly toward them and leaving. Randy said that we are "not being anything, we're just ourselves as kind people." We don't know how to be anything but nice to people and treat them with respect.

Every service call starts with a thank you for being with our agency, and we're here to help you. Every day, each person in the agency in both service and sales contacts five clients to say a sincere thank you. The inconvenience of doing this makes the client feel important. The gesture is professionally unconventional in an age when heart to heart connection is fading to automated online marketing systems that sterilize the capacity to connect.

To win at selling today, Randy understands that his agency must be compassionate and present to the issues that his clients have. First, he pays attention to his A+ customers and their dream solutions desired and imagined instead of looking at the competition for strategy. Randy says these dreams have to be part of the equation for competitive positioning. He calls his process "strategic client pruning."

Randy had this say when we met last:

> "When we say we understand, the other person knows we're just saying we do, but we don't. We must locate and develop client needs outside of our experience and expertise by engaging questions. When we meet a new potential client, we want to know what brought them here. Not why they're here, but what happened in their lives to bring them to this point in time. This backstory will help us understand what we need to do for them and what areas to explore in giving help. To perform this, we must be able to function beyond the role of a programmed sales-person. That relating with ourselves is primary to helping others. We need to quit trying to appear more than we are and come to terms with our limitations, showing up as a whole person with

curiosity, and engage with playfulness. We will bring the humanity back to insurance this way."

I love this paragraph you just read. Doesn't that inspire you? Randy says that when his team operates from this place of service to others, clients will introduce them to their mothers! It's a fun joke Randy says to measure how we're doing with client influence.

CHAPTER 6

A TABLESPOON OF HUMILITY

"Mistakes are made by people who know too much."

Incompetence is annoying, but overconfidence is terrifying. Entire wars, societies, and perhaps our planet disappear because of overconfidence. Overconfidence overlooks the best place to start something. It is a disease of experts who claim to know what is real. And it stuns the good preparation, and resourcefulness. The best place to start anything is by having a clear inventory of the present situation, good bad and ugly, including yourself. Constraints are an inevitable part of achieving anything.

Having a clear understanding of current reality involves a generous listening to what is going on. Listening this way leaves out editing the present situation with concepts and thought, instead redirecting using one's quality of awareness, to seeing where one stands looking at it, and where everyone is standing whose involved. To see where everyone is involved, even the most marginalized in the system, it involves open-hearted listening with compassion to see the world in their eyes. This shift is called occupying a 3rd person orientation to the world around you.

Despite the possibilities for epic change which arise from this shift, past success has left bad lessons. Past frameworks (overconfidence; certainty) gives rise to the blind-spot that the ego neglects to notice. One then guards their own ignorance out of fear of being inadequate, especially when the certainty is married to one's identity. As success continues, there's a rising sense that whenever the party's over, the hangover can be endured. The United States is experiencing this right now confronted with the debt ceiling. Bailing the world out has caught up to their success. Being the hero to affirm one's existence can put you into exhaustion to prove your importance.

Friends are negated, lost, unappreciated because so much success makes the future seem like it'll continue the same way, despite the ineffable nature of things to never stay the same. As the supply of success goes up, the demand for building new capacity for appreciation and gratitude begin turning toward complacency. Vulnerability turns off, and supply lines to success become a thing of the past. As you hear this, you're seeing how this has come back to haunt you, others, and even whole civilizations like the Roman Empire coming to an end.

This dynamic resembles the archetype in economics of supply and demand. Demand always rises to match supply. Expenses always rise to match income levels. When income reaches a substantial level, something shuts off. People do what they do unless there's something more compelling to do. Like income, time is like a vacuum. When not having a place to go in life (a goal, vision, direction), anything will rush to fill the space. Boredom is so dangerous for entrepreneurs because often times messes pop up to re-interest one's attention.

So why can't confident people articulate an accurate picture of the present situation? In a word: pride. We simply fear to look like a fool with humiliation. We fail to take inventory of our true capacity. Instead, we wear a false persona to mask actuality and genuineness. And this is why smart people don't learn.

An alternative is to come to terms with one's incompetency. Take identity away from failure, so it can be used as an asset. This is possible by heightening one's quality of self-awareness. It also involves the choice to be true to oneself.

If you say you know, then you don't. But if you know you don't know, then you know. What is there to know? There are three levels of knowing.

Level 1 is embodied knowing. This is the knowledge that is in the library, stored, shared, and taught. Level 2 is tacit knowing. It is the knowledge that has no remembrance of how it came in. Lacing your shoes, putting on your clothes, speaking your first language, putting your car in drive, all of these you know but don't remember how you came to know; you can't explain the process of assimilation. Level 3 is the knowledge that is not yet embodied. It is knowledge waiting to come into form, emergent, and pregnant.

Level three is the primary knowing. It is referred to as knowledge available at the moment of action. It is a reflection in action, gained through evocative energy. It is tapped by making space for it. Letting go is a useful way of becoming available for this knowledge. It is where experience reveals self-knowledge. And the quality of awareness you have regulates the reception of such knowledge like this.

The creative process is the most prolific structure for primary knowing to be drawn forth. The creator must be able to remain keenly aware of her present situation to see from inside the system in which they enact. When I say system, I am suggesting a greater context from which the creator withdraws from the past (letting go) and operates from the present moment from this place.

Being smart isn't from embodied knowledge, being smart is one who understands they are a small piece of a very large complicated picture. Ineffably, people are dependent upon and must rely on others to see what they cannot alone. Being smart is having a tablespoon a day of humility, and a cup of values and aspirations to follow into the day as a companion.

When we open our hearts and get personal about what matters to us, that is when we find what is universal between all of us. Many of us are preoccupied with power. We see ourselves as inadequate and seek ways to offset it. But in the endgame, we're all the same in this sense. We all have doubts about ourselves, shame, and guilt. If we didn't, we wouldn't appreciate what has meaning, what connection does, and where we find the voice of the whole within the groundwater of our being.

How can we be more of ourselves to be competitive in growing our business? This question is one that organizes a great deal of my work as a coach. Of all the answers here's what I can say: By articulating our personal gift and making it the central story of value creation through a conversation that inspires consent (choice). All value creation comes down to three aspects important to one needing help: Direction, Confidence, and Capability. What motivates the need for help and dependence on teamwork as the choice to create a future far bigger than in the past. Challenges and obstacles must be eliminated, opportunities must be captured, and strengths must be bolstered, in taking aim to create the desired future.

The central story of value creation is the compelling motivation for others to refer you, follow you, buy from you, to be led by you. It is the story of the particular conditions of your relationships that inspire your personal gift for help. Think of the dynamic like the gravity between two objects to come together. This is not only front-stage with clients, referral partners, and potential clients, but with internal customers and team-mates who depend on you for help. This compelling motivation is most likely going to happen when the "fundamental relationship" is established.

The "Fundamental Relationship" is a combination of personal gift x an ideal client x a transformative conversation x an intrinsic desire to make a difference. These elements, when placed in confluence, give rise to a creative pattern of order, where energy and information flow patterns unfold into more opportunities and growth for everyone. Life enhancing qualities arise from the application of one's personal gift (a superior skill they have a passion for).

We place personal gifts within conversations that can restructure people's motivation to create what they want. The greatest gift we can offer someone is the ability to sustain their accomplishments, so they don't backslide. If the self-knowledge of this is placed at the center of one's awareness, the whole is enfolded within it, as it unfolds into conversations where helping becomes possible. A sense of soul service becomes possible, where the one giving help is brought into their highest quality of expression that is accessible. "Helping" in this sense is giving someone something he or she can't do for themselves. This help is not based on someone not having enough or lacking capacity, but what could become possible from the helping process.

Service is the work of the soul. *Meaning* linked with service is the language of the soul. These two in combination bring forth the voluntary energy in the helper. One gives value just for the joy of it. This is important to point out because this energy is evoked not because it makes the helper feel like a hero. The helping process is offering one's truth independent of a need for adulation and affirmation of their existence.

If the helper is preoccupied with their sense of inadequacy, with the negative belief they aren't enough, comparing themselves to someone else, then the helping relationship is polluted by one's power hunger, instead of giving power to another person. In other words, don't be an expert, in fact, no one is when giving real help. We're all just making it up as we go along. So, you're better off just showing up in the truth of who you are---welcome everything, and expecting nothing, without your identity or ideals of self-perfection at stake.

The basic helping process begins with someone asking for and someone providing help. For this to happen, the one needing help must suspend their own knowledge of needs to the degree that the provider of help can define the needs with them. An example would be a doctor prescribing medication to him/herself versus depending on another doctor for help.

When the helping person is open, they can use all their organs of perception to bring their wisdom into the service of others. This wisdom is composed of knowledge not yet embodied. It has not been acquired yet, but instead, it is information awaiting arrival from emerging future possibilities which are waiting to enter the space. Making space is the process of letting go---of judgment, of cynicism, and of fear. A fresh outlook like this would characterize what it means to be fully present in the service of another human being.

The helping process is actually the learning process. They are the same. Invisible help is when the one giving help uses humble inquiry, starting with a blank canvass to ask for clarity and information from the one needing help to learn about their current reality in comparison to their desired conditions they seek to create. The challenge for the one giving help is having all the answers. The challenge for the one needing help is knowing what they need firsthand.

If prescribing the help stems from any pre-existing knowledge (the past) within the giver or receiver, their overconfidence, and experience short circuits the need to humbly inquire. This requires suspension. It is to place all the certainties in the bleachers and come forth with a beginner's mind as if you're maintaining your inexperience only to be led by curiosity. It is to be friendly with the mystery that encourages life to unfold that which the future is needing right this moment and trusting it. To do this, the intellect is bypassed to wiser attention. This wiser attention is made to stay with the present moment fluently, without adding interpretation to it.

This would be akin to a doctor prescribing medication without a diagnosis. Prescription without diagnosis is abusive. The learning process is motivated when structural tension is brought forth by the conversation. Structural tension is a powerful principle because it is nature's law to seek resolution when the tension (like a rubber band stretched) is formed between where a person wants to be in contrast to where they actually are. Where they actually are may be unseen until humble inquiry unearths the existing structure motivating the current behavior.

Structure influences the path of least resistance, where energy is most likely to end up. For example, the riverbed shape influences the flow direction of the river. Or the building you're in shapes the path back to the door. The human body's structure shapes the way the blood flows within in. By structure, I mean a flow pattern of energy and information. The whole inextricably is contained within the parts of it.

Motivation is structural. We know this because there are two types of structures: ones that oscillate (move forward then back) like the structure of a rocking chair, and advancing (move forward and continue going forward like a car from A to B). When a person has an underlying belief, fear, assumption or competing goal, the structure they're in tends to pull the person backward toward the concept or belief rather than forward them toward the goal in mind. This is because there's something more senior is at play like at riptide or headwind that is of greater force than other units (goals) within the structure. Human beings are a complex species. We carry forward a database of experiences from the past that habitually bring perceptions, interpretations, and expectations to the present moment. We edit ourselves, our reality with these, and the behavior of others by seeing life through our concepts, assumptions, and generalizations. These could be called mental constructs or models based on conditioned thought. We often are walking the path hypnotized by our own context around things that we take in, and these shape our behavior rather than our choices.

Our constructs are most often ideals of ourselves, or expectations of what *should* be, or fears that something might turn out a certain way. From these, we make attempts to create the future instead of creating a future. We forget to refresh our awareness to occupy the present moment, where our biggest future possibilities await us, and we can listen to opportunities ready to begin at any time. Instead of acting in an instant, we relegate ourselves to preventing what we don't want. Problem solving then replaces the creative process.

In the helping process, it's important that in giving help we learn to see and think structurally, picturing what the other is saying as we listen respectfully. As we humbly inquire, we wipe away our comparison thinking to our database and just listen with a blank canvas. As we inquire into what is going on for someone, we begin to see the underlying structure at play like a can't miss. We see perhaps that the person is more inclined to live up to their standard of perfection or a way to be rather than creating the values that matter to them. We see how they obligate themselves to deserve first what they desired by complicating things and getting in their own way to offset their negative concept of who they are. They seek self-acceptance instead of seeing the truth of themselves, the good bad and ugly. To see and comprehend the interior condition you cultivate is key here to the encounter.

The giver of help (you) probably knows his own strengths and limitations, and is able to allocate his personal gift in the direction of the invisible help that becomes visible through the conversation. The conversation to understanding the one needing help and getting to their real needs is probably more helpful than the solution itself. This is called a "transformative conversation." All business is a network held together by a transformative conversation, and little ones on many levels that compose it. When the conversation on the outside is the one on the inside, a brand is discernable. An executive replied after this conversation that it was the first time he really 'thought' in six months. Just the process of inquiry inspired him to pull back, consider what he really wanted, and also consider where he was in relationship to this. He began to see new courses of action motivated by the structures coming into play.

RESTORING HUMANITY IN PERFORMANCE

"The way the client was given our work was nothing short of exceptional," said Donna. She went on to describe her most extraordinary moments of the team doing amazing acts of generosity and service.

"At the age of 42, I wasn't afraid to let go and trust my team members because I could see them in their truest form. We knew each of us had the seed of giving rather than taking and this made all the difference."

Mom's funeral was a moment of truth for Donna to reveal the best of life's nuances. Being mom's daughter was about participating in life in all its personal and professional aspects. It was always mom's desire to see Donna take the helm but do it in her authentic way to drive successful change. The new sales volume requires nine new support staff and two sales managers, and it was Donna's finest hour to send Mom off in her celebration of life and do so in staying true to Mom's 40 years building and outstanding sales force.

"What would mom want me to do now?" Donna expressed how important it was to follow her heart-felt passions for the business mission and how it served the world. "Providence" wasn't only the Company name but meant the connection to the divine in all decisions. "A good strong leader is strong enough to be open, weak, and vulnerable, as she is a human being. Being a human being is the first step to becoming a leader." Twenty-eight managing leaders circled up were nodding their heads like admiring allies, as Donna went on to describe mom's legacy going forward. Donna was reading some of mom's best quotes throughout her lifetime to imbue the best of her traditions.

August 22nd, 1993. (Mom's Notes)

We were facing the biggest challenge yet for our 4 escrow business units. Everyone was struggling with his or her needy voice to be identified and affirmed as knowing something worthy of affirmation. There we were acting as if we weren't needy, pretending, faking with our heavy knowledge-base of how to look at things and what we should do. Everyone in the room had a certain opinion like religious fanaticism with untested certainty trying to convince everyone they're right. Not one person was asking questions.

We were stuck. There we were sitting on our answers, jumping to conclusions without any understanding of what was really going on or what brought the situation to pass. Everyone was seduced by the hunger to be the hero with a craving for problem solving. I could see where all of this was going and called a break. Fifteen minutes in return from the bathroom, I asked what conversations were overhead outside the conference room. Everyone was locked into his or her points of view, ready to fire their ideas out as if to be competing for a jump ball to be right. Nobody was anywhere near his or her potential here.

"Stop!" I shouted. I slammed the palms of my hands on the desk. Everyone looked up in shock. "Do I have to scream to get you to think?" "Does anyone here have any idea how to depend on each other to work through this challenge?" I could see hidden, latent potential in each soul in the room yet none of them had tapped into it. Everyone was convinced of his or her opinion and approach. I could see my setup when I asked for solutions, not complaints. Boy, little did I know what would happen with this ask!"

"What is really important to us here?" The room went silent with my question. "What are we trying to accomplish in this matter?" "What are we living for that is important to us?" Being a citizen means to be involved on an intrinsic level by choosing an outcome we deeply desire. This was another path than where everyone seemed to be attending. I wanted everyone to enter the world of desire, not the intellect. I could tell that what really mattered to us wasn't in the room yet. We hadn't understood what we were really doing here. This lack

171

of sensitivity was short circuiting our potential and kept us away from trusting our teamwork.

There is a collective level of what is going on that influences at a level that only together we can access. Instead of looking at ourselves, we were there standing side by side realizing loneliness that we had not registered. Like learning to cooperate, we needed one another to embolden and imbue what we together would come to know immediately as our truest work. This had very much to do with reflection.

What began to come up as I tapped into what was important to us was an outcome that stood beyond what we had imagined in the past. The more we internalized our search for self-improvement, the less capacity we had to listen to each other in our different points of view. Locked into our individualism each of us was seeking to be noticed, to be special with an idea of a self that needs affirmation to become real. Unfortunately, no light can get in when we project something into the night sky. We miss the stars because of diffusion.

A self-indulgent, "Me-first" orientation ruled the room like a bunch of heroic egos gone wild. Ruthless ambition was put ahead of asking for help. Receptivity was far less than willful action to think communally. I started to see where to go toward a "We-first" approach. Our underlying general opinion about one another was we were each too dangerous to be trusted. To share our thinking with another partner is so scary that we resign to operate from relative truth to operate in the world. Defending and armor the heart is a way of preemptively striking against this perceived danger.

"What is really going on?" When I asked this question, everyone stopped thinking and talking. Debating became interrupted by the need for seeing things more carefully. Being fast and manic in our approach is expected. We are rewarded for speed, and yet slowing down and understanding the problem and the source of it could position our help in a much greater manner for the customer.

"What is this speaking to us?" The problem itself wasn't about eliminating it, rather, using it as a powerful source of education. We were about to lead something out of our talents non-adjacent to our operating entirely from what we already know. We were facing a new way of learning from the future by doing. And the knowledge coming from what seemed to be appearing for us had a natural inclination to be poised as some greater fabrication from threading each strand together.

I noticed when asking these deeper, profound questions, people felt respected. Just asking the questions implied that a greater leadership potential was ready to stand in the participants.

But I could see how the concentration on ourselves was obstructing a truer, more real conversation with each other and with our customer. "What is expected of us?" As much as we were convinced we knew our customer, we really did not. Our own assumptions denied us access to understanding their true position. It was as if we had to be the citizen, not the doctor. We were being asked to live in their world and grasp what we were about to do.

Richard turned to Angela and asked her to help him understand how she concluded that the customer had changed their mind. Angela played back what she heard, and Richard added on more to clarify his point of view. This was the first glimpse of the team learning to learn. Instead of selling opinions and debating, Rich and Angela were coming to seeing what could be going on dependent on each other. In the middle of their exchange, I asked them where this was going. Both expressed a "squeezing it out" type dynamic as if to give birth to sense-making together of what is going on and what is important about it.

The interaction became contagious as I saw others in the group compose small groups of various formations to inquire into what each was considering in his or her reflections intimately. After several minutes a quiet calm came over the room as if closure was bubbling to the surface. I was suspended in slow motion somewhere between asking for the content and leaving it where it was already there living in presence with us.

We had glimpsed together how our habitual ways of thinking and acting toward each other no longer served us in being a real team. Outside these places, a natural, common caring had arisen, and a will to help arrived as if to be a finer quality of expression we all knew was leaving no one out. Like an orchestra, we knew the tone required to play the music we were making. It was as if the music was being written as we were playing it at the same time.

We were teasing out a pre-existing fantasy as we were interacting within a flow of interdependent, elaborative, psychic energy. Rather than say our hard reality, we remember that too was a fantasy, to re-open the flow of psychic energy. The whole room began to shine like a light with enthusiasm like a deep, profound, unexpected partnering that felt great much like the relativism of band member playing off of one another. We were blessed. It wasn't our expertise that we needed from one another; it was our humanness that connected us in new ways.

THE BEGINNING

The question of where you start from is an interesting one. Where does the creative process begin? You begin with a blank slate. You start with nothing. Creating is a process which begins separate from what you know. Knowledge is the storage material of your internal database. The internal database is composed of what you know and expect things to be, based on the past. When starting with this, you are not creating; you're repeating something. This is why "achievable goals" don't work. An achievable, realistic goal is an attempt to protect you from discouragement! By reaching for what you already know you lower the chances for failure. Yet all your thinking is drawn from the past, from fear, in an attempt to predict the future rather than create one. And by doing that you remain the same as you are now. The purpose of a goal is to change behavior. What would you need to learn or unlearn by setting a goal you proved you could reach?

Sales managers and organizations chant that they must have a sales system. This usually includes a process to level out the different skills in the sales ranks. If the newest and weakest is selling to a laggard or conservative buyer whose difficult, losses incur. However, today this isn't necessarily the case. As you're probably picking up by now in this book, the capacity for emotional intimacy, connection, and safety is the foundation of a helpful process. No sales system can replace the humanness that far exceeds the expertise when it comes to building a relationship. If someone can't trust you, they don't buy.

Having a helping process is necessary, it's just insufficient. Knowing how to sing is necessary to sing professionally, but if you can't connect to the song or the audience listening, nothing moves. There "ain't no soul" as the saying goes. And it's the source, the inner place from which the performance is arising that creates the itch to listen and engage with the music. The artist is coming from the love invoked by the music they're making and the spirit for what is felt when received. Selling needs engineering, control, and process, but without the heart, it's dead. Enthusiasm is what people love to be around. This is why we go to concerts or theatre. We love to watch people loving what they do because it's attractive.

THE MAGIC HELP FROM YOUR STAY

Practice the capacity to *stay* in the experience of the other person's story. Stay where they are, not where you want them to be. Creating safety is about setting an unforced space with gentle curiosity and inquiry. The content (what you're selling, what they're wanting) is an excuse to hold the process for relating. As you take the person in, put yourself in their shoes.

Pay attention to the following as the buyer opens up:

1. What struck you within the story they're describing in their experience? When they describe concerns and challenges, what grabbed you? This is your next jump off point to trust and enter.
2. Do not position yourself to know something they do not. The implication of knowing something is that it commands obedience. Your knowledge is your enemy. Instead, your curiosity infers emptiness and vacancy.
3. Conserve your ignorance and stupidity. Trying to know what you're talking about excludes your trust fallibility. You're making all this up as a go along.
4. What could be possible impact of the personal experience? Good? Bad? Construct your curiosity questions to understand the impact this experience is having on who and how?
5. Do not help the person, trying to help them suggests they're helpless. They're able to help themselves. When you honor the helper in themselves, you let go of replacing it. And you get focused on understanding them in ways that enhancing their comprehension of themselves, their situation, and what is emerging actually stages the opportunity for seeing what to do and where to go. Don't get in the way of things.

CHAPTER 7

SLOW

When your piano is out of tune, the music sounds flat or sharp. We can't harmonize with the sounds because they are dissonant and tense. Much like being out of tune, our interior condition can equally go off balance and become full of noisy thoughts.

The quality of any connection with anyone begins with the interior condition of the intervenor. In this case, you the sales practitioner must practice quieting your brain down to help the mind become active through it like a peephole looking into a line of sight.

Quality in action selling begins with attunement. This is the practice of putting aside the doer and cultivating close contact with your innermost being. The place to begin this practice is through intentional grounding and silence first thing in the morning. Many sales professionals love to walk, run, workout, and do something active. They consider this to be their quiet time for reflection and attunement. They gather what is going on outside and integrate four conversations all at once, slow, not fast. To them, *slow* is the new fast.

Our lives are encumbered by a whirlwind of information, social media, entertainment, tempting experiences, people, rules, expectations, striving to meet our standards and ideals to be someone, and all that. We can slow down by using our single biggest leverage point: our levels of awareness. I'm often asked how to slow down in the middle of things. The idea of getting away---going into the silence, a getaway is often the vaccine to such a hectic life. Yet we don't have to be on vacation to back up and see what life is saying to us, what has meaning in what we're doing and reflect. Reflection is a skill, not an act through convenient circumstances that line up just right. Reflection on action is one thing, but reflection *in* action is available to each of us if we just use our quality of attention to be mindful---to be the doer observing what we're doing. Without our use of this quality of attention, we lose the opportunity to see new sides of what is real, we disconnect from our capacity to empathize and be touched by those around us, and we cannot integrate emerging future possibilities that arise in the now. Space is not given to us; rather we give space to what is present in our lives. And when we do, a new field of power opens for us to learn, live more fully, and create out of the emerging order of what is here and now. We must set the stage for this space-giving to all things and as we come into understanding through new seeing and insight, compassion and acceptance, integration and emergence, we are involved in our own evolution as become conscious of our surroundings in use.

GENERATIVE SPACE

A powerful teaching that came out of this is about unrestricted movement. Whatever we make space for can move. When we let others live as they are (respecting) outside of our habitual judgment, we help whatever they choose by consent to move. When we seek to confirm our certainty of thought, despite its invalidity, we leap anyway and forget to see that our judgment reinforces the behavior we think is independent of our influence. If you've ever held a judgmental opinion of someone, just watch what plays out over time. The enactment of your belief goes live as an active ingredient in locking them into a pattern that we fail to connect back to our thinking. When we suspend our certainty and make space for disconfirming realities, it creates space for new movement. This explains why any new level of understanding leads to something new becoming possible.

A HOLDING OPEN SPACE AS A POINT OF ENTRY

The internet has begun causing the extinction of time for thinking and reflection. The world has gone off the deep-end on action and left in slow time in the dust. What is it like to help someone by figuring things out together? Most of the problems your prospects have are caused by quick fix solutions to surface issues.

You might be surprised that you can slow down time. Your levels of awareness can increase the qualitative attention such that it transcends how time is experienced. When you're more aware of what is going on, what you're creating, and what matters to you shifts the way you experience time. Your intention informs where you place your attention. Having a place to go helps you integrate where you're going with elements showing up in where you are now. You might look at it like holding a 3D image. You see here and there as one emerging wholeness. And to know the whole, it is seen in the expression of its parts. A "fractal" is a representation of the whole without losing its true form. Remember the Russian nesting doll with large to small versions. Each one is the same in form as the larger, yet it is a smaller representation. When you move down into deeper levels of awareness into what is emerging, the micro becomes an aperture to the macro. This is a place where the past, present, future is altogether, and what might emerge becomes visible. As you do things, you see some new aspect of reality. To understand the whole, you have to try to change it as a continuous cycle of deepening in action. This is called "reflection in action."

Look back at your three most recent meetings with new prospects or clients. How many questions did you ask? A question expresses an act of vulnerability. You pause the habitual mechanism of your head and act from your open mind of curiosity and wonder.

HOW TO SLOW TIME DOWN

The future is uncertain. You can't have it your way, ever. Half of life is coming to terms with just how powerless we all really are to manipulating life. We are on its terms. And yet we have choices to make about how we intend, attend, and connect within our present moment moments. What we fear the most is just how free we all are to choose. We can rethink our lives at any time without any reference to the past. What matters to us comes and goes from one thing mattering before to not mattering now. We are in constant flux with this question.

We don't want to be controlled by life despite having no control. So, we mentally construct something called "time" to avoid being controlled by it. We use our model of time to protect ourselves from the uncertainty of the future. Yet the mystery is alive and full of virtual possibilities that await us when we let go of having control over it. What presents itself is just at the perfect moment, as if the future needed it right now.

Being the observer is having the integrity to tolerate ambiguity, volatility, uncertainty, and complexity until grey becomes a clear path. The clear path is born of yielding vision, clarity, understanding, and agility like staccato steps over sharp rocks. We press long enough to feel the sharpness but light enough to move toward another stepping point.

The skill of separation starts with opening yourself to something you don't know. In fact, you don't know how you know what you know. The only verification to knowing anything is what presents itself to be true right now. Separation isn't automatic for you because your brain is wired to make sense of things, even if it lies to you. You see what you perceive. Your thoughts distort, contaminate, and fill in gaps with theories and non-facts to make it look like it knows, and yet there's another companion hanging out in the same place called awareness.

If you ever wonder what scientists say about using our full brain power, it's about turning your levels of awareness into a highly tuned vigilance watchdog on the brain's tendencies to get mechanical.

The fundamental ingredient to holding space is trust. Trusting the unknown isn't friendly to the brain since it suggests something that threatens survival. Uncertainty breathes danger. The brain alerts the nervous system to prepare for an attack by drawing adrenaline from the glands and activating a stress response.

The body is preparing for something around the corner to fight with, flight from, or freeze when it arises. Holding space is the room to let this go. It isn't that fear is the constraint, it's not touching the fear itself. Fear itself is good. You wouldn't be scared if you didn't care about you and didn't want you to get hurt. Fear is out of respect for your survival. It's a good alert. But relating to it is a whole other story. Receiving fear requires steadiness, stillness, centering, and breathing right. The nature of fear isn't permanent, it comes and then goes away. The knee jerk reaction feels discomforting. True fearlessness isn't the absence of fear, rather, knowing it all too well and cutting the cord to more generative urges with full attention.

Observing and meeting whatever arises inside requires letting go of comparisons to our ideals. Ideals steal relaxation by comparison thinking. We fill in what we'd rather be doing by "should's" and "ought to's." Downtime makes us panic, anxious, and nervous because we feel out of sorts with our ideals to be producing, working, fighting, and being responsible. We define standards of perfection and attempt to live by them such that downtime is negated. This is often why slow time, reflection, and meditation get sidelined to the frenetic pace of life. We consume and clog our time up with staying busy instead of putting a priority on rejuvenation, reflection, to become a lot less busy.

SIGNIFICANCE

One of the concepts in time management is a principle of simplicity.
"Not everything matters the same." Being overwhelmed isn't because
we have too much around us, it's because everything has equal
meaning. Well, what if you propose that's true---what if everything has
equal meaning, wouldn't we be on attention overload? Some time
management pros would say yes, but not if we learn to make space
for anything, in fact, we can better assimilate what is significant by
offering our full attention to whatever is arising no matter how small or
big it looks to our sense of what matters to us. Because we move
through time as nothing stays the same, context is in motion. We
make sense of things as we go along. What didn't matter before may
matter as things progress and unfold, and yet what once mattered
doesn't matter now as something else does. We live in a world of
constant flux where the order of things is in constant conversation
with our interior world. Do we make everything significant or not? That
is the question. How much power do we give life in its organizing
character, and how much power do we take into effect?

As Steve Jobs said in his Graduating Class of 2006 Keynote Speech:
"Connect those dots." We make sense of things after the fact after
things have gone by and then we translate what they meant when
arriving here and now and seeing the relevance. These integrations
are revealed by walking and moving, not sitting and watching only.
How we learn is both an active and receptive process. What I think
Jobs is implying is to make space for something we must leave out.
Barbara Sher describes this as "wise innocence" when we remember

the must of having an intention, and yet the must of leaving out the blank spot, the parenthesis for life to give us what we need as we move along.

Perhaps it is the combination of feminine and masculine imbued in our way of being---the masculine is the doer, as the feminine is the listener capturing more deeply what is being realized or taken from what is going on. Perhaps these co-exist much like holding a 3D image with our attention and intention in a constant dance of change. We are available to the new, as we are obedient to the intention we choose. We can change our minds at any time as things become clear along the way. There are no rules that apply to what we must or must not do; our choices are up for grabs at any moment. This suggests that having a sense of what mattered before is helpful because we are in constant comparison with what moves us now compared to what moved us before. We can relate with life on both terms simultaneously from the inside out. We can reset our attention qualitatively to reset our intention qualitatively to have something inspiring or moving us to be the centerpiece of organizing our lives. The term I often use for the way these terms stay in use is "quality in action." Ken Bast, a colleague of mine coined the term, "the enlightened doer." Awareness-based creating might be another way of putting it.

We can operate from this as the basis from which we come at helping others (selling). The seller learns to have SLOW conversations.

THE FOUR CONVERSATIONS

Let's explore SLOW in the four moving parts when you are influencing another human being in meaningful ways: self, life, other, work. The first is the conversation around the self. There are two selves, the current one and the future one that is becoming. Their current self has two sides: the weaknesses and strengths, while the future self has one side only: the dormant or potential self that is emerging and unfolding.

Strengths and emerging qualities of themselves are what excites them, while weaknesses are qualities that limit or disturb them. Unrestricted visibility to these qualities in itself is a great source of helping another human stage a starting point for a significant change effort. This one could be organized by what resources are required to position the strengths and emerging self to come into being while the weaknesses are managed or no longer a constraint. This liberation is so powerful in helping another human being mobilize your highest potential to come out. So, all of this content—the current and future selves are actually sources of motivational energy from which the person is organizing the effort. They seek to make contact with their highest future possibilities (future self), taking aim with the strengths (their best current self) they have to apply. Removing weaknesses and reinforcing strengths are both access points for helping another person. In fact, much of your leadership, confidence, and creativity will spring from from how you match your helping process up to these qualities.

186

The second conversation is the one the person is having with their life. Everything included, and nothing left out. They live within an entire spectrum; a web of life in which they exist within a network of relationships. This web of life supplies the context in which certain features in their life define what moves them toward something. The third conversation is between them and the "other"; "other" being close and near relationships, their teammates, associates, their customers, their support systems personal and professional in which they give and receive inputs. And the fourth conversation is work or wealth. Wealth is the confluence of spirituality and commerce living together. Another way of putting this conversation is "opportunities" that they desire to reach because they matter to them.

SLOW conversations contain the seeds from which a transformative event can emerge. The self is the greatest weapon any leader has to create change. The distance between their current and future self is a pathway of giving oneself to their highest future possibilities standing in need of them. Connecting another human being to their future self is perhaps the greatest access point to feeling alive. Many leaders are in such turmoil or running so fast; they bypass reflection. Cutting ones' self from reflection is like severing the meaning, service, and mystery of the soul from any moment. It is "soul-loss."

IT'S ABOUT PEOPLE

People buy people, through connection, not products and services. If you ask the last ten customers why they buy from you, they'll tell you what it is about you that makes them trust you. There are habits you have that influence their ability to give you their loyalty.

Usually, Dan starts every presentation with his PowerPoint. He likes using it to present the same process every single time. Dan prided himself on how consistent his presentation came through in his appointments. Dan was doing presentations, not having conversations. I encouraged Dan to explore another dimension of his conversations. Next time he starts an appointment, I asked him to get interested, instead of looking interesting. Despite his fear, he was comfortable with his own ignorance and tried my idea.

Next time Dan asked the prospect to describe what they wanted to create as if five years from now they had what they love and want most. When Dan asked Elliot the question, Dan looked at his watch, and after thirty minutes Elliot was still talking. Dan was stunned how much detail he retrieved when asking Elliot about where he was going in life and business. It felt as if no one, not even his wife had asked Elliot to describe his truest desires. The description included how Elliot aspired to spend his time, use his money, and deepen access to relationships with his children and how his fundamental values flowed naturally throughout his business day.

As Dan stood still, listening as if a blank slate, Dan could feel a swelling presence from within. Elliot began to get emotional, and as tears streamed down his face, he described his life as an alcoholic, unavailable, motion-less for the last 20 years and longed to create a meaningful life. How did one question open up all this intimate sharing of information and bonding? As Elliot wiped away his tears he said, "Dan your financial planning services around pretty good, what do we do to get started?" Dan hadn't said one thing about himself, his products, or his process. What Elliot got was that Dan's efforts would be about *Elliot*, not Dan. This made all the difference.

Dan's next appointment started with a distinct stillness. Instead of his habitual presentation method, this time Dan started with a blank slate, to learn more about the future self the person he was influencing wanted most. The generative power of a pregnant future desired from aspirations became the starting point from which all direction, capability, and relationship Dan would bring forth.

The power is in the curious mind. When you begin from nothing, you encounter a sense of wonder, empathy, and understanding that gives space for something new to arise. Making space for wonder, curiosity, and understanding struck Dan profoundly because it was the first time he truly felt his self, imbued in a heart-touching act. After his appointments, people said it was some of the best reflection they had ever had, and the clarity of direction was greater than any problems Dan could solve.

Dan was so excited to share with me (his coach) about his new influencing. I encouraged him to go into the next conversations the same way but add another element. Dan asked Ben where he was now in relationship to his future self. Ben started with the challenges. He described the obstacles, barriers, and concerns that he wanted to remove to bridge to his dreams.

As Dan took in these data points, he could sense the swell inside to help. Ben described his best opportunities from his current position relevant to his vision. These three opportunities were what Ben wanted most for his future self. Again, Dan made a note on several ways he could enhance this. Then Ben went into what excited him most today that he wanted to reinforce. If Dan could help by removing the dangers, reaching the opportunities, and reinforcing the strengths, just imagine the difference possible for Ben's life and his family? Dan began seeing his work in a new light. He had forgotten the salesman and found himself awakened to a new type of "helper."

Dan felt like he was ready to spill with solutions and answers, but he remembered the conversation is what he provides. A transformative conversation is one that is SLOW. The future self becomes the anchor from which all decisions, actions, communications today are to be made. Then Dan noticed that the conversation expanded into key relationships that the buyer needs to produce this future self. Life itself is the current reality as a living breathing frontier—that which is welling up now. These are qualities that are concerning, opportunities emerging, and strengths to conserve and reinforce. The work conversation is about the time and productivity the person intends to have and the conditions they have now. Dan knew that with the SLOW model, all value creation inspired him to provide direction, relationship, and trust, and creativity in co-creating a future the buyer truly wants. That joining the buyer in their SLOW journey made Dan an indispensable resource for bringing great enrichment, support, and essential expression to making the most of grace and transformation in their life.

BUYER PRECONCEPTIONS

Alignment is a key concept in SLOW selling. It is the ability to understand the buyer in their own truth by listening to their listening, and how they relate with and integrate their own experiences. Buyers live in three possible orientations to suggest how they organize decisions, actions, and communications in their life. The first is the orientation of the reactive-responsive. They toggle between a first and second person orientation. Part of their behavior is organized by what they know as well as living from what they don't know. They can move from subjective to objective levels of attending to what is going on because they are comfortable with their own ignorance and find themselves curious, to honor differences. They have basic access to an open mind, using their awareness to suspend their voice of judgment. Buyers who are mature tend to live from what they don't know because they're not attached to their certainties. These buyers are easier to approach because they are astonished and happy to explore differences. These types of buyers are called "Explorers" while the buyers with certainty are called "Pacifiers." Pacifiers tend to see what they expect and already know. Pacifiers can be so asleep to alternatives that they have latent needs for help. They just sit in their lenses and filters, letting their conditioned, habitual thinking drive their behavior. If they feel safe, they may be willing to explore potential demand for help.

A special version of the explorer is the Tipi-toer" because they don't want anyone to know they are exploring something else. People have belief systems with such certainty that their identity is married to this.

Once buyers go live with a solution they care about and in pursuit of it, they become "hunters." Hunters are buyers who have recognized they need help and knew what help to expect. A special version of a hunter is a "Networker." Networkers hunt only through friends and contacts to regulate strangers.

Beyond 1st and 2nd person perspectives, buyers who operate within a 3rd person orientation are great listeners and tend to be interested in others rather than being interesting. These are curious buyers with an open mind, whose movement is inspired by seeing through the perspective others have in their community. They are "value creators and early adopters." These buyers want help with how to make a difference and how to help others win. They organize from "them" or "other." These buyers like to get things done via collective and social intelligence levels. They are great delegators, using their reverence for the gifts in others as mechanisms to authorize people with responsibility and ownership. They are not rugged individualists like Pacifiers, they are team leaders, who see dependence as the key to getting things done.

PACIFIERS. A buyer/leader who has a pacifier in the mouth nice and comfortable, operating with continuity and a sense of certainty. They are living a reactive orientation to life in a 1st person perspective.

EXPLORERS. A buyer/leader who at times might tippie toe around people knows they're interested in change but haven't acted upon any new ideas or directions. These buyers are comfortable with their own ignorance. They have more questions than answers most of the time. They toggle between 1st and 2nd person perspectives.

MOBILIZERS. A buyer/leader who is actively creating the desired state. They want a future that is possible by removing dangers, reaching opportunities, and enhancing strengths that excite them now. They live in a 3rd person perspective, focusing on their desired creations, not themselves.

VALUE CREATORS. A buyer/leader who is actively seeking to help others be there for themselves and others at their very best. They live entirely from a 3rd person orientation, leading a cause to enrich others by being interested, rather than interesting.

HOLONS. A buyer/leader who is both part and whole, which leads from the emerging future, with courage, compassion, and connection to wherever goodness and wisdom can expand. They live in a 4th person perspective, letting go and letting come, with confluence between their inner intention and the universe's will. They are generous listeners.

HOLONS

A rare type of buyer is one that you've probably come across less frequently. They are teachers whom others seek advice from, mobilizers and diehards who evangelize new ideas and upend the status quo, and skeptics who test the validity of great ideas and conclusions. They are warriors, lovers, and magicians in the fullness; you might say "kings." They live in a 4th person perspective and make decisions based on a profound intuition or inner knowing. Their relationship with you draws upon something aesthetic to their senses activate a felt sense connected to a social body that is collectively accessible. These buyers have extraordinary sensibilities that connect you and your help with an emerging future possibility they trust is coming toward them. These individuals seek relationships with characters participating in a grander scheme of things that draw upon their concerns for the greater good because they remember they are soulful people are so are you. These buyers move in the direction of wisdom and evaluate decisions from a wider, grander will that is of higher intelligence than their own. Their faith is in the quality of connection with you, and the content comes forth from it. They see the world as God does, using their sense perceptions as they conserve acceptance and legitimacy such that other people feel loved. And they enjoy intentional silence and grounding, using interior stillness and meditation to meet whatever arises. They integrate their experiences such that everything is energy to be used for awakening.

These individuals are called "holons" from the Greek word "holos" meaning part and whole are one in the same. These individuals are so present that any formative forces are purely not yet embodied matter that is dormant, ready for something new to begin. These individuals are capable of seeing differences, sensing the value in others, as well as trusting context in motion from here and now as divine construction. These holons are able to listen so widely and deeply that their entire being pre-senses emerging possibilities ready to be born, and set foot into that unknown territory, such that moving in by walking unfolds mystery into making. They are devoted to change, to harnessing and harvesting disruptive change, and love to drift outside the familiar into new ground. These are the true innovators. They have shattered the falseness in their image. They aren't preoccupied with power or needing to feel noticed or special to offset their inadequacy. They have accepted themselves as human beings to incorporate cosmic intervention into their design structure. Since this is the case, they don't need to net others in what they disown in themselves. As sentient beings, their attention and intention are clear minded and clear hearted. They see without judgment or criticism, internalize what has heart and meaning, and welcome the outcome they desire without attachment to it. They make room for wise innocence. This is the part of the story beyond their intention for a result that plays out as the universe desires it, not them. Serenity is given its placeholder in the grand array of things. This surrender to a larger will involves the capacity to let go and let come. They live from the emerging future, not the past.

As you read the different orientations and buyer typology, you probably are self-evaluating which orientation you tend to organize movement from most often. The figure below illustrates the four

195

different perspectives and other elements that are worth remembering.

Explorers are on the verge of defining their lives in service to others. Their stage of learning is how to let others change them. If they learn how to trust and lower their cynicism, they can grant ample amounts of power to others to move them into action. Explorers are learning to work with compassion and understanding. Hunters and networkers are the serial creators who move by their chosen intention. They don't have the plurality that a holon incorporates. Holons are radical co-creatives, who sense the influence of the whole and act from that place with emerging design powers coming from inside and outside. External and internal purpose align like the confluence of two heartbeats into one field or frame of reference. Will and willingness work together to forge a way forward that is both serving a destiny as well as choosing to create what matters to them.

VALUE CREATORS

Value creation depends on the inner place from which the seller is attending, listening, and acting. This is the main point of this book. It's not about what sellers do, or how they do it, but rather the source from which the come from—the beginning.

When I asked one of the top sales producers what problem was with his #2 guy, he gave me the main reason why he was so far below him on personal production. It wasn't about the level of action. The guy was getting in front of people—generating interest and setting

196

appointments. But he wasn't connecting with them. Why? Because he wasn't giving value for the joy of it. I was at first stunned by this observation. But he was spot on.

He went on to tell me that his number two guy was all about himself and getting the money. He wasn't concerned with what served his clients, he wanted the material wealth and winnings of big money, and for this a certain quality of being, an animation was missing from this persona that turned people off. He seemed insincere, slimy, pushy, and irreverent. The guy was in it for the money and the money only. No heart.

At that moment I opened my eyes to see this was a universal matter. All around me I could see the money guys and heart guys, and the heart guys had most of the business, and the quality of connections were far different. Their manner of service was innovative, full of enthusiasm, and fun, while the money guys wanted to create a system, a team, and a business to run by itself while he made big money. Which do you think is more sustainable? Which would you want to be a part of as a team? Which would you rather become a client of?

Value creators seek to add value first before expecting anything in return. They give for the sake of it. Holons are serial creators, value creators, and expanders of emerging future possibilities that arise in the now. When you encounter a Holon, a generative dialog can help both you and them arrive at answers to their needs and your role in their next passage. Creators (Hunters) and Value Creators are all about creating a future they desire for themselves and/or for others. Explorers are willing to construct an alternative future that you help them see with your help.

Future based questions are important to the hunter. He lives from his future self and wants help blasting any obstacles lying in his way. He wants to reach opportunities that matter to him and reinforce strengths that expedite his success.

Explorers don't have a clear future yet in mind. They need help getting their head and heart around one that matters enough to change their direction. As they envision this future they seek to create, they can gather a clear picture of the current state they have now in comparison, to see where to depend on help to close the gap. Your role is one of wingman in co-initiating a vision together, one that they choose after getting your help in choosing a direction.

A quality of leadership you might spot here is called "respecting." This capacity is to revere and respect the differences between you and others. Respecting is giving space for the "other" instead of being reduced to the "object" position of needing to be something made for you. Respecting is handing another human being ownership of their own life. It is a position of non-interference. Another way of describing this step is "redirection."

There is a great teaching in Zen comparing a stick when thrown at a dog compared to a lion. When you throw the stick to the dog, the dog without hesitation runs after it and goes to pick it up. But when you throw a stick to a lion, first the lion pauses, turns its head to see where the stick came from? What is the source or person who originated the throwing action? Like your head, you jump from zero to hundred into thinking, such that your assumption governs you without looking to see who is there. When you pause and take a breath first, you place space between the sudden habitual thought and the one having the thought. You separate from the thinker and thought. This space in between is called redirection back to the inner source from which the activity is originating. Respecting is a redirection of netting another individual in judgment and letting them be just as they are right now. When we get trapped in automatic thought, we leap into inferences instead of seeing what is actually going on. It's as if we react to shadows and phantoms that are projections of thought, rather than what is actually there.

One of my experiences that vividly illustrated the process of redirection was a shirt that I choose to wear in front of my wife. She suddenly told me to change my sweater. What she didn't register was the argyle pattern on my t-shirt looked like the ones you'd see on a sweater. Her eyes fooled her as she leaped to tell me to change. She realized after verifying what was going on that her eyes fooled her. She saw a sweater, not a shirt.

LIFE AS THE COLLECTOR CONTINUES...

Early in life we learn and store our experiences into a database of concepts, beliefs, generalizations, knowledge, and models of the ways things should look. Our education system inserts a covert belief in our psyche that having knowledge is power, as if we become better people by what we know. Education is pointed to avoid a sense of inadequacy by knowing something other people do not. This marries our identity to a collection we keep from the past.

What's the problem with this? Creating. When we create something new, relying on our database limits the creative process by what we already know. A key aspect in the creative process is the capacity to report current reality just as it is, not through our collection of concepts. Our collection edits what we see through our biases because we compare it to what we know and lean toward consistencies rather than differences. After a while seeing what we know dulls our experience instead of making life interesting and honoring these differences. There is sterility and staleness to operate from our collection. In fact, a few years ago, I heard an entrepreneur attempt to convince me of the nobility of lifelong learning. As if to collect action figures or trading cards his pride was identifying his worth by how long and far his learning could carry him. To him, unlearning threatened his belief that his collection symbolized a superiority over others with less learning over great distances. Anyone who questioned his level would offend him because he took it personally.

Unlearning can become linked to one's self-preservation. People convince others and themselves that knowing nothing makes them a better person. Attempting to appear as better people, they purge everything they know. Their new model of themselves as better people is justified as one who suffers less when judgment is missing.

Their self-propaganda is the clean-sweeper of anything they think is true in an attempt to subscribe to a person with a higher mind. The approach asserts that knowing less will change their attitude toward life's course. By comparing themselves to others, their ideal of a don't know mind confirms their belief about themselves that knowing too much is dangerous and they must do mental house cleaning to affirm their ideal is for real. Yet, hiding underneath they are deeply judgmental, and feel inadequate to show it.

Perhaps the underlying concept they're attempting to bypass is people disagreeing with what they know. What's often interesting is pretending not to know something, which is based on the premise of knowing nothing, they know will make them a better person. They still know something by trying to appear they don't know anything.

Buyers are also full of mental theatrics. Today they learn from a variety of sources what to do---the internet, other sellers, friends, social media—a super-flow of information informs their notions of what to expect. This explains why their resistance is lack of clarity. When they resist getting help, their knee-jerk thinking pops up and comes in use. Relying on their models of what they need and what is going on, sellers despite their best efforts are edited by the buyer's biases. This is why sellers today have a different role in being agile to spot this early on and change their approach accordingly. Sellers have to out-sell the habitual thinking and models that buyers filter decisions through. This requires a re-engineering of the pre-existing notions and gaining trust and credibility in overriding the old with a new way of seeing and depending.

This is to keep the buyer clear that the new concept from which they see what they need isn't manipulation, rather it is meant to be ultimately their idea to take. Sellers aid the pivot of the outdated thinking to an updated view of what the buyer needs. And making it safe to enter this shift of mind is the work of a great seller.

The first step is beginning with the original idea the buyer has in mind and understanding it. Second, the seller invites a gentle severance from this view by looking into a potential set of possibilities that were undiscovered before.

Seller: Joe, help me understand how you see yourself using the help of an insurance agent?

Seller: Joe, is there anything else I should know about your expectations? Very good. Let me tell you about someone else you might be interested in that also was needing help. When he first insured his home, business, and car, he knew his premiums had to be contained. Then he had a painful vision of one morning getting his hot coffee and doing 80 mph up the 405 fwy, and suddenly the coffee fell over, spilt, burning his legs—he looked down to attend to the burning sensation as the car veered toward the center divider, and just when he looked up to pull the wheel, kaaabooom! He hit it and rolled over several times thrown from the car. Lying there, four other cars slammed into his as he heard the people screaming ejected from the front windows as the shattered like dreams being lost. As if a drone was hovering over the scene he began to see the faces of the mothers, babies, and fathers, and friends bleeding and dying on the pavement after the collision. The gasoline smell alerted him to a question: Would his insurance pay the parts of the cars, or the hospital bills and funerals of the victims?

Buyer: I see how fragile life is, and I'm not far from this risk either. I drive that freeway every day and not paying the bills of those poor souls would cast a shadow on my guilt forever. I couldn't live with myself knowing I didn't do what I could to bring them back to a normal life.

The logic in this conversation is outside the door and emotions, compassion, and concern is raising the buyer's blood pressure. The seller has clarified a powerful picture the buyer can live in for a moment and relate themselves to feeling the pain of it. The buyer and seller together really feel the depth of the story. The seller's deepest conviction is to never underinsure anyone. His conviction is to only insure someone right, instead of collecting their money only to lose later on. The grace, kindness, and reverence to see as this story as the seller does, helps the buyer connect with the seller from the heart. Resistance is always lack of clarity

CHAPTER 8

PRESENCE

Zengetsu, a Chinese master of the T'ang dynasty, wrote the following advice for his pupils:

Living in the world yet not forming attachments to the dust of the world is the way of a true Zen student.

When witnessing the good action of another encourage yourself to follow his example. Hearing of the mistaken action of another, advise yourself not to emulate it.

Even though alone in a dark room, be as if you were facing a noble guest. Express your feelings but become no more expressive than your true nature.

Poverty is your treasure. Never exchange it for an easy life.
A person may appear a fool and yet not be one. He may only be guarding his wisdom carefully. Virtues are the fruit of self-discipline and do not drop from heaven of themselves as does rain or snow.

Modesty is the foundation of all virtues. Let your neighbors discover you before you make yourself known to them.

A noble heart never forces itself forward. Its words are as rare gems, seldom displayed and of great value.

To a sincere student, every day is a fortunate day. Time passes, but he never lags behind. Neither glory nor shame can move him.

Censure yourself, never another. Do not discuss right and wrong.

Some things, though right, were considered wrong for generations. Since the value of righteousness may be recognized after centuries, there is no need to crave immediate appreciation.

Live with cause and leave results to the great law of the universe.

Pass each day in peaceful contemplation.

We underestimate the power of human presence. The value it has is huge for the person being listened to, as well as coming into contact with the present moment for you the listener. Listening happens from three places within you: Your head, your heart, and your body. You stay present to others and stay balanced in your intelligence.

When you listen from your head, you listen for content, story, and cultivate your wisdom, clarity, and discernment. When you listen from the heart, you hear the emotional flavor, to cultivate compassion, love, altruism and understanding, and empathy. When you listen from your body, you cultivate the capacity of intuition and presence. These three are always accessible at every moment. When you operate from all three, you get greater access to your own wisdom, higher levels of intelligence, and balance. Most of all you're able to access greater value available to use to help and serve others.

NOT ENOUGH

When we are preoccupied with not being enough, helping others goes out the window. The fact is *we are never enough*. But some of us can't register just how powerless we really are. We have no control over life. It is a wildcard. This eternal truth is too honest for those who are so hurt and bruised in their negative beliefs of themselves that they can't serve others. Instead, they manipulate them as objects to offset their preoccupation with power. Somewhere in their hopes of having better human potential, they attempt to use the world for themselves instead of participating in the world to enrich it. These are takers, not givers. And they can cloak themselves behind the face they show you.

They are liars, manipulators, and narcissists who haven't come to terms with their own power, and the power of the impermanence of life. They seek power over others to reduce their internal story that they're a horrible person. So, they seek methods, social fancies, materialism, competition, domination, and any symbols of power they can get a hold of to gain mastery over their petty little sense of self. Many people in the entertainment business, unfortunately, operate from this orientation. It is all me, me, and me, self-absorbed in human potential, thinking and growing rich, and acting like a person who is all that while they aren't in fact anything. This is the world of the ego.

DEPENDENCE

The ego is afraid of dependence. Its goal is to lower risk and
vulnerability by maintaining a twisted version of you in order to live up
to your ideals. Welcome to the costume party. What you wear, how
you look, where you live, how much you make, all of these social
status symbols have captured you prisoner to feeling like someone
special. You associate power and adequacy with these ideals by
defining yourself by what you do, what others think, and what you
have. When you attached yourself to these symbolic forms of power
that you assign self-importance, you're blind to see the abundance of
divinity, creativity, goodness, love, and blessing in other human
beings around you. You consume yourself being the center of
everything in your life building process. It's tough trying to get others
to notice your power, especially when you lose it. True power is given
away.

As you mature in emotional development, your aspirations and values
begin to float to the top of your list of organizing features in your life
building process. You find yourself leaving an old chapter of making
powerful impressions to being nobody and creating something that
matters to you. Who you are appears to fall away like burning down a
building, with something new rising from the ashes that matter such
that you long to create it. You move from adolescence to adult
maturity by relating with the world according to what touches, moves,
and inspires you. Meaning, service, and taking meaningful leaps into
uncertainty replace mastery, competitiveness, and individualism. The
part of you that wanted to get above everyone else is washed away

like foot prints in the beach sand. And your comparison thinking that measured you against other people and your social status scorekeeping burden up as well like a flaming paper blowing away in the wind. The past is history.

Voicing

Your truest leadership voice is the one that conveys what really does matter to you the most. It's important to hone your relationship with this voice as the primary organizing structure in your life building process. Voice the following:

1 – What inspires you right now
2 – What amazes you right now
3 – What touches or moves you right now
4 – What challenges you beyond the familiar to grow and stretch
5 – What activities give you the most energy

These five reflections tap into your levels of aliveness and enthusiasm. When you reflect and voice to yourself and the world these inputs you compose content that makes creating it worthwhile for its own sake. These five bring you into touching your own wholeness.

It's important to trust these ingredients like a touchstone. They are quintessential features to liberating your gifts and signal a destiny standing in need of you. With courage, alacrity, and trust you let these reflections ajoin cosmic design with interior purpose. You are master and servant, adaptive and creative as your entire being is called to the task. The fusion of both the bigger will and our own is the deepest source from which you let go and let come everything waiting for you. Everything the future needs is given to you this moment.

When you connect your own voice with the macro voice (larger will), you become incandescent, emitting light as a result of being heated from the inside out. This incandescence is like a radiant glow around you that others tuned in like a radio tower receive your transmissions. Holons are those who have developed this keen awareness and inner knowing.

THE FIRST CONVERSATION

You are in many conversations all the time. Most often you're in the conversation with yourself. There is an inner dialog with you running how you pay attention and interact with the world around you. The majority of your inner conversation is dominated by the past. This is because you have accumulated a lot of information from your experiences about you, about the world you see around you, and the way you interpret and add meaning to what comes at you. So how you take in and influence the world around you is primarily organized by this conversation with the self. And this conversation has habitual reflexes when the past defines what is going on.

When you say "your self" you're suggesting something that is yours. You've composed it. But when you say "the self" it's suggesting something separate from you that isn't yours, at least not yet. You actually live within a bilateral internal conversation between your current self and the future self. But most often what orients you to the world is your current self that you've composed. One third of your life you spend most of your time trying to help the world not see a part of your current self that isn't acceptable to you. I say one third because I have hope for you that you will make a fundamental shift from all your attempts to call attention to yourself, to organizing your life around creating what matters most to you. By comparison, when you attempt to put away, deflect, hide, and deceive by living inside a false to affirm your significance for a while, you obscure your capacity to connect with what most matters to you and live from it.

How you organize your life becomes an interesting matter when you're preoccupied with who you are. When you come from the notion that you are inadequate, the natural attempt is to cover it up. Your attempt to offset your shame and fear of humiliation is to make manifest ways to solidify an acceptable identity in what you do, what you own, and how others see you. And this identification with these things is made worse by society norms around power and success. I'm not saying that you have to go live in an ashram and live a menial poor life to be holy. There are many phone holies afraid to confront the truth of their egoistic propensities. I know because I played that game during more formative years in my late teens, early twenties. I tried to look for myself in other people's eyes. For a while, I wasn't sure I could find it without this. Boy was I off base!

Self-Improvement

You cannot repair the problems with yourself, but only outgrow them via the pursuit and manifestation of meaningful urges. I find more people agonizing over who they're not, and what's wrong with them, and heavily programmed into self-improvement. They attempt to affirm to themselves they are someone different with self-propaganda and self-manipulation. They over-monitor how they feel, their self-esteem, and their sense of worth that it short-circuits their capacity to create what they want. And the human potential industry takes these to the bank with great marketing! But most self-help actually enahnces about 20% of the ones pursuing it. The reasons why this rate of return is so low is because self-help people don't tend to have their attention on what they seek to create. They lack the honesty and accuracy of themselves to not be at issue with what's wrong with them in the realm of the creative process.

From 1st to 3rd Person

This week:

Please keep your voice of judgment in check. Start your VOJ (voice of judgment) journal and name and write down the lenses, biases, and concepts that you hold of

1. others (their intentions, their person, etc.)

2. you

3. what is going on

then test each:
1 — is this true?
2 — how do I know for sure it is true?

3 — what would happen if I didn't believe it?
4 — whom would I be if I didn't believe it?

Then if you stumble upon an alternative motive follow it, beneath judgment lies the open heart, not the armored one.

When you suspend mental models (VOJ) you begin to see how your thinking has been participating in the enactment of what is going on. Your levels of awareness can help regulate your concepts and offer you an alternative way of bringing your self to the world.

THE THIRD CONVERSATION

How do we learn to take things in and let them go fluently? We have a front door and a back door, and yet we forget we have these.

In 2014 I was in a hurricane in Baja California, "Odille." To not blow the house down, we opened the front door and the back door to position a stream of air to run through it fluently. We gave the air nothing to push up against but gave it a place to go. I often think of our relationship with our experiences like watching in a white room what comes in and what goes out. Like turbulence on an airliner, what might rattle us eventually goes away and dissipates. There's a tolerance and intestinal fortitude in relating to life this way. But as we do this again and again, we develop the capacity to remain in the present moment without grasping or running away. We can learn to welcome everything and expect nothing by keeping aware of our regulating our default patterns to avoiding the past. We can access our capacity to stay without editing our experiences.

What is life affirming for you? You probably have an idea what qualities in your life now bring you into feeling alive!

THE SECOND CONVERSATION

When we try to push away, medicate, or run away from our pain, we create more. We isolate ourselves from allowing meaningful connections that fill our hearts and enlarge us. We don't find out what we can from spiritual practice. Our pain is our roots and our teacher if we only just face it and be with it.

You will spend your time on this journey through life suffering. When you lower your attempt to deny it, you give rise to your capacity to choose what matters to you. As you attempt to repress and shove down your hurt, your pain becomes a wound with a scab on it. The manifestation is putting armor around the heart by reverting to cynicism and contempt to disconnect from others.

When emotions are blocked and unexpressed, it is hard for us physiologically. Our immune systems break down, and we become less resilient to disease.

SHOULD A LEADER CARE

Some leaders I've coached don't care much about what their organization does or the people in it. They see their business as a cash flow machine to fund their lifestyle and retirement. Money is their primary metric.

The missing piece for these people is involvement and engagement. Despite making great money what wears thin over time is their reverence and enthusiasm. They seek to be involved more in what they're doing to make it last. Like a love relationship when a spouse's contributions feel great, lack of reciprocity shuts it off. Relationships and businesses that last depend on the care and concern of the business leader. Second, what you care about usually brings you into being creative. You learn by creating things that matter to you.

Our restaurant business "ZEN" had ups and downs in money in the first 24 months and during seasonal periods when tourism was down. It was at these times we had to recall why the business mattered to us to push us through these barriers.

What is "IT" for you

You cannot manufacture love. It is inherent in you to receive and generate love. Generative love is the place from which you create for its own sake. I haven't found any higher or nobler reason to create than this source. What gives you the most energy is what makes the biggest difference that matters to you. It is a law of spiritual economics to stay in touch with this like keeping in a freeway lane without swerving.

INTENTION ( )

What is that? It is the empty space you make for what emerges in addition to your intention. Life is context in motion. Every moment is a frontier---a conversation shining in through the cracks from an emerging future possibility waiting to be born.

What brings you into aliveness? What a question. Something----a thought, idea, a thing, an experience, a vision, a dream, a person, a moment, an insight, a touched heart. We live within a web of life---like nods and hubs within an emerging network where a living, breathing frontier of potentiality seeks us in parts of the whole. Everything is integrated into everything; nothing is compartmentalized. You grab your next insight or tool from the time with your daughter on horseback. Kids jumping on the bed remind you to live uninhibited such that you jump in and play.

BE---DO---HOW

You might see these synonymous to spirit---orient---process. If we begin with being, then we are using current reality and the experience of it as an informing place from which our future is signaling our gaze. We are imbued with inspiration (in spirit) and act from that place (do) by orienting ourselves to our deepest intention that is blended with a greater call for action as we figure the path out as we go along with revelation. Just having a vision and plan isn't the essence of creating, rather it is a more direct immersive relationship with our surroundings that bring us into contact with defining features that aim our way. It is our state of being that penetrates us and taps our deepest knowing like a sacred hideout with our hearts. These itchy features are born from what has heart and meaning for us to scratch with such a generative love and concern that our maker instinct compels the creative act. We cannot NOT act. Self and Whole become one 3D

215

image like an implanted sacred project that brings us closest to our best work and self.

Your being is coming from nothing. Your being begins from nothing, not the opposite of something. Your being is the one who is attending to the present moment. If the quality of perception (awareness) shifts, something you do is motivated, and as you act from this instance with faith, your next action is evoking learning from a future unfolding into reality. Something is seeking you to come forth, act from that place with trust and faith, and meet whatever that possibility is. I find this to be the essence of living dangerously—where meeting the mystery life has at every moment helps us meet a grander array of potential. Our most inner knowing comes to the surface to meet this emerging future to bring us toward it by inviting itself in, positioning itself with crystalized vision, and evoking action in good cause.

D. H. Lawrence said, "I can never decide whether my dreams are the result of my thoughts, or my thoughts the result of my dreams." I've been inquiring for ten years on this question: "How are things I'm creating coming into reality?" From where do our creations come into their beginning? It appears to some degree they are governed by the existing structural dynamics. This is how you step away and relax when you create outcomes. You can backup far enough to see the existing system in which you are enacting from a larger whole. Jerry Garcia said, "The song plays the band." To retrieve the emerging song, you release your grasp and let go of control to the underlying structure quelling from beneath like an invisible hand. It reminds me of Mozart's short answer to his admirers when asked where he got his music; he replied, "I listened."

Fitzcarraldo

n. an image that somehow becomes lodged deep in your brain— maybe washed there by a dream, or smuggled inside a book, or planted during a casual conversation—which then grows into a wild and impractical vision that keeps scrambling back and forth in your head like a dog stuck in a car that's about to arrive home, just itching for a chance to leap headlong into reality.

This is the essence of the sacred project inside you that is the life-activating principle and purpose written on the tabloid of your soul to awaken and realize. When you place your gifts in the direction of this, there is no decision to make; you simply must do this with deep conviction. There's a saying in the Eastern Tradition, "follow your Dharma."

When tension seeks resolution, the relationship between current reality and vision of the outcome establish the need for equilibrium. While they are held via an intention with conscious attention to the present, it's as if mystical experiences, strange coincidences, and mysteries become apparent by themselves. It's as if an embedded, underground field of creative order and energy was coagulating with matter and mind and animating you.

When both current reality and vision are the same equilibrium is restored. In the meantime, there are delays, assimilation, and a learning process by doing things that bring about new responses and adjustments as you go along. The natural structure inclines you to bring current reality toward the vision to make them equal. This is why creators know when nothing appears to be happening, this is a natural moment in the creative process. Something not happening is in itself a significant place to be. And giving space for this space is also an inherent part of tension seeking resolution because new mental capacities and resources are internalizing within the motivation of the structure governing change.

One thing amateur creators learn early on it is how to regulate the energy with this dynamic. Early on, some creators attempt to push things along faster and forcefully despite the structural governance. This is like blunting a knife by over-sharpening. At its basic motivation, the creator is attempting to offset a fear. He has a determined view of the future that looks either optimistic or pessimistic and attempts to predict the future this way, rather than putting his faith in the elements that incline him to create it. This faith comes in many forms—faith in his intention, ability to learn, in his relating with others, in what the unexpected wildcard of life will bring---the honesty the professional creator develops is that he is at rest with the unknown of what is unknowable. He is not at issue with trying to predict or control the future by learning from it as it emerges. He leaves space, vacancy in himself for seeing new things as they come toward him. Through reflection, he has the antidote to changing his history. This involves a consistent, keen awareness kept on staying fluent with current reality. The creator refines what he sees now in relationship to where he wants to be. And it is this relationship that generates the motivation to create, experiment, learn, adjust while reflecting in and on the action.

Reflecting in and on action are two key sides of reflection. The "on" part is the past while the "in" part is in the instant moment. Knowing what matters is the key to reflecting in action. Reflecting in action is learning by doing. But the past isn't the only source of learning. Instead, the future is made of disruptive change, like context in motion in a state of constant flux where one must be able to develop new ways of constructing the intention he has from what he sees, and sensing what is wanting to emerge. Setting foot into this is the essence of leadership because faith is the future. Faith is placed in front of knowing. The creator starts with nothing, learning through unlearning, as he goes. He evolves and creates all at once in a dance of change between attending from the best inner most source and operating from his deepest intention that he must bring into reality. Intention is a constant conversation with one's surroundings. Our experience offers up information from which we reflect and grab meaning by listening wholeheartedly.

CHAPTER 9

BEING CAPTURED

A missionary has a reason for being on her mission. A company has a reason for existing. You've probably wondered at some point in your life line what your purpose for being in the world is? What is your place to take in the ecosystem? What does the world see in you for you to ignite responsibility?

In early times in Japan, bamboo-and-paper lanterns were used with candles inside. A blind man, visiting a friend one night, was offered a lantern to carry home with him. "I do not need a lantern," he said. "Darkness or light is all the same to me." "I know you do not need a lantern to find your way," his friend replied, "but if you don't have one, someone else may run into you. So, you must take it." The blind man started off with the lantern and before he had walked very far someone ran squarely into him. "Look out where you are going!" he exclaimed to the stranger. "Can't you see this lantern?" "Your candle has burned out, brother," replied the stranger.

Planet, people, purpose, and profits are interconnected in a creative web of life from which you take your cues. It all begins with noticing where you put your attention---not the future, the past, you, or what others are thinking or expecting. You stay in the present moment to be captured by the defining features that bring you into full being. There is a reason these are in this sequence: 1) Planet (wholeness;

220

wise attention), 2) People (connection), 3) Purpose (intention), and Profits (continuity).

How connected are you with what is going on in the world around you? My guess is you aren't getting up in the morning connecting your drive to "sell" within the context of what is trending in the world today economically, sociologically, ecologically, and spiritually. Everything you see around you is a potential source of significance for your mission. I say this because facts and data are sources of reflection as to their meaning to your relationship to your true self and work. This is suggesting that your mission or purpose organizes itself via your connection to the world around you.

BEHIND THE METHOD

There are tons of sales methodologies out there---Spin Selling, Solution Selling, Consultative Selling, Selling the Invisible, Insight Selling. These are all great in terms of having a structured process. But the technical without the spirit is like a machine without a heart. Insights come from learners, not performers. Seeing differences comes from open-hearted bravery and social development and trust, and integration by seeing and acting out of the whole - all levels of comprehension become available in the present moment, depending on the inner place from which your listening happens.

The technical/mechanical piece is excusable when the connection is first. All the methods are worthless and useless for helping others if you aren't connected to the other person first. Connecting requires the capacity to listen and accept the other as a legitimate other. Connecting is an inner place of compassion and understand that only the open heart can access when cynicism falls away. Always put connection before content. The helping process is a living system of intimacy out of which responsibility emerges.

Connecting is finding the most significant places for goodness to prevail and rise up. Connecting begins with perception. Any method when brought on initially is manipulation, not connection. It reduces the other (the buyer) to a mechanical, lifeless conversation devoid of confidence and creativity, which are the hallmarks of a transformative conversation that gives a place for methods down the line. Tools are useful, but the source from which you sell changes everything else in its way.

In a retreat with doctors, each one of them wrote a sincere wish for the other in doing well. As they got to know each other over the course of two days, their reverence for each other's gifts, style, talents, and overall way of being dramatically increased in visibility. One doctor stood up with tears saying that it was the first time that he actually felt the awesome surge of others truly, sincerely wanting him to do well by his gifts. He said that the influence of being truly seen in his truest self and work was the essential component to him approaching his most cherished and desired future with full commitment.

Behind the method, every doctor found a place in themselves of deep humanity and concern for others to heal. They said they had forgotten

222

this primary source of effort when all the programming, requirements, and rules diffused their true sense of participation and involvement in their work to help others. Through reflection work, they had reclaimed a lost or hidden part of themselves as the vital additive to their work and realized that once a doctor is converted into a "performer" of the method, they had lost their humanity in practicing medicine. How much creative fire were they sitting on for so many years? One doctor mentioned that when they blocked this authentic fire from getting expressed, it led to depression and disconnection from their true purpose. Most of the doctors in the workshop started seeing the consequences that played out when governed by the fear of staying true to themselves. They had compromised and lower their standards to a system that trapped them into robotic lives. Many of them said they had forgotten their own permission to remain human beings.

THE PERMISSION TO IGNORE

The best effort is the effort to make less effort later. This is the secret to multiplying your time. It takes time to make it into more time. It takes time to get out from what's happening to you, and into what you choose to do with the time you have. First, you 1) need to think long term---what is significant for you later, and 2) focus attention on what remains after you ignore things that don't matter now. Permission to ignore requires you to be aware of what really does matter most to you. If you don't have a place to go or a sense of what matters to you, anything will come into your attention and demand your effort. You are in control of your own levels of dread! You are your own bouncer at the gateway!

Ding dong the dread is dead! How to stop dread starts with DEAD = delete, eliminate, automate, delegate. These four give you the leverage to clear to the decks for action. Since you're going to be in different requirements the future needs, your not-to-do list is more critical than your to-do list. It's not how much can you get done, rather, it's how much you can permit yourself to ignore and stop postponing your refusals.

You go through life trying to say *no* less and say *yes* more. Any time you say yes to one thing, you are simultaneously saying no to an alternative. There is opportunity cost with every decision you make. Choosing is about making a full selection. You focus on what matters most. And as you consider this moment to moment, consider what matters in combination with what will multiply your use of time. Multiplying time means eliminating debilitating tasks, automating processes to lower stress, and delegating to others by developing them into areas of superior skill that give them energy.

The best delegation is elimination. This means simply declining, stopping, not doing something any longer. The second-best delegation is automation. When you make a system, you make space because you've put something on autopilot. Now you can get to where you want to put your time and effort. You leverage your time and making the effort now to have less effort later. You're freed up to live on-purpose and access activities that make you feel alive and create the most value for the world!

Delegation is bringing others around into their personal gifts. You develop people around you, such that their competency is so ready to be trusted that your needs are authorized to be handled confidently. Their abilities are authorized when they are passionate about the superior skills that qualify them to deliver a high level of value to meet your needs. This is a fundamental relationship when their personal gift links with creating value. Can you imagine what it feels like to be coached by a boss this way? To be developed in ways where you love what you do, and do what you love? How reliable would a team member be when plugged into this?

TALENTED TO BE TALENTED

Being good, brilliant, even genius, the best in the world at what you do helps forgive many things you ignore. Ignore putting attention on improving your weaknesses, or just focusing your strengths.

Instead, know where you want to be and tell yourself the truth about where you are now, the good bad and ugly. Truth is an acquired taste. This motivates you to become resourceful as a learner through repetition until your skill level matches where you want to be.

Yes, know your limits, and know your strengths, but organize around where you want to be, and where you are now as the organizing principle for directing your focus and attention toward building the future you seek to create. That requires you to take your identity out of the learning process, to use failures as assets. You don't plan or expect to fail; rather, when you do, you get information you did not

225

have before. You can use it or get discouraged. Moreover, you will get discouraged.

When you do, remember that at the beginning of learning anything knew, you'll look like a fool. Human potential supporters suggest "focusing on your strengths" to bypass the painful process of practice until you're great. Nobody avoids practicing. Doc Severenson, the gifted trumpet player, practices every day at 85 years old. Swimmers and ice skaters practice diligently every day to move closer to where they want to be. Tennis players stay warm every day to keep on their game and play the level they seek, and serious singers vocally warm up twice a day because it's part of their creative habit.

The standard of difficulty isn't what organizes action, you do, or instead, your choices do. Whether you think it's hard, belief in you, fear failure, these perhaps are there, but creating anything doesn't require pushing a psychological view into it. If you talk shop with creators, their concepts and all the head stuff is left out. When I asked one of my restaurant franchise clients how he learned the business, he replied, "I just started a business." When you create, you begin separate from what you know. Otherwise, it wouldn't be called creating, it'd be repeating. *Creating* is learning something new that didn't exist before.

The process happens in three stages: First, germinate a vision they seek to create and assimilate new learning as they go along through to bring the creation desired into reality. They adjust the process as they go, with strategic actions until the actual state of their creations is the desired state. This third stage is called completion. Unfortunately, many human potential thinkers make it psychologically based, when in fact professional creators don't use the creative process this way. That means your attention to building, learning, and creating such a high level of competency at one thing is your best advertising; take aim with it.

If you want to learn to master the creative process, coaching is a great way to accelerate learning. However, you must be talented to be talented. If you don't recognize where you are---what your talents are during the process, building competency is negated. The coach helps you discern where you want to go---the result you want to generate, rather than a problem you want to get rid of. Then describe the current state---where you are proximate to where you want to be, without exaggeration or minimization (denial). Then you construct actions in service to the higher choice or goal that you choose to do on behalf of what you want. Activities that serve the outcome I call "informed actions." Intention backs these actions. You find that when you create by intention, you're more involved in what you're bringing to life, especially your life building process.

Focusing on finding who you are is different from recognizing your current talent level. In fact, seeing where you are can be very hard to stomach, you might not be excellent yet at what you're creating. When you focus on who you are (whom you're supposed to be; your ideals; positioning your identity) you handicap the creative process.

This is because creators who are active do not focus on themselves, they focus on their creations. An example is how a mother focuses on bringing her baby into the world instead of how she looks or what kind of person she is. Keeping your identity in check takes some strong practice to get the hang of, but each time you create something successfully, you find yourself less attached to your status (whether you're a good or bad person; your worth; your esteem) and more able to refocus your attention on what you seek to create.

One of the neatest aspects that intrigue me about the creative process is that things begin when you say so, not because of the circumstances. You're not obligated to create anything, but you create by choice. Creating begins with love, and that which you love enough to bring into life then becomes the subject matter of the creative process.

You can rethink your life, your business; everything is up for grabs at any time. Second, you can see where you have talent, and even a passion for it, but that doesn't require you to make money at it, or even build a career with it. You can do nothing with a recognized talent and create something different. It's your call. You can desire something and decide not to build it.

To create or not create, that is the question. Society puts social pressure on us to live our passion, and to force ourselves to build a work-life around our talents and gifts. Some people do, some don't, it's a question of choice. We fuss with all the existential mysteries like who we are, instead of creating what matters to us. We are the only species on the planet that is preoccupied with this! Leave the mysteries to be mysteries and organize your attention on what matters to you. Instead on fixing what is wrong with you, focus on creating what matters and building the talents you need to create it. Take aim with your gifts!

Moving from a reactive orientation to life, to living in a creative one, living by a life plan is the best way to achieve and bring into being your highest dreams and aspirations. Are you ready to become the predominant creative force in your life? It's a fundamental question. Are you talented to be talented?

PERSONAL INVERSION

Creating a better future than the past starts with the opening of a crack from within. Following that crack requires us to let go of the old and "let grow" something that we can sense but that we cannot fully know before we see it emerging. This moment can feel like jumping across an abyss. Now we leap, we have no idea whether we will make it across.

As human beings, we are always on a journey of becoming who we are. This journey to ourselves — to our Selves — is open-ended, full of disruptions, confusion, and breakdowns, but also breakthroughs. It is a journey that mostly is about accessing the deeper sources of the self.

Knowing who we are is impossible if we direct the beam of observation away from ourselves and onto the exterior world around us. To discover true self-knowledge, we must bend the beam of scientific observation back onto the observing self—that is, back onto its source. Francisco Varela described this as the "core process of becoming aware." His three gestures of suspending, redirecting, and letting go mark the process of opening one's full perception in relating to the world, and organizing from these places of most potential. The places of most potential are coming into knowing one's deepest intention, connecting to the social field in connection with others, and attending from the whole which informs where one's goodness and purpose is ready to emerge. As the access to these places of potential come into awareness by suspending, redirecting, and letting go, creations come forth, deep sensing of something needing you pulls you toward a future standing in need, and a sense of one's true humanity and soulfulness that animate one's quality of action. This dynamic is the essence of "awareness-based creating" to operate from the inner place from which you take inspiration into the creative process, the intention being that by connecting to one's emerging future self to create what matters most, and the sense of service to others to create value for them for the joy of it. The continuous pulse of these access points through becoming aware, opens doors from which creations emerge. But more importantly, the creative act is imbued by the highest quality of expression that one can occupy at any moment. The creative process infuses intellectual, emotional, and ontological intelligence into a dynamic balance.

THE EXCELLENCE TRAP

There is a natural trajectory in the sales producer or professional's career where they get so good at something that a tremendous level of interest comes from raving fans. What happens along with an uncommon skill that is first among equals is being too busy. Busy is the killer of:

Hope. When activities and tasks consume you, there's a sense of doom that comes over you. The future looks dimmer because you're caught in a myriad of things coming at you from all directions.

Credibility. Nothing is more unnerving than being invalidated by someone who's not present and rushed. It's a big turn off.

Connection. Busy is the connection killer. When your head is full of loose ends, you cannot connect with others due to a lack of access to focused attention and alertness.

Progress. Busy can become so consuming that you have no time to think or even plan the future. Often the thrill of so much activity negates space to think of the bigger picture.

Presence. Feeling things are unfinished is very unsettling. Trying to go on vacation with a head full of incomplete to-dos is a bandit for rejuvenation and balance.

Your sales career depends on being a whole person. Your best relationships rely on you to be happy, alert, and present in your life. The better you get at what you do, the less likely you'll maintain the capacity to live in your life. This leads to hopelessness, depression, and stress because you cannot get to anything new. Moreover, the enthusiasm you have for what you do starts to fade as well as the fascination.

Making less effort and having time for things—people, activities, experiences—doesn't come from the outside, it starts from the inside out. The path to simplicity and mobility is accessible when you make a fundamental choice to stop being busy. Stop doing the tasks and activities that make you overactive. This is an important decision to make right now. Instead, select the three things you're going to focus on every day. Second, be your own bouncer. Schedule your free time a year in advance. Pick how many days you're going to take completely free and subtract these from 365. The remaining days are to be divided between maintenance days and high-performance days. The first is for preparation, delegation, reparation, and systemization. The second is for selling. You sell for a living. Your best relationships are those you get in front of, help, and create value for, and listen for new and essential ways to enrich. This also includes those you won't put effort into; not everyone is right for you.

Selecting your ideal clients and ridding the duds is like losing fifty pounds of heavy weight. When you combine the stopping activity with those relationships and replace them with ones you choose to spend your time on growing, and you stop giving attention to being busy, you find yourself more available and present to think, plan, be present, and amazingly other people come toward you. You're more attractive when you're available this way, like a magnet for others. This restorative process is an incredible makeover from one whose trapped by a world of task and people who bog them down to one who is incredibly excited and alive with the kinds of opportunities that you're born to reach, and time spent on activities that generate desired results instead of being busy. Again, make no room for being busy, go cold turkey, stop being busy. Moreover, make no room for dud clients, cut them loose. The releasing and letting go the phenomenon of letting come what really excites you, focuses your gifts in the right place.

Your best creations and performances
arise from creating an unforced space.

If you're creating at a forced pace, then you're not creating. You're reacting or enacting out of someone else's goals or expectations not your own. When you turn yourself into forced performance, you take your humanity out of creating. This is a significant danger because your humanity is the unique quality in what you create. When you bypass reflection, you miss cues presented to you to learn and adjust in responsiveness to what you're putting together.

When you free yourself from your concepts, ideals, expectations, and anticipation, you can live in your actual life. Current reality can have your direct access to what is going on without editorial, just news right now. Moreover, the story is coming and going, in and out, up and down, moving with you or against you. Life is like a wildcard.

So, what this means is that your capacity to hold space is key to creating, relating, and learning. How do you hold space? You time block it. Time blocking is a technique to align your schedule with what matters to you. It is a free ticket to do this, and all it costs you is time to make time. You make an effort to make less effort.

Blue sky time is what I call time for doing nothing, reflection, looking at the past, the present, and considering future possibilities that are arising now. When you leave a city and head out into the desert or the mountains, you find yourself in a reflective state of mind. The natural vistas and open spaces speak to you such that you can hear *you* as well as what is going on around you with greater clarity and definition.

"You are wired for sound when outward bound."

What draws you into the world is a fuller comprehension. Distanced from it, backing up far enough helps us see and sense connections and integrations. Silence speaks. It is not boredom; it is a swelling presence embracing whatever arises. Silence teaches you acceptance and legitimacy. It is an invitation to peripheral listening and reflection on what was produced, what is going on now, and what appears to be coming next. Your brain isn't geared to do this, but your heart and body can.

Your nature is to hold space using your levels of awareness to shift the source from which your listening and attention arise. You aren't just seeing, but going beyond your five senses into a 3rd and 4th person orientation.

Objectivity is helpful because you report a more significant aspect of reality than your habitual thinking sees. Your heart's perception is one that holds space for voices other than your own---as if everything has a significant place to take. Nothing left out. Moreover, with faith, you leave room for non-adjacency. Reality isn't under the command or control of what you predict; instead, it is an emerging, animating flow of information not yet embodied within you. Not-yet-embodied information is like entering a sea of possibilities abound. Life is in the business of unfolding and creating a new experience. What you choose to conserve continues as life unfolds.

THE PATH OF LETTING GO AND LETTING COME

Unpluggability is to undo first your dependence on what you know from having direct access to your current experience. Unplugging from your voice of judgment allows you to see insights. Insights are visions of reality without editing it with biases or concepts. As you access this, it expands into what moves you. You let what is occurring change you with internal rapture by sensing it with your heart. However, you must unplug from the voice of cynicism that armors and defends your heart from wounding. The interior shift is a conscious intention to connect, be available, and listen from the heart. As you enter the animation that comes through this organ of perception, you enter the dimension of your open will. You unplug your voice of fear from broadcasting what is around the corner and let it be there without obeying its forecast.

With judgment, cynicism, and fear unplugged, what's kept? Like a clear voice, you decouple from what you know and enter the unfamiliar with alacrity, courage, and openness in all aspects. You are ready for anything, expecting nothing. You are open-hearted with bravery, porous to allow what is outside to move your touch you. You let go and hold space for ambiguity to the degree that what is ready to be born is let come. You listen with all access points open to the emerging future possibilities as the beam of what you see, and sense is bent back to your emerging future self and most authentic work.

You are informed by the sacred as to what stands in need of you to mobilize it into action. There is no decision to make as what to do and bring into being, and what you need to do is obvious. You unplug to nurture what is crystallizing where goodness and wisdom are whispering to you for expansion, like a seed watered to tendril. The release, the surrender into what is ready to come is the natural cycle of dying, beginning, and continuing of context in motion in constant flux.

As you step into this territory, the aperture widens to give you clarity through walking. You know the path through forward motion, taking significant leaps into uncertainty to unfold your next step. Leading and learning become one process of meeting the future as it informs a clear way forward. Volatility, risk, and ambiguity yield vision, understanding, and the agility to move where the tidal currents ebb and flow, as faith in action enlightens the doer. Intention mobilizes effort, while the unknown mystery offers new hope.

CHAPTER 10

URGES

We have urges of all kinds.

There you are driving along and suddenly you see McDonalds. That Big Mac is like an itch you must scratch. You pull over, drive through, and order, and gulf down a great tasting meal. The urge is satisfied.

What is an urge? It is a strong desire or impulse. You see something that looks good, and you want to possess it. You gotta have it and satisfy your eyes. This is temptation. You urge to feed yourself and feel good. If you feel bad, you desire to feel good. If you lack importance or adequacy, perhaps having that thing will give you a boost in position and status. All these wants are based on one common denominator: immediate gratification.

We lack the intestinal fortitude to hold space for these types of wants. We don't know how to separate from our feeling states. We don't know how to separate from our urges to devour what our eyes want. We don't know how to divide our ideals and unwanted beliefs. We stink at holding space for these and instead give ourselves to the roaring river of sudden temptation for temporary relief, status, and cravings. The present becomes a source of impatience.

Then there's the urge to avoid or remove pain. Break-ups, losses, mistakes, negativity, death - these are part of life. Life has suffering in it, and yet, you're not here with the intention to suffer more. That's self-betrayal like putting your face in a boxing glove.

So what urges exist in addition to these? Love. We desire something that matters to us for the sake of it. We create music out of love, films out of love, write books out of love, relationships out of love, buildings out of love, almost everything around you was made from a loving, generative urge to bring it into being. You love creations before you bring them into reality. What you imagine stimulates your ardent desires to bring these creations from virtual to reality. It begins with composing and germinating a compelling urge via an envisioned outcome we genuinely want to bring into being.

Why do creations made from love for its own sake succeed? The generative love is what brings you to go all the way and last over the long haul. It's about distance. The impulse urges come and go like vapor in the wind, but conserving something loved and establishing an intention out of it, the resilience is at its strongest to outlast setbacks.

However, you are deeply flawed just like all of us. Nobody is without the short-term impulses. Like the Titanic myth, you try to segment your life, section the whims off, but the fact is the hole in the boat is a hole in the ship. The reality is it is going to take you down. An impulse may be private but it's never personal. Your little deviations may be individual, but they will influence you and others in your life.

The only antidote to the possession that your eyes urge you to jump and grab at is generosity. Nothing makes a more significant impact like your attraction to cheap sex or gluttonizing good looking fast food than giving to others. Enriching the lives of others shatters the self-enclosed system to keep what you possess and have it yourself. What you devour is masking the vulnerability required to offer yourself in the heart to loving, appreciating, and giving to others.

Every time you give, you break the bonds that armor your heart. You can give without loving, but you cannot love without giving. If you're falling into patterns that gratify your immediate urges, give more. It's a signpost that you're closing off your heart by loving oneself, and this will never actually quench the thirst you long for---the joy of giving value and help just for the pleasure of it. This is the nature of "service." It is the path to the work of the soulful person that you are down deep inside you. Moreover, yes, your wholeness includes all the downsides, the lust, your impulses and all—you have thorns on your rose bush.

As Randy walked past the sign outside Charlie's office, he stopped to read:

Integrity is the antidote to the lust of the flesh
Generosity is the antidote to the lust of the eyes
Humility is the antidote to the pride of life
Faith is the antidote to fear and doubt, that you expect God to use you
and bless your life.

Respect — Reverence for all of life
Honesty — Sincerity
Supportiveness — offering service to others
Kindness — Gentleness

Randy asked Charlie why each of these was posted on the wall. Charlie said the first four are what his father gave him at 15 years old, and the second four are what Charlie dedicated to his son Michael at his 18-year birthday celebration, as virtues to live by to create a happy, satisfying life. Randy wrote down the second four on a note and put it in front of his place at the dinner table. His family of six passed the letter around the table and last to receive it was David, Randy's 16-year-old son. Before anyone could comment Randy jumped in to tell why each of these mattered in a powerful anecdotal story of his own life. Each virtue Randy attached to a dynamic sequence of events that brought these to the top of the table in his current life.

Randy went on to describe a moment of learning "respect" with his wrestling coach in high school. During hell week, his coach would setup the training grounds in consideration of neighbors, nature, and noise. All three mattered in balancing the training layout to fit within the homes around the area, the gardens and plants in the hills near the running trails, and the noise level required not to disturb the peace. Even though the men were high voltage in their running, climbing, and calisthenics, the coach was always balancing sensitivity around the training area to the dynamics going on. Every area where snacks and waters were consumed, a great cleanup left the space clean such that nothing was left in nature. No training went past 9 pm to keep the noise level low for the households around the track and field.

When my client Gary told what it took to get here in his career, his description conveyed a massive sacrifice. There was no growth without change and loss, grief, and depression. They don't call it "labor" for nothing. It is painful to bring into being something new. Just ask a mother giving birth to a new baby. The struggle, the difficulty---when these are accounted for, people bond together. Gary went on to describe the word humility:

Humus — "of the Earth" or "of the ground" or "humor—laughing at yourself"

If you get criticized enough, it breaks your tendency to try to look good. You start listening. Because people are often giving you criticism to hear something more than you know. The fact is most of the time don't agree with things *you* even do. If you learn to laugh at yourself, you'll never run out of material. You're no different from any of the critics around you. You make mistakes, and you will make them. However, *you* are not a mistake. The key is not taking errors personally.

What is it in you that you are afraid of? The fear of disapproval from others makes you contract into a small sense of self. Praising others is sincere when you stop disowning what you have in yourself and let it be there. You don't have love yourself. You can't because it wouldn't be real. There will be parts of you that can't stand. What's the matter with that? Nothing. You like parts of you, and other parts you do not. Leave it there. Be fluent in what this is. However, trying to use how others see you to offset your unwanted beliefs is an attempt to belong.

Expertise is the enemy and the reason why smart people don't learn. Emptiness is courageous, and it's the place from which you can enter moments of life. The most defining moments most likely will come from moments when you're making things up as you go along. The less you know, the better, because you 're available inside you to listen to what's different than what you already know.

I see leaders motivating their decisions around the standard of ease something requires. In the creative process, learning comes with discipline, tolerance, and building skills by mistakes and experimentation. Being able helps, but the creative process is the best way to become skilled from unskilled at something. Moreover, the best way to learn is by creating an outcome you care about. So what if you cut the cord on the standard of easy, and choose outcomes you want based on how much they matter to you, then look at your current reality, what skill level do you have now, be accurate. This implies, whether burdensome or not, the path to the outcome motivates learning how to create it. If I choose to create a restaurant, I start separately from what I already know. Creating it will require business skills, culinary skills, and so much more to bring the vision I have into reality. This approach sets the stage for what to learn and

243

where to learn. However, the key is taking your identity out of it, to use failures as an asset. Because creating is an iterative process of learning by doing, building capacity intensifies until the vision of the desired outcome comes into focus. This is also why short-cut strength focusing can be a bad idea because learning something new is 1) refreshing and energizing and 2) required to create the desired outcome. You don't need to see a shrink to learn to play the piano. Delegating everything is silly, Mozart didn't delegate all the deep practice and skill building to mastery. Michael Phelps didn't transfer his most laborious effort to level up his swimming to generate 8 medals in one Olympic game! These achievements demanded different choices in service of creating the outcome, and this learning process is the creative process, they are the same. It requires an ongoing motive to continuously improve by immersion and adaptation, to resolve where you are in relationship to where you want to be.

Each goal you set and create has its own process you must learn to bring the target into being. That process is left to trial and error. Your journey reveals to you what to change and where to change. There are no copycats. You find that your diligence to remain in taking significant leaps forward into uncertainty, dreaming a great dream, and making it happen you will learn as you go. You don't need to overestimate or underestimate yourself for any good reason. You come by yourself discerning your abilities and inabilities by unlearning and learning during the creative process.

Do not hitch your size of yourself to the extent of your dreams, don't make it about your identity. When you focus on what you want, not what you need, indeed what you *want*---setup a learning process to learn your way to it. You learn 1000 ways it doesn't work. This is an education, not failures. Failures aren't dangerous; it is the fear of it that hurts you. Being dead in the water is your unwillingness to risk failure.

According to your faith, it will be done unto you. Faith is expecting God to use you. Hope is determined, persistent, and not letting go and compromising your big dream. You keep your head down and moving forward. You live into by grace.

After 15 years at winning as a financial adviser, one afternoon, Rob got the call. His top client dropped him like a hatchet. Five thousand dollars per month gone! Rob was so discouraged that he began to question his career direction. His bell was so wrung that he was ready to get out of his career entirely or do a significant overhaul in reaction to the sound of that hatchet dropping down.

What does it take to discourage you? Who's going to leave first? You or the problem? You don't know how to give up or quit! You outlast the problems by keeping on keeping on to creating. You eventually outgrow the problems by having bigger business to create.

Vince wanted everything he put out to the world---an image of himself he tried to convey as always polished and fancied to be better than he thought he was from the inside. Vince's unwanted belief of himself motivated his portrayal of perfection to lower the burden of his inferiority on others. No matter what was playing out—during the ebbs and flows of life Vince couldn't give him license to show up whole---as a human being. It was as if Superman was without kryptonite as the perfect person.

His need for approval was screaming for real intimacy and belonging, but his model of himself invalidated the vulnerability to stay in his truth.

Vince craved for positioning. He created a forced space to boot any sides of his personality that were deemed unattractive, moody, emotional, angered---as if he cut off the frequency to his part of his humanness. Moreover, Vince ensures that people couldn't get close to him. Defending against any sudden stirring or turbulence, he would smile and wear a phony face of synthetic niceness and composure. This omission of himself brought people to keep their distance.

The distancing to Vince meant he wasn't perfect enough, so he poured on the fanfare and acted happy all the time to never be a bummer. Forcing a positive attitude all the time seemed to Vince to seem fraudulent to himself. His lack of self-regard worsened, and his ideals and false standards of himself only imprisoned him worse.

His girlfriend Marie invited him over to meet her mother, Toni. At 82 years old, she was fascinated with ragdolls, in fact, she knitted several of them per month meticulously adding details to their outfits and their accessories. Toni's bookcases were filled with poets and great Spanish writers of the past. Moreover, her collection of novelties from her travels were artifacts suited for long conversations on neat topics.

Then Toni brought out her photo album to replay the early years for Vince. It was the best of times and the worst of times. The photos of her parents during the great depression were heartbreaking, and she said her father died of a sudden heart attack due to financial stress.

Vince stared at the lost look on that little girl's face within a week of her father's death. At 18, she found art as an outlet to focus her energy. Toni mentioned how ambiguity, unpredictability led to accurate comprehensions in the creative process, and that the content of the art she created brought her to realize it was ok to stay fluent in what was going on. She told him that art taught her to hold space for whatever was coming and going including her emotional ups and downs.

Toni said she felt shame for the first time when her mother told her what was wrong with a painting she had put her heart and soul into creating. Toni took it profoundly personally and concluded she was inadequate. She spent the next five years trying to outlast her mother's criticism. Her mother came up short in meeting her own expectations and ideals and used Toni as a scapegoat to dump her regrets. "Regrets tell you what matters to you and where to go next," said Toni. Then she said, "Guilt is the aftermath of a mistake that you can use to learn from, but shame is when you are a mistake."

Humility after the depression was about remembering that you're not better than anyone, "You have strengths and shortcomings. If you can admit them, and learn from them, you have humility." Toni went on to explain that taking on your inferiority is maturing into someone who is capable of comprehending things, people, and patterns because you're so not preoccupied with showing off and impressing people, so you can honor, respect, and listen to them as whole people. Toni said that when you cast your nets on others to get adulation, you reduce them to objects. Vince was burning from the inside as if he'd ingested hot salsa.

I have designed outcomes and plans I want to create because I genuinely wish them out of love for them to exist. Making them happen involves creating them, acting, making choices now on behalf of what I want. What motivates these choices is the love I have or what I want because it just matters. Ok, so that's making it happen, but what about letting things happen? What about the part of me that has no clue of what is to come toward me? Life is the business of creating life.

The future hasn't happened yet, and the past is the past, it's history. So how do I play making it happen along with letting things happen? One urge is creative, while the other call is receptive. We must treat both as valuable sources for creating. Too much of doing nothing is so passive that life drives by and you watch it. Too much creating is so narrow that we miss the present moment that is summoning attention to something new and different to awaken us.

CONTENTED CREATOR

So, what tends to come out of ourselves when we aren't satisfied or fulfilled with what we have now? Deficits. We compose our desires upon scarcity. What makes matters worse is that our society is full of biases about defining ourselves by what we should have. Our own solo voice of what we want to create is outlawed when we give obedience to what others think in combination with our status. Creating changes then originates from living up to feeling a sense of adequacy against others who look less than us. When you define yourself by what you do, what you have, and what others think, you're no longer available to be yourself. You sell yourself out to compensate for a dangerous matrix of individual differences that lead to judging ourselves against ideals that make us feel small and invisible. We build a sense of contentment around craving for power and adulation to offset the unwanted belief system we form around our comparison thinking.

The cosmic joke in all this is that our belief of what gives us power and affirmation of our sense of importance and value is folly. It's a hallucination. None of the internal rewards can be accessed substantially because after it all is acquired none of it genuinely quenches our thirst. We claw and fight to be seen, and yet the people seeing us are all to mastered by the same self-consumption. We deprive ourselves of space for humanness and incompleteness to strive for perfectionism. And to this end, we will often make incredible sacrifices and risk so much for the status and domination.

Focus on outcomes, not rewards. Let go of what you get from what you do, and instead focus on the outcome you desire to create. When you shift your focus to result, you make space for the imperfections along the way when the path isn't there to satisfy you. Bad days compliment good days; they are a part of our lives. When you focus on satisfaction, you pull away from what you're doing until you "feel inspiration" or "have the best mood." That isn't what creating an outcome is about, your focus is on the result, not yourself. Remember, people focused on themselves make lousy creators.

ROJITO

Life brings insights and opportunities of all sizes and shapes at any time. It was our French friend Claudia moving back to Paris who offered her thirty-year-old little Ford car to us. The compact car was tiny yet arrived in perfect timing because my wife said her Ford SUV was a gas hog and difficult to find parking.

The little Ford we'll call "rojito" or "little red" in Spanish would last us a month on one tank of gas.

My wife knew that our housekeeper Janet needed a car. She left her house each morning at 5 am to ride two buses to reach our house by 8am. Then going home, she did the same at 5pm, to get home by 8pm. Janet didn't have the income to buy a car. It was obvious she needed the car more than we did.

Two little kids and her husband were without a car. They hadn't been to the beach or drove to work all their life.

We gave Janet the car. She was imbued with joy and positive regard for us and the same week she took her family to the beach. Sitting at dinner time, my wife shared a photo of her little two-year-old boy in his underwear laughing happily on the beach. It brought tears to my eyes as she said, "Look what we get to do, look how much joy this family has because of us." Janet could drive to work, leave home and get home a reasonable hour, and she could take her family to enjoy things.

This is what being alive is for....to help other people create and enjoy experiences that matter. This is the essence of selling. It is the vital act of assisting others to get what they want, just for the joy of it. Janet offered to pay me back in return, but we remained clear in our hearts to give her the car.

No payment could have replaced the intrinsic reward I felt looking at her son Leonardo's picture laughing and smiling on the beach. That transformative little boy's joy changed my life.

THE DYNAMIC URGE

Veronica, a 54-year-old sales rep making a million-dollar income admitted that her drive was animated by her fear of running out and being poor. Her image to keep herself the person who regularly uses their wins and victories proves to her how safe she is from slipping into oblivion, like an addiction. If she takes a break from work, the apparent risk feels so violating to her because any moment to sit out and balance her life meant a race to the bottomless pit she ran from all her career. As she became aware of this primary motif, she questioned whether it served her going forward because of the contradiction with her values. She felt inside of her different bottom lines emerging, such as her longevity, emotional intimacy, inner peace, and fun. Her heap of savings was to be invested in a year-long sabbatical to deliver herself back to life and reclaim a lost a hidden part of herself that she wanted to restore. After a year away and slowing down she never returned to her sales career, and instead took the remaining money to open a K-12 school for kids. She said that slowing down helped her find her bliss and brought her to see that money buys time. The liminal period of the year renewed and reinvented her sense of hope and true aspirational desire for a future that mattered to her for the students her faculty would develop. She said that she's the happiest in all her living years and seeks to now create a necklace of charter schools throughout the United States and Canada to bring kids closer to their gifts and teach them how to use the creative process.

Veronica followed her inner voice pulled by a dynamic urge. The urge itself is brought forth generatively to bring something into the world as it is imagined. She is now doing what her precious life spirit is fully engaged in creating. Once she caught a glimpse of her emerging future during a night out with her two best friends, the pathway to children's education was the itch she had to scratch, and she always remembers the fast-track sales person with no time for life compared to the entrepreneur-school creator filled more by her urge than the financial rewards. Her spiritual pay was the involvement of bringing her call into reality.

A Zen Story

Ryokan, a Zen master, lived the simplest kind of life in a little hut at the foot of a mountain. One evening a thief visited the hut only to discover there was nothing to steal.

Ryokan returned and caught him. "You may have come a long way to visit me," he told the prowler, "and you should not return empty-handed. Please take my clothes as a gift."

The thief was bewildered. He took the clothes and slunk away.

Ryokan sat naked, watching the moon. "Poor fellow," he mused, "I wish I could give him this beautiful moon."

CHAPTER 11

CONFIDENCE

This is the story of the lake and the three big fish
that were in it, one of them intelligent,
another half-intelligent,
and the third, stupid.
Some fishermen came to the edge of the lake
with their nets. The three fish saw them.
The intelligent fish decided at once to leave,
to make the long, difficult trip to the ocean.

He thought, "I won't consult with these two on this.
They will only weaken my resolve because they love
this place so. They call it home. Their ignorance
will keep them here."

It's right to love your home place, but first, ask,
"Where is that, really?"
The wise fish saw the men and their nets and said,
"I'm leaving."
You must just set out on your own.
So the intelligent fish made its whole length
a moving footprint and, like a deer the dogs chase,
suffered greatly on its way, but finally made it
to the edgeless safety of the sea.
The half-intelligent fish thought,
"My guide has gone. I ought to have gone with him,
but I didn't, and now I've lost my chance
to escape.
I wish I'd gone with him."

He mourns the absence of his guide for a while,
and then thinks, "What can I do to save myself
from these men and their nets? Perhaps I'll pretend
to be already dead!
I'll belly up on the surface
and float like weeds float, just giving myself totally
to the water. To die before I die."
So he did that.

254

He bobbed up and down, helpless,
within arm's reach of the fishermen.
"Look at this! The best and biggest fish
is dead."
One of the men lifted him by the tail,
spat on him and threw him up on the ground.
He rolled over and over and slid secretly near
the water, and then, back in.

Meanwhile, the third fish, the dumb one, was agitatedly
jumping about, trying to escape with his agility
and cleverness.
The net, of course, finally closed
around him, and as he lay in the terrible
frying-pan bed, he thought,
"If I get out of this,
I'll never live again in the limits of a lake.
Next time, the ocean! I'll make
the infinite my home."

PONDER AND CONSIDER

Which fish are you?
How did the wisest of the fish get away?
How did the half-wise escape?
What happened to the foolish fish?

The first fish got smart, and said to himself, "Don't underestimate
what you're actually up against. If you're going out to sea, don't forget
what the open ocean can do." This way he could be responsive and
alert always to changes in conditions. This is a powerful principle as it
pertains to a life skill. It is what the first fish does. Yet, the first fish ran
away like the human condition to run, ignore or divorce oneself from
reality. The second fish dies back into life. This is a great example of
courage. I'd rather be this one. The third fish simply crumbled in fear
and lost his way. His bad decisions conditioned him like we do as

humans to avoid the past with regret. If you see the past with regret, think again. When you choose a worthy goal, you get to choose what parts of the past to bring along. The best of the past are skills and achievements. The present is often a source of impatience, and yet you can learn from an emerging future by staying longer, and listening deeper, being "inter-wise." And the future is giving you everything it needs in this moment. It is not a source of frustration but rather, a direction to learn and consider.

Two aspects that position the capacity for learning are 1) having a place to go---an intention they genuinely want, and 2) having a clear picture of the actual state in comparison to where they want to be, always. Keeping over-confidence in check is a form of demonstrating humility. *Reverence* is the capacity to see both positive and negative aspects to what is there---the risks, the pluses, and minuses without minimization or exaggeration. Without reverence, preparation would be shut down as well as an appreciation for what is significant. If I'm not reverent to the people around me in my life and their gifts, that's a severe loss of visibility.

"To see what's going on" is so noble that it helps leaders access a greater part of themselves through the work. They create as art. In fact, when this motivation is what motivates the work, it becomes work with a capital "W" Work! These leaders act from this place everywhere they go, personally and professionally. I've studied their behavior extensively, and to this, I chose to share my findings with you the reader. I've outlined eight key points in this brief to help you understand how to apply *reverence* in your daily living as they do.

What you see is what you get. There's an old saying that when a pickpocket sees a Saint in India, all he/she sees is the Saint's pockets. When we look with a pre-existing judgment, it's like loading up what we see into a net to confirm what we know and want to see. The model we hold (filter, lens we edit from) isn't an issue; instead, it's when we forget we have a mental construct at play is when things get complex. I liken our pre-judgmental thinking to shadow boxing. We tend to see phantoms when we see what we perceive from our pre-existing beliefs that we hold as true. Without question what we construe as fact, we act on non-factual data without careful reflection or further understanding. This is disturbing oneself. To decouple from the domination of our habituated thinking is to cut ourselves loose from the grasp of the automatic mind stuff, and see with new, fresh eyes. What we can take in is fuller, bigger, more real than our relative truth that limits our full spectrum of encountering new possibilities where alternative future might be seeking our gaze, to come into being.

There is a leadership capacity like the second fish to meeting reality directly without hiding, ignoring, denying, or exaggerating what is in front of you. You can soften your edges into it. One of my first encounters with *respecting* was diving with a Mako shark in open blue water. Although it wasn't comfortable to admit, I was forced to become fluent in registering the nature of the shark. This fish can tear me to shreds in seconds. As I observed it, I looked for signs of aggressive behavior. I was moved by the pure power of this fish in how it cut through the water with its sharp snout and thorny teeth. All at once I could feel the world and its footprint on limiting its subsistence. Fishing boats would net these sharks, keep only their

257

fins, then throw them back to die a miserable death. My primal fear of their ability to kill me was paired with my open-hearted compassion for their livelihood. I could see a future ocean like a dead wasteland devoid of life. I turned to this sense and felt a need to treasure and cherish these creatures. I felt a powerful urge at that moment to help the world know of their tragedy.

When we register what is true, we are changed by it. This brings us to be more resourceful and try new responses. We use the energy of our restrictions to awaken our sources of creativity, innovation, and courage. We can participate in life such that we enter a level of consciousness where love meets this honesty. We suddenly come to terms with how powerless we are in the web of life.

My Mexican father-in-law Fernando had thirteen children. As the man in charge of customs in Guadalajara's import and export process, each day he kept his head down to do what was needed on behalf of his children's needs. Each attended universities, became successful in their own path, and led great lives. How was never at issue, simply the daily disciplines of bringing forth the forces needed were organized by his acceptance of his current situation. Like it or not, Fernando was braced with courage to meet his commitments. Unforeseen forces always seemed to come to his aid in the more dire moments, "saying," you do your part, and I'll add mine. The universe is a friendly place, and very helpful, when you're really going for something you must do, and figuring out how as you go. Fernando always took care of his friends in need, and his generosity always seemed to provide him support from people he helped along the way who felt gratitude for his concerned heart. In some mysterious way,

Fernando's capability to thrive with confidence was imbued by his never-ending faith in making a difference and concentrating daily on marching to what mattered most to him, which was his family. I was reminded of the hotel manager in the documentary-based film, Hotel Rwanda, with his agenda to keep people safe. Moment by moment, he remained responsive and with agility, he yielded mighty bravery showing faith in every action, and letting go of the outcome. Our experiences guide us, not just what we shoot to attain. If we conserve learning in our momentary living, we listen and act from a place of letting go, and letting in future possibilities that are somehow seeking us, to come into reality. Papa Fernando lived his life on this tenet with a full deck of faith to play the cards he was dealt, without reducing his confidence when discouraged. He would repeat these words to me: "Start with what, and let the how come, just make up your mind, commit yourself with courage and go." Don't hesitate, act and learn what is next. This is the essence of reflection in action. Maintain your inexperience and start with nothing."

Something alive lives inside the mystery of life, and this is where the presence of the soul lives. However, when you attempt to take control of life and attempt to master it, you trade this mystery for mastery. This level of control is at best folly.

We are preoccupied with the tendency of our brain to explain things. We coordinate ourselves by default to create or understand things consistent with what we know, to describe something as truth. This innate thirst to explain things keeps us preoccupied with existential questions that are unknowable. Who are you? Whatever opinion you hold of yourself is one thing, but you will never know in fact who you are. You will never know yourself.

As you move through time, you shape yourself by your experiences and shape your experiences by yourself. You exist within an ongoing flow of conversation with life and conversation inside you. This conversation is never fixed. What comes and goes is a continuing process, despite our cravings, to form distinctions and compare things to what we know. We attempt to claim correlations between differences from the past to the present. Moreover, what is made true in the present is observable independent of biases born from the past. Information is not yet embodied when we meet the present fully. Therefore, validity is made in momentary acceptances, not by comparing what was before to edit what is going on now. You realize that in the actual moment you are living in a combination of different domains: your intentions, your relations, your emerging surroundings, your beliefs. That world in which you live is appearing with you.

I was 17. I was returning one late Sunday afternoon with my friends Shane and Christopher from a weekend in Big Sur California. Christopher sat across from me in the music room with a gaze that was as if God was seeing into me without any impurities. The three of us took a sacred passage through hot springs walking naked in meditation. As I look back at the years with these friends, it was experiences like these, the music, the soul tones that fostered a sense of total acceptance, unconditional love, respect, and holding space for being genuine with trust. My friends were taking sensing journeys into the wilderness, learning the ways of nature and eastern traditional anti-stress practices such as tai chi and qi gong. This opened my eyes to see a way of being in the world where I'm present, indifferent to the dominant outlaws of fear, shame, and resentment. Meditation was a way of knowing that I could meet whatever arises, this cast of kindred spirits and soulful people were like a balm of peace to cross the bridge into my adult life. Rather than mastering life by control and acquiring power, I became interested in the unfolding moment as my teacher. One can access their own wisdom through intentional stillness, silence, and reflection. When you meet life this way, the mystery is the presence of the soul.

My lifetime friend Shane took his life at 47 years old on May 4th, 2017. Had I not been nurtured by the cast of teachers earlier during my years with nature's help, meditation and reflection, I would not have been able to meet the conditions of my friend's death. The past often prepares you for what is coming without you knowing what is coming. It is a trust that everything is going to be ok, and that mystery is the gateway to this eternal truth. Everything must change. Nothing stays the same. Every moment is seeding the next moment, and if captured, noticed, and processed in reflection, the future seeking what is given to you will become what it wants to become. You learn to meet anything and expecting nothing, no matter what shape it comes into your life.

Rainer Maria Rilke, the famous 19th Century German poet wrote about rising to meet such realities, in all shapes in and sizes in his piece the Bell Tower:

Quiet friend who has come so far,

feel how your breathing makes more space around you.
Let this darkness be a bell tower
and you the bell. As you ring,

what batters you becomes your strength.
Move back and forth into the change.
What is it like, such intensity of pain?
If the drink is bitter, turn yourself to wine.

In this uncontainable night,
be the mystery at the crossroads of your senses,
the meaning discovered there.

And if the world has ceased to hear you,
say to the silent earth: I flow.
To the rushing water, speak: I am.

Sonnets to Orpheus II, 29

Any attempt to take control of life and master it leaves the mystery out of it because you're scared to face what little you know. What you know has formed an identity for you in which you've found homeostasis. You probably think you can get it all done, in fact, you take pleasure in the sudden hit you get from getting things done because it affirms your sense of being industrious. However, as I said, you're too busy being busy to do what could make you a lot less busy. This is a state in our coaching situations we call "F-State" meaning "Frenetic State." It is the incessant frenetic-ness that is often at the root of the inability to solve the problems with a level of thinking different than the thinking that caused them in the first place. That, on the one hand, we have a set of activities that create our constraints when we fail to stop and look, while we have another set of activities to remove the constraints we create. It's like Pandora's box. The way out is via a fundamental shift of mind or "metanoia", as it is called. Here's the Shift: <u>The only antidote to changing this is through reflection</u>. Reflection means to slow down by walking with your intention and attention fully clear. We're not victims of the system; rather, it's a *system of the victim*. It all begins and ends with thought. To be aware of what is going on, and see things objectively with "reverence."

You must go slower to go faster. If you're not mindful and paying attention now about what you have and what you want, it affects the way things look later. This explains why getting to something later is very unlikely to happen because you've forgotten how busy you'll probably be then, despite the necessary lie that you'll be free. No one is any less busy later than he or she are now.

If you want to have less effort later, you must make an initial attempt to get it. This speaks to the "law of short reverse" which explains why bending your knees a few inches more leads to jumping upward a foot higher. When a quarterback steps back three more steps, the calibration and precision of the throw are ten times more accurate. It's like a slingshot effect; the more you pull it again, the more intensity you have available.

We play the game of life as if we're a mouse in a maze trying to find its way. We lower our standards far too often by tolerating things that

263

get out of touch with our desires. Your relationship with life circumstances moves you like a victim living in a reactive orientation, and you're left with the option to respond better next time. In fact, most of our education is built on this narrative: *getting better responses to what we know is going to come up*. Going through life like this is a waste of your life gift. It is an orientation that you've fallen into and live from because you don't know another way forward.

In the *quality view* of time you can do something far different with time and change the value you gain from it. In the quality view, you manage your energy by making better choices. The quality view of time enables you to trust your decisions better because what you choose by intention and conscious attention motivates new behavior. Having a place to go (know what matters to you) directs your use of time qualitatively. However, in the quantity view, you manage your hours in the day, which isn't enough. Without knowing what matters, time acts as a vacuum, with space to fill up whatever rushes to fill it. You do what you do unless you have something more compelling to do. In this case, it's easy to invite emergencies. This makes it hard to trust your decisions. So alternatively, when you don't make them toward a place to go, you make them by better responding to what life brings.

You cannot stop the clock, it is impossible. However, you can slow time down by how you choose to involve yourself in what you're doing. When you focus your attention on creating one thing, your relationship with time seems to change. Hours pass, and then you're amazed at how fast the time went. Your levels of awareness regulate whether time seems quicker or slower. When you're externally paying attention like a panorama view taking it all in, you're stimulated by the here and now and what is happening around you. Time slows down. Therefore, you can't wait to get to your destination in the car. Kids ask us, "are we there yet?" because of this external attention. When you're internally focused and concentrating, you're focused like a zoom lens. Time appears to speed up---the way you experience it is to lose some sense of where time is. So, if you want to slow down, focus attention broadly and externally. If you want time to speed up focus attention narrowly and internally or externally.

Now let's add something to this: Intention. Let's say that as you pay attention, your intention is awake as if listening behind your attention like a timeless eye behind the eye. Example: I want to buy a Mercedes Benz. Throughout the day I see them everywhere. Why? Because my intention is informing my attention. When we have a place to go, our aim is placed at the center of our awareness, and we tend to select subject matter in our environment that coordinate with it. Our choice informs our awareness. Therefore, setting goals and paying attention when we choose them tends to cause a cognitive reflex to what is consistent as well as inconsistent with it. At times it feels like passing through a time warp or a mystical experience.

Now let's add something else to this: Attention. Let's say that aside from setting your intention, you mindfully pay attention to what is going on---without editing it. Instead of interpreting, analyzing it, adding meaning to it (by conditioned thinking), you begin to commit your attention to see what is going on—compared to the intention that you set to create. Where does your relationship with time come into play? You authorize the time necessary to move from where you are

265

to where you want to be. Example: I intend to learn French and speak fluently in a conversation (intention). Today, I can pronounce basic verbs, but I don't yet understand others when they talk. The day I took my car for repair a French couple was waiting in the hallway. They began speaking French such that I could grasp what they said. More shocking is that they are both French teachers. How did this line up? Are the stars aligned? Not at all. It's the principle of *structural tension*.

INVISIBLE HELP

When I chose to be fluent in French and observed where I was in my current state with it, something almost mystically presented itself---1) hearing French I could understand and 2) meeting French teachers in the oddest of places I'd find them. These coincidences are more frequent when you position what you want in contrast to where you are now. Something within that gap is naturally seeking to resolve, and it's obvious I'm not the only one who is doing the resolving myself! The difference between what we have now and what we want to create is the armature and engine of the creative process, structural tension. I have nature stacked in my favor to succeed when the contrast between my intention (what I want), and what attention I bring to what have now! Nature is a powerful ally.

Time passes in connection with the eternal by way of positioning a structure which coordinates a resolution in favor of what I create. This is not the law of attraction. I don't need a state of mind, vibration, or self-manipulation through positive thinking. It is not the cosmic drift inside me where I must touch the sky to allow bliss! In fact, just the opposite---being faithful to where I am compared to where I want to be. I take meaningful leaps forward into the uncertainty. Structural tension is what governs nature's ways to move the path of least resistance from where I am to where I want to be. It's like having a success ally on my side!

Positive thinking is positive lying. The more I could tell myself the facts of my current stage of French; the more resourceful the universe became on my behalf with invisible help. Unforeseen forces came to my aid and dramatically shortened the time to acquire French!

Time lapses like these require us to have the flexibility to tolerate the discrepancy between the current and desired states of our creations, as the tension is resolved through action and invisible help. What summons that eternal is the love and honesty paired together---what we truly desired juxtaposed to what we have now. When we're intent by a choice to create what we desire---we turn on our concentration and narrow our focus. Time passes quickly. When we remain keenly aware of where we are, by comparison, time passes slowly. Slow and fast co-exist in circularity as we pay attention without the mental constructs that distort how we experience time. Music writers and authors often describe this dynamic as they move in a creative flow between where they are and where they're going. Nuances and sudden improvisations are trusted and bound by structural tension. The path of least resistance is positioned to go where it's easiest to go---in the direction of the result.

We learn and unlearn on our way to our destination. We open a dimension of space for the new to enter. This timeless eye can see this. It recognizes our own seeing as just editing from thought. Rather than see what is projected onto reality, it sees directly and opens our heart to understand what is there with greater depth and compassion.

As we move, we unlearn an old identity that we hung onto, as the direction ahead is made for us by walking on the path. You listen as you fail your way forward. Successful failures help you unlearn, learn, adjust, and tweak, to build new capacity. As I learn to snow ski, and fall, each time I re-enter by getting back up, I'm inheriting new information. It's like scratching a lottery ticket. We have to scratch and scratch until it comes.

And without conceptual limits on what truly matters and what we truly see, resources near and far can make our use of time on-purpose, almost predictable miracles come about on the path. Nothing is to be expected, and everything is valid. I don't know the mechanics precisely of how this works, but it's like a light bulb; turn it on, and it works! Knowing what matters makes our time validated and valuable (quality) by what is essential. Our mind has bigger business to attend to when we're aware of what matters, just like a dog with clear instructions. Without a place to go, a dog would poop all over the house and chase trucks!

Wanting to be happy isn't what I hear people wanting most. They hunger to feel involved with their own lives, building something that matters to them and learning and unlearning, to create it. This involvement is where we can touch the bounty of life, and touch eternity before life runs out. Reverence is the awareness tuned by our intention and attention working in common cause. You can't control your fate, but you can choose and remain in service to your destiny with reverence. Your destination is what you conceive to matter to you and move toward it. Creating what matters is like a sacred project.

For example, if I choose to be healthy that is my destiny---create optimal health. My fate is what'll be going on when I get there. This doesn't imply that you should give up and let life take you wherever it goes. Life is a wildcard, it will take you wherever it does, and that's the way of itself. It's called nature. However, if you fall into believing you have no power to create what you want, that's the assumption from which you operate. Moreover, you'll probably coordinate your responses to life to give in and go with the flow to resolve the concept you hold that you're powerless. You put away your intention when your belief makes contact with you and you comply with it. Defying it is when you choose to organize action from another motivation--- Destiny!

You choose to be the predominant creative force in your life---that you organize your life around what matters most to you. This is a fundamental choice. Everything is up for grabs, and you can rethink your life as if you started over again creating your life as art. This orientation to life not of the reactive, it is of the creative. It is a placement of power on creations you seek to bring into the world, instead of improving yourself. The orientation is one you probably already know and don't know you know. A woman who creates a baby and brings her child into the world innately lives in a creative orientation. Her awareness of her loving intention to deliver the baby into the world is compared to the stage of growth the baby is in along the way. Her intention *and* attention work in common cause to create a miraculously successful birth event. She is a creator; the baby is her creation. Reverence for the baby is a 3rd person orientation, not 1st person. Nowhere is the story of "me" for the mother in the baby. The mother isn't the main character in the story. She creates the baby out of generative love and empathy and attends to the baby by setting this intention into her awareness.

When you assume someone has answers for you, you put them in an ignorant position to feed his or her ego. What makes it worse is when the person is looking to affirm their importance and appear better than they think.

No one has answers for you. They have questions for you. Items come from curiosity and wonder, instead of answers which come from certainty. There are no experts; everyone is making things up as he or she go along. Helping someone is about having them come to the answers together, not you, not them but instead the relationship. The mode of interaction is one of trust, such that cultivating a don't know stance is safe and constructive to becoming more intelligent together than apart.

If you're someone different at work than home, you're out of touch with the eternal. You live a life of always running out of time, wanting 40-hour days instead of 24. The fact is you have 24 hours in a day like everybody else. You live in a neighborhood of scarcity, where time is an adversary because of the view you hold, and the terms you're on because of this view. In this quantity view, time is a mental construct of the world to avoid being controlled by it. Even if you had free time, you wouldn't use it because your belief that you have no time is made real by the negation of having the opportunity to enjoy even when it's staring you in the face. Without this free time, there's no renewal to think about your thinking, reflect on what matters, and position yourself to spend the time better moving forward. You're too busy being busy to do what could make you a lot less hectic.

"When you waste all your time attempting to fix what is wrong with you, then you discover that in your attempt to manipulate yourself, it has made you a lousier creator. Putting out fires makes you an arsonist."

When you waste all your time attempting to fix what is wrong with you, then you discover that in your attempt to manipulate yourself, it has made you a lousier creator. You're more preoccupied with your identity and your power than the reverence you have for creating what matters to you. Therefore, you may be able to fix yourself (your esteem, your stupidity, your self-love, your confidence, your beliefs) and still may not have what you want. Make self-improvement a hobby!

Simran

Unchecked, our habitual perceptions shape what we see. When we change *how* we see, what we see changes. If I see the divinity in me, I see the divinity in you. This suggests a circularity to come into full being. Simran, a powerful term used in Hindu doctrine was mentioned earlier in this book. Remember, this quality describes the capacity to see one's inner light, and therefore illuminate it in the other. When you dare to be seen just as you are, you're not preoccupied with power or inadequacy. You see all your parts, both positive and negative qualities. Seeing your positive sides becomes intensified when you stay true to what matters to you. Your comparison thinking holds you against a set of ideals. These ideals went live in your head when you concluded something about you disqualified you from the love or relationship with others, so you hid your secret-self down deep below the radar. Deception or camouflage is a form of fakery to help you offset your preoccupation with an aspect of yourself you deny the world. Anyone finding out how dumb you think you are might prove that your suspicions are correct. And anyone finding out how foolish you are might reject you and cause isolation or humiliation which you fear genuinely. Approval overcomes you like a slave to belonging, except the world is relating with a mask, not you.

Several human potential approaches push that self-love is the antidote to this vaporizing this false self, yet how can you love something that you don't enjoy. Love isn't manufactured or synthetic. Our marketplace is loaded with discouraged people who've concluded they are the problem. Their proposed answer is to fix flaws and quirks that denied them access to meeting expected success.

I suggest self-honesty instead of self-love. Coming by yourself honestly is a radical idea that doesn't ask you to pretend you to love yourself or force your acceptance. Why force acceptance of who you are? You don't need to affirm who you are not to be someone better, because lying to yourself sets you back. Who but a person who is insufficient constantly would need to propagandize to themselves constantly they are better?

We have a bad habit in our society of linking self-esteem to the creative process. Self-doubt is the enemy, and to create, it requires we overcome it. What's funny is when you read the bios of more celebrated achievers or famous people. Almost all of them had confidence issues, had terrible self-doubt, yet they created great things anyway. Their creative process didn't depend on their identity. They were able to take the positive sides, their talents, and gifts and apply them. Their weaknesses and doubts weren't an issue. They were registered merely, then left alone. They didn't create what mattered to them by self-improvement. They mastered the creative process, and one aspect of that involved seeing current reality accurately. This required them to evaluate themselves honestly against the outcome the sought to create. Like learning piano, you must assess your current level of competency to see where to adjust and improve on behalf of the playing level you seek to create or the music you attempt to write or play. Like learning a language, take stock of your current level of fluency in the new language, as the key to knowing where to learn and go next.

In the domain of creating a successful relationship, one experiences their ability to make a secure connection, build trust, meet another's wants and needs, listen, communicate, and co-create a loving and committed long-term courtship. The relationship becomes the subject matter of the creative process, as the current connection is brought to the desired relationship one seeks to create. In doing so, one recognizes qualities in himself, as if the link was a mirror reflecting back conditions and properties from which the individual can learn, build upon, unlearn, and grow. We naturally seek to build links for this reason—to experience parts of ourselves that we depend on others to access. We touch deeper parts of ourselves as we deepen our intimacy level, making it safe to share truth-telling together.

When Farah, a transformative leader in the banking industry saw how women in business could be liberated by their ability to choose where to place their efforts, she acted. Without disqualifying herself or questioning her compelling urge to create something, she sprang to her contact book and started connecting with women she knew about a TED Talk. There she was asking her hand-selected leaders to come and speak at a special luncheon. They all readily and gladly agreed to participate. Moreover, when she asked her banking team to support the effort as a marketing push for entrepreneurial women, they gladly green-lighted the project.

The event was about to begin, and Farah began clenching her fists with nerves about to open the talks and introduce herself. She'd been working for days packaging her speech and envisioning the way it would all go down. Then, as she turned to face the crowd, it was like a shot of strength went down her spine and she tossed out her entire speech and said, "well, I'm not going to go with my prepared speech, my name is Farah, and I grew up in Buffalo and moved out to California..." and everyone started clapping and cheering for her bravery to just show up and be herself. She was connecting with her truth and without fail her words found her. She described the experience as losing herself and seeing herself, and as she laid it out there, everyone was enjoying themselves and laughing at what brought her to the event that moment. All she did was tell the events that took place and how she moved through them. Then four other speakers led their talks, and the final one with stage four cancer touched on the rapture of life itself and the blessings we all have in us to give to the world.

The room was in tears with this grand finale speech that brought people to their most profound joys and sentiments. Within hours after the event, Farah saw emails of gratitude pouring in. They all were so moved because Farah gave them her truth. All they wanted was her honesty to tell it just like it is. Farah found herself opening a door into a new frontier, one where people listened to something in her that she was getting to know. She remembered the ability to choose what matters to her. Moreover, that if she did, it sent a ripple effect outward across vast distances. That life is up for grabs, and you can rethink it at any time.

Nothing disqualifies someone from this capacity to choose. She said that it wasn't how she made others feel their potential by her talk, but that others had a profound concern and care for others in the presence of her speech. She made everyone feel care for everyone else. It was this moment of opening their hearts and faith in seeing the light in others that moved her to the core. Farah was connecting to her most essential self and her most deep work. She recognized that what makes her feel alive is what belongs to the world.

One of the principles Farah learned was that to open the door to full possibilities and potential, it starts by suspending her conditioned thinking. Leading up to the event she argued with herself about not being good enough, not having what it takes, and that everything would turn out horrible. As she heard herself, she didn't turn away. Instead, she met these thoughts. She remained separate from them. But she knew she had more significant business to attend to. She fostered her choice to show up to what she wanted to create and set

275

her deepest sincere intention as to what outcome she wanted. It was a generative love for the idea she was rallying for. To learn how to make it happen, she kept keenly aware of where she was in comparison to where she wanted the event to be. This unedited objectivity helped her determine needed resources, navigate key decisions, ask for help, and depend on teamwork to bring the event into being.

It was after the event when Farah reflected on the defining features, the context from which she knew what she had to do. She felt these women---their limitations, and their potential. She heard their voice and placed her awareness in their conversations---with themselves and world. She could feel in her heart the need to lower their suffering and liberate them. Even though other groups had similar dynamics, what was significant for Farah was the way she saw these women, and how it resonated with her. She learned that strength is resonance. Where there is a dynamic urge there's always strength. People often define their strength on their skill, but Farah determined her strength on what this experience meant to her, and where that energy was ready to take her forward.

BILL'S WAY HOME

His parents lived the jet-setter life. Bill's dad owned an insurance agency with nine locations and 78 people working for him. Dad took the family on great vacations all over the world and put Bill and his brothers in the best schools. One night in 1983, Bill remembers his dad emphasizing what was required of him. Whenever dad invited company over to the house, he asked Bill to wear his happy face. The family meeting before the invite laid out a clear plan to project an image. Other than the parties, dad and mom were around yet not around. Dinners together were distracted by TV shows, and just hanging out and talking was overridden by something to do.

When Bill was 14 years old, he finally saw his dad cry in church after a powerful sermon, but after that dad held in his emotions. Grades to Bill's dad Larry symbolized whether you were a good person or bad one. In fact, in 10th grade, when Bill's progress report had a "D" in biology, Larry marched down the school and darted into Bill's classroom. He grabbed him and yanked him so hard that Bill's shirt tore. Yelling behind him like a wild dog moving a cow, Larry's insults and contempt echoed throughout the H Building. As Bill stood in the school counselor's office like a beaten animal, Larry paced and belched yells saying how much of a loser he'd be in life with grades like this. Larry felt the grades meant a lack of appreciation for his family heritage and the pride of his last name. "You're not a Garrison." Larry left no room for Bill to discuss reasons why, nor examine what's to be learned from this.

It was safe to be truthful with dad because his conditions were so strong. Larry was committed to shaping Bill into the performer he must be to meet the world's challenges as Larry saw them. At 18, Larry was divorced by his wife, Bill's mother, Julianne. That year, Bill's younger brother Chad committed suicide. After weeks of terrible fights and drag out arguments in the house, Chad elected to end his life because he felt responsible for his parents coming apart.

THE LIFELINE

During the morning of the retreat, Bill was asked to build out a lifeline of his life journey to get to this point. The facilitator asked, "What brought you here?" The question wasn't about how, but what events shaped what brought you to this point in your timeline? Then the trainer went on to say that various persons entered your timeline at key moments to supply something to you. Bill started to see the faces of people who were his supply lines all his life. He felt a huge surge of gratefulness in his chest for their contributions as well as sorrow for those who passed on. The trainer spoke of people whose shoulders we each stand upon to get here, and that forgetting their contributions is missing an opportunity for gratitude and humility. "You are a person who speaks from many voices that have gone into you," the trainer said, as Bill listened closely.

When Bill started the consulting business with Jim back in 1994, Jim was the wiser one while Bill had the swagger to go out and bird-dog new business. However, when Jim asked Bill to pass the clients over to him, Jim scared them off. At times Bill would kiddingly call Jim a "jerk" or an "asshole" beneath his breath until one time it set Jim off. He went on a tirade, telling Bill that he must feel beneath him and used these subtle verbal attacks as a sign of showing his insecurity. Unfortunately, Jim was spot on. Bill was doing male banter as a form of getting "one up" on Jim because Bill was preoccupied with Jim's dominant ability and experience. Bill felt internally intimidated by Jim and used these words as ways to project Bill's inner disapproval on Jim. "I'm just mirroring back to you Bill what you think of yourself," exclaimed Jim. Jim was the rough and tumble type; he loved confrontation. As a consultant, he was known for "gutting" people and insulting them to ring their bell when their ego flared up on him. In fact, Jim was so direct that people often wanted to fist fight and punch him for his hurtful comments. However, after the flare-up, people got that Jim was toughly empathetic and using his roughness to get people to see a destructive part of themselves that was troubling.

There is an ancient, inspiring short story coming from the sacred land of Tibet. I don't know who wrote it, but one thing is sure: its message is profound.

Long, long ago when the world was young, and the tiger walked with the deer, there was a wealthy king who had four wives. The king loved his fourth wife the most and adorned her with riches. He also loved his third wife and was always showing her off to neighboring kingdoms. However, he still feared that she would leave him. His second wife was kind and considerate and his trusted confidant and advisor under challenging times. Wife number one was devoted and loyal, and although she loved him deeply, he was not as interested and tended to ignore her.

One day, the king fell ill, and the truth dawned that his life was soon to end. He thought of the luxurious life he had led and feared to be alone when he died.

He asked his fourth wife, "I have loved you the most, endowed you with the finest clothing, showered gifts upon you and taken great care over you. Now that I'm dying, will you follow me and keep me company?" "No way!" she replied and walked away without another word.

The sad king then asked the third wife, "I have loved you all my life. Now that I'm dying, will you follow me and keep me company?" "No!" she replied. "Life is too good! When you die, I'm going to remarry!"

He then asked the second wife, "I have always turned to you for help, and you've always been there for me. When I die, will you follow me and keep me company?" "I'm sorry, I can't help you out this time!" she replied. "At the very most, I can help with your funeral."

Then a voice called out to the king in his sadness: "I'll leave with you and follow you no matter where you go." The king looked up, and there was his first wife. She was so skinny and undernourished. Greatly grieved, the king said, "I should have taken much better care of you when I had the chance!"

In truth, we all have four wives in our lives. Our fourth wife is our body. No matter how much time and effort we lavish in making it look good, it'll leave us when we die. It'll be burnt, buried or chopped up for the vultures and wolves or feed the worms.

Our third wife is our possessions, status and wealth. When we die, it will all go to others. It will be divided up.

Our second wife is our family and friends. No matter how much they have supported and loved us, the furthest they can stay by us is up to the burial site. Even if they enter the portal of Death, they and we must walk alone into the *Bardo Thodol.*

Our first wife is our mind stream, often neglected in pursuit of wealth, power and pleasures of the ego. However, our mind stream is the only thing that will follow us wherever we go.

THE FEMININE ENERGY

At age seventeen, Bill was visited by his mother's best friend, Lorraine. Lorraine was a free-spirited actress with an open heart and mind. She had a regular contemplative practice while staying at Bill's home. Every evening Lorraine would burn incense and meditate with beautiful ambient music emanating like the smoke of a Nag Champa incense stick. The scent carried into the living room where Bill would follow it to her room. Lorraine always welcomed Bill to sit quietly and let go of anything he was thinking about. She explained that letting go and observing rather than thinking allowed him to experience a different way of seeing things. Instead of being ruled by the context of his thinking mind, Bill found he could access a more open, empty state from which he could relate with life. Lorraine explained that listening is part of the creative process. To listen, you first let go of your judgment (downloading the past into your thinking mind). She called this "cultivating a don't know mind." Lorraine had a way of always looking at what is going on freshly without distortion or edits, and said she'd learned to do this from her acting classes when intentional stillness was the starting point before performing.

THE RETURN

Bill went to see a new potential client John Sanchez, President of Rancho Restoration, to help him with his financial situation. After several meetings to discuss John's retirement plan, it became clear that Bill needed John more than John needed Bill's help. Their meeting up was not by accident. Like chess, something bigger was moving the pieces of his life around. John Sanchez devoted his life to restoring prisoners doing time for the worst offenses. Bill was fascinated in what brought John to do this work, and what he had learned from all his interactions with these people. John would speak of how deep the pain would run in gang-related inmates. They had poor role models and did horrible things because they had no sense of who they were, and what mattered to them. Their lives were nothing and causing harm to others became a destructive way to ventilate the pain and hurt they carried inside all their lives. The negation of love, acceptance, and encouragement had cut them deeply, and that doing bad things had been their way to retaliate against the neglect.

One of the topics Bill became most interested in was the topic of what John called "re-seeing the light in oneself and others." John told stories of inmates who had lost touch with the good in others. Their belief that everyone is out to take, and nobody cares because their way of rebuking themselves to be nothing. Part of the rehabilitation back to their true nature was to reacquaint themselves with the light within them---that they are, beneath all the rubble, loving beings, capable of giving love and receiving love. Forgiving themselves for their stage in the journey was one step toward returning to the light. John explained that when giving a trouble-maker uncommon grace, acceptance, and legitimacy, the quality of being light helped the one being observed become it. And if they saw the divinity in themselves, they could see the same gems in the hearts of others too. Rebuilding the trust in this light was the return to becoming alive again.

John said:

> "Find a place of rest in the middle things and plant a tree there in a forest of your life, Bill. You are here to use this wild and precious gift of life by placing your gifts in the service of others. Find a home to park this gift. This home isn't static but moving. It is to find a seat in a dream of your own of being part of building the life dream of others. Let go of all your rules around this and be free to listen. Listen to others' hurts, dangers, opportunities, strengths, and all they aspire to create with their own life. You will never go hungry; you will have inner rewards and external rewards if you listen, become essential, and serve others from this place. What you find within yourself belongs to them, as you're to show up to give this to the world through all you are. This part of you was lost or hidden under the rubble of modern life but never left you. Your journey is to rehabilitate this life force among things and meet the heartbeat of life as it deserves you in service to your gift."

"What a wallop of a reflection," Bill thought. He knew of his personal gift: verbal agility. He could naturally speak words from a deep place within him and trust these in natural order to come through him. People admired Bill for his capacity to access this connection within himself to convey his ideas and make them attractive.

John went onto explain to Bill that when we lose sight of this gift and leave its domain within all we are and do, we depend on others in unhealthy ways for meeting needs that we are responsible for fulfilling within ourselves. We cannot love others as a legitimate other because they are objects to fill the emptiness that our disconnection to our personal gift leaves us empty. We cling to addictions, depend on others and lower our standards, and fixate on what is wrong with us. This is not the way.

John told the story of Nelson Mandela, after 15 years of torture in prison, said he didn't know who love anymore. So, he elected to love his guards. After that, the turnover rate in prison was the highest ever because the guards couldn't bring themselves to torture Mandela anymore. True resilience is an uncommon grace. Mandela going to higher ground to love his guards motivated them to do the same toward him. Mandela had no conditions prerequisite to loving. Love is the act of accepting the other as a legitimate other.

ANOTHER THING

After Ed hired Jeff, it seemed that it'd all come together. Jeff coming from UPS brought the swagger and people skills to get others excited about accounts receivables solutions. Jeff could earn a high commission from each system installation after enrolling new business clients in increasing their cash flow from their slow-to-pay clients. Ed's company provided a third-party collection presence to prioritize payments for businesses that wanted to get paid faster. The first ninety went incredibly for Jeff, in fact, he won the sales contest and was the hope to win the next. However, suddenly Jeff's performance dived. Ed couldn't figure it out. After dinner together with Jeff and his wife, it was Jeff had a side gig to earn income steadily.

Jeff was trapped between depending on his other gig, while he built his book of business. The speed and impact, aggressiveness and commitment to making it were neutralized by his fear of unsteady income. Jeff wasn't an economic adult yet.

Frank was a multi-millionaire with a philanthropic heart. Early in his career, he found himself driving his financial investments hard, setting and meeting production goals, and going after new levels of income with new entrepreneurs to fund.

He learned to let go after hanging on with dear life. "You learn to walk a path with your palms open. You allow others to lay their palms on yours. When you go, don't grasp their hands, let go, and release them, for someone else is ready to enter in their place."

When the giver comes toward you, inherit him. I say this to you because there is now or will be an inflection point when the taker side of you (ego) transitions to (eco). It is the natural order of your life building process from adolescence to maturity, and it can happen at any moment during your lifetime when you're ready. It is the collapse of having to prove you are somebody, to living the being you are, as nobody else but yourself. It is the moment you come to terms with power. You are no longer living inside your role (as a husband, business-person, father, etc.), you are living from the soul. You outsmart constructing a self of what you do, what you own, and what you've done. You stop buying things you do not need, and stop impressing people you don't like. Because when you think you lack power or think you are inadequate, you shift your way of being to an impersonator of what is worthy of attention and love. That version of you is false. It doesn't listen and plays others the fool. When you collapse this face, what rises from the rubble is a new one, a truer one that is your nature which at its core is divine love, acceptance, and legitimacy. You are a loving being at your heart, like a flashlight in the dark shining from inside to outside. Rather than shine the light on yourself, you shine it on all you can affect. You yearn to influence, enrich, move, give, and stimulate the lives of other people. It is a dynamic urge you were born with and surface when you are ready to give up the false self-system.

Your true role in sales is offering help to people who need it. Help is providing something to another they cannot do for themselves. And by helping those in a way they truly know and learn they need it, you can change lives. You are a hope dealer. Your help gives people the confidence, direction, and capability to take delivery of a better future than ever before. And if you don't take advantage of the opportunity to do this, what waste of the gift of you. The gifts you have stored inside you don't belong to you, they belong to the world, and your purpose in life is to create the potential for these gifts to come to the aid of what stands in need of them.

These gifts you were born with, and they have been trailing you, nagging you, they live in your deepest whispers inside yourself, and you've always known in some way or another than one day your time will come to bring them out. If you look behind you, these gifts haven't ever left you alone; they tap you on the shoulder constantly asking to come out. Open the door NOW! This is an invitation and a warning.

You can make a lot of choices in life about what to do with your time, or who to spend it with, or where to be, but this aspect is not a decision. You must do this. It is what you were given this wild and precious gift of life to use it for, and you must. It is the sacred project you came to this world with, the seeds of your unique strand of your DNA, and when utilized, your life will have no more music in you left to play when you're on your last breath! So, get serious about this. It is your initiation to allocate your best self, and true work to whatever calls you stands in need of you and matters most to you.

You can transform suffering in others. When you do this, your life is filled with heart and meaning. Years ago, you could follow a sales formula, a process to do this. It was re-usable again and again. Today, methods can become very limiting because selling has become more organic. It is all relational. The quality of connections made equal the quality of the opportunities. Even more is the quality of listening that gives rise to powerful relationships out of which business is done. This explains why emotional and spiritual intelligence is just as if not more necessary to selling than the intellectual piece. You could say it's like selling from the right brain where rapport, context, connection, creativity, collaboration, listening - all of which involve people skills - are what it takes. People don't buy from machines; they buy from human beings. Moreover, the one thing a machine cannot do is create. Creativity is what makes us the possible human.

This idea of letting go of structure, process, and something to hold onto can be scary, mainly if you've been selling one way for some time. However, if you do, what will go with it is the whole notion that you are a salesperson. You must be there for yourself and others. When you do one, you do the other automatically. This is because what you love to do is what belongs to the world and what the world is waiting for you to do. You cannot validate the true quality of what you have in you to give the world until the world echoes it back.

When the world listens, it's telling you something you're giving or delivering is essential. Your dependence on this echo is forever the origin of your expansion of higher capacities in your creative process. Relationship validates the origin of your most essential self. Patterns of interaction give rise to your exact properties. When you express love for a client, for anyone, you are essentially bringing yourself into the love that you are.

There's so much that comes with the programming of "being a sales-person." This is composed of what we should or should not be. However, when you decouple from the costume and norm, none of the old rules apply anymore. You're free to create with liberating new energy. Life is always asking of you to let go.

You don't have all the answers nor should you. There are no experts, like the rest of us, you're just making things up as you go.

UNDERSTANDING YOUR AUDIENCE EQUALS RELEVANCE

Your buyer today has four critical conditions in a world that is more volatile, uncertain, complex, and ambiguous. Your buyer is living in a world of flux. The context in his life is always in motion. His plans shift like swift ocean currents going in the other way. In these conditions of modern life, the buyer has been living with four conditions: 1) Confusion, 2) Isolation, 3) Powerlessness, and 4) Frustration.

In response to this new world, your opportunity to heal and change the buyer's life is in how you translate his experience of volatility into vision. You must find ways to move a buyer from a reactive life to a creative life. Moving from reactive to creative starts with a sense of direction and choice. The power of choice is the antidote to a belief that one can't create what they want.

People don't care what you know until they know you care. Understanding and compassion are vital to helping the buyer feel understood and essential. These two human needs in everyone, if not met, shuts the buyer down from hearing what you have to say.

LIVING CLOSE TO DEATH

Death reminds us how fragile life can be. You can be here one day and gone tomorrow. Life is so precarious. Stopping death is an impossibility that we all share. No one has control over this, yet we are all the same in our fate which is to die. Death is imminent.

You die all your life. You've been killed and come back to life as you evolve. You were once this, and now that. You are always in motion, just as the context is still breathing new and defining features that motivate you. Opportunities enter, challenges enter, and people enter, just as others leave. It is the ongoing saga of a life unlived and then lived. Life lives you as you create the experience you love. The only verification of what is true is now.

You are doomed to make choices. You are the chess master and the chess piece at all at once. Something more substantial is moving the parts around as you are choosing what matters to you as you go along. What once mattered may not matter anymore. What doesn't matter now might matter later on. You will change your mind regularly. Your experience will accumulate. You will edit what is going on out of this database.

To create your life as art, you will establish and act from three connections that are the backbone of this book, and the place from which your helping process prevails when selling. First is to establish a relationship with your emerging self---the essential one that seeks you now to come into reality. This is called the vertical connection. It is to align your behavior and act from a place of your deepest intentions (what matters most to you) as the rudder in the water today. This is authentication instead of conformism. Second is the horizontal connection between you and the other---to act from the place of empathy and understanding. To actively accept them as a legitimate other. This is to love instead of control or manipulate. The third is the now. You act from a larger field in which your inner knowing and highest good is called to action. Selling is bringing yourself into connecting with these three as one single quality in action.

To access these three connections: self, others, and wholeness, it requires several capacities. First, is you from certainty to curiosity.

The practice of suspending your voice of judgment by letting go of categorizing and learning to think. Categorizing is when we resign from observation and convert inferences into apparent facts. We walk into a room and immediately slot someone in a category and act from that place. It's like dirt on the window. What we fail to see when we habitually think this way is that our categorizing reinforces the other to continue how we look at them.

Fran believed Julie was disengaged. The rest of the team would stay more extended hours showing total commitment to tasks because Fran saw they cared more. When Fran labeled Julie, she elected not to include Julie in meetings to discuss plans and reflect on existing critical problems together. Being cast out, Julie began to think the team didn't value her opinion. When Julie elected to go silent, Fran's bias about Julie was confirmed even more. Fran continued to disconnect from her and withdraw.

The cosmic joke here is both are inaccurate about their assumptions of each other's intentions. However, we see how assumptions can confirm biases when at play within systems like this were interdependence is active. What could be possible of Fran saw her own seeing and what plays out when falling into her own certainty about Julie? What would Julie be able to do and contribute by suspending her certainty that her talents weren't valuable to Fran? If we're all thinking about what the other is thinking, this is the cosmic joke!

Aaron was angered at a prospect because he appeared like a stupid knucklehead when disregarding Aaron's solutions. When Aaron categorized Brad this way, he shut off trying to understand why Brad was reluctant. Brad saw Aaron's harsh move to cut Brad lose as cruel and selfish. Aaron had cut off helping Brad any further after giving up on Brad's stupidity. After careful reflection, Aaron suspended his model of Brad's behavior and reached out. First, he admitted why he had given up on Brad, and asked for a second chance. Brad agreed. Aaron shifted his focus away from his bias toward Brad and elected to inquire into what made Brad reluctant about Aaron's original solution.

They spent a half hour going into the backstory, and what was real for Brad.

As Aaron continued to listen not just to Brad's words, but to Brad as a person and his point of view, Brad started to feel safe within the acceptance level Aaron brought forth by his curiosity and generous listening. After forty minutes of playing back what Brad said about where we were in his life, and his concerns, Brad had talked himself into solutions that Aaron could help him implement. Brad then asked Aaron to help him and asked what next steps would help get started with Aaron's financial planning process. If Aaron had made the meeting at first about Brad, and his situation, and his desires, Brad would have felt safe to discern his current reality and goals, and Aaron would have had success early on.

ACCESSING SOURCES OF CREATION

I'm often asked to reflect with clients on where creations come from. To create is to be alive. Every moment is establishing itself and has a place of potential significance via how you relate to it. Every moment is a living breathing place to receive the direction wisdom is coming from. The essence of this direction is what this book is helping you take in. You do not perceive the world we see; we see the world we perceive.

This is a great example of why a woman will perceive differently than a man, why a lawyer will see differently than a poet. The place from which we look is generative. When you interact with your environment, you bring forth an awareness which if heightened can see how one sees. Instead of seeing an object, we redirect our awareness back to the source; the perception that is bringing the object into existence. When we indirect directly with reality, and bring forth awareness, we access something open. We encounter a sort of "field of power" from which specific patterns of energy and creative order are naturally self-organizing.

The social reality is a living system of interdependence from a certain favorable of connection brings us into understanding. Our capacity to make space for differences helps us experience our creative process that emerges when two or more people connect in a social body. This horizontal connection when intimacy, verification of each other through another's eyes, and our capacity to listen with empathy, help us learn to use the energy of this collective intelligence that seeks to express itself through our relating.

This implies that sales is not about cultivating a need for products and services and conducting a purchasing process to acquire them. Instead, sales are the process of learning to live together in a helping state from which an atmosphere of trust informs a setting for value creation. Value creation happens by coming together in ways that clarity of needs become recognizable through a particular mode of open interaction. Intimacy is the capacity, to tell the truth or be true. Intimacy requires trust and safety. The exchange of information depends on this dynamic. When truth-telling is highest, value creation is able.

When we start to appreciate the real nature of human perception as a living system, it has huge implications to how we get along and work together. The process of value creation becomes redefined by a spirit of being together and living together. We make space for each one of us seeing reality as they do with sensitivity to differing views, acceptance, and legitimacy. Reverence such as this is perhaps a part of our loving species that knows how to do something we don't remember enough. Amnesia is the most significant limit to this capacity.

RECKLESS RESPONSIBILITY REVISITED

Our human potential audience has socialized you to believe that you create your life. This notion suggests that you are the enemy and if you could master yourself, life would be Shangri La. That if you could fix your issues and quirks, everything around you would respond favorably.

Let's be clear that you do not create your life. You aren't that powerful and don't need to act like it to get ahead. Trying to beat life is wasted energy to your ideal of power used to offset your preoccupation with having no power. Despite all the work on yourself, you fundamentally are trying to respond better to life, instead of creating what you want. The difference has to do with orientation.

Life is a wildcard. Sometimes the universe cooperates with you and sometimes it does not. Circumstances come in all shapes in sizes: good, bad, and ugly. When you orient yourself to the creative, not the reactive, you're able to establish separation. Separation is a skill in the creative process that requires you to separate from your emotions, your issues, your circumstances, much like an artist would back up to see an entire view. This isn't about disconnection; rather, it's required to establish connections. When you practice separation, you can pull back and see your own seeing---as mental constructs.

Moreover, you can experience your emotions to be emotions. You can learn from these because your identity isn't married to these. They do not define who you are.

You're never prepared and in control of your life at all because you cannot predict the future. So rather than attempt to control life because of your assumption that you're in control of it all, let this notion go. It's just you trying to acquire power because you fear not having enough. It's is so freeing to remember that life is made of impermanence. Unexpected things will occur---people will come and go, money, opportunities, as well as miraculous occurrences, synchronicities, and more. You're ready for anything, expecting nothing.

Because self-improvement is about attempting to control one's life, when things go wrong, it's easy to blame oneself for what they did to cause this or that. After all, the notion is that one creates (her) life. Moreover, when life shows up unexpected, you habitually turn to yourself to work on your flaws. You think life is your own reflection. If you thought this was true, you'd be blind to see what is going on, and only look at what you project onto it. There's no separation.

Reckless responsibility is a good recipe for depression. Since I create my life when my life has gone wrong, what's wrong with me? Here's another one: "It must be a reflection of my thoughts?" We've given thoughts a bad rep. Yes, we do fall into habituation with our judgment. We fall into living from mental constructs downloaded from the past in order to make sense of things. However, these don't necessarily create our reality as if our thoughts are the main character in the plot dooming us to our beliefs becoming true. This suggests that we are the center of our own universe, and everything is in orbit around us! I call this reckless responsibility.

And people who obsessively focus on what's wrong with themselves are lousy creators. I guess they've never read the bios of famous people who created notorious achievements. Almost every person had negative thinking, pissy moods, doubted themselves, and had low confidence as well as setbacks. They weren't busy working on themselves; they were busy creating things that mattered to them and learning how to get it as they went along.

Remember, when we assume we're the problem, we fail to see what else is going on. It's like learning a new language and not seeing where we are in the process of becoming fluent. Pointing the finger back at ourselves for everything affirms our existence and helps us feel in control when we are not. If we cannot separate from what is going on, we can't get leverage on what to change, and where to change, as strategic choices to create what we want. Learning to play the piano doesn't require seeing a shrink, nor does learning a language.

We've all had others criticize us or not like us. Being ourselves is a process of making enemies as well as new friends who reinforce our true self. Some of the criticism is worth listening to because it may be useful, but you're not in control of others' perceptions, expectations, and interpretations from which they lens everything.

When professional creators talk shop, they don't bring in a psychological view. They leave it out. This way their own psychology isn't at issue. Instead, they learn from mistakes and successes and make tweaks to their capacity to create their creations they desire. Whether they succeed or fail, it's doesn't define who they are.

When my client Eric asked me how to create his own business. I replied: "you learn by creating a business." There are no right answers. There is no recipe for success. Each goal you seek to create requires its own learning universe of trials and errors to get it right eventually. It's like a process of elimination. Moreover, we love to insert tricks and gimmicks to attempt to shorten the learning cycle. We chant mantras like "don't reinvent the wheel" to apply fixes that later backfire when the approach worked for someone else's goal, not yours. If you carefully examine what 'creating' is, you notice that it is an intentional process of causing something desired to exist that did not before. You create separately from what you know.

However, since most of us aren't fluent yet in using the creative process, we default to human potential approaches such as positive thinking and willpower approaches that at best are short-lived and backfire later. If you want to work on yourself, make it a hobby. You can organize your life around creating what matters to you. What you do with yourself is another matter entirely. To create or not create, that is the question. You can work on better reactions and responses to life like a mouse caught in a maze of circumstances, or orient yourself to your choices and focus on creating what matters to you as your life building process. You can create your life as art.

Positive thinking is positive lying. Believing something will happen is delusional because you cannot officially think it until it exists. Professional people who create understand this principle all too well. They don't require believing in their creations before creating them.

Instead, they attempt to see the current reality of their creations in contrast to the desired state. They begin creating with love for the creation first, decide to build it, then learn how through action taken in service to their higher choices. This provides them with a clear pathway as to where to place their attention, what to improve, and where to further progress. The creative process is a well-motivated learning process. The process evolves in ways that are very rewarded as you go, and even more rewarding when you get to live in the universe of your creations that now exist after you create them.

Without keenly remaining aware of what is going on, creators lose the natural tension-seeking qualities that incline their motivation to resolve the difference between where they are and where they want to be. As they harness this engine like an archer stretching the bow to power an arrow, they keep their identity outside to utilize failures as assets. This is the main reason why working on themselves becomes hazardous to their creative process. They attempt to fix everything in response to their failure, instead of gathering new information and using it to organize new and better actions to foster the development of their creation.

Selling According To...

Selling in the 1st person orientation is far different than selling the 2nd or 3rd. First person is imbued in the sale being all about the seller and his self. The self is either current or future based. Current based self is that which is composed of the past, while the future based one is yet to become real yet. Either the seller has attempted to be someone important or on the way there, and the sale is another point scored on one getting more masterful and competitive. The 1st person seller is the controller of everything-the outcome, the process, and personal effectiveness.

The Game

"Do you want to live an impressive lifestyle or create a fulfilling life?"

You drive around your net worth. You're probably convinced that to play the game of selling you must look like you're powerful, capable, and successful. You eat at only the finest restaurants. All of this pretending puts tremendous pressures on you to spend more and more money, buying what you don't need, trying to impress people you don't like. You may be in severe debt because of it. This whole phenomenon of looking good and being noticed while trying to keep up financially is called "pimp factor." You buy the nicest clothes, driving the nicest car, and live a lifestyle to keep up. You fear being thought less than substantial. Yet, having an impressive lifestyle is different than creating a fulfilling life. Having a big home to entertain guests puts demands on your hours and efforts at work. Having your kids in the nicest schools and having a big roof over your head traps you in a constancy of work pressure that is out of balance with your values. You are prisoner of your own machine, trapped by the fear of humiliation, isolation, and poverty. Your ideals of perfection drive your hard work, while you miss the moments that really matter.

MONEY MONEY MONEY

Money is awesome. I appreciate money and enjoy having money to create what I want when money is needed to create it. As businessperson, your mission, values, and aspirations will depend on money coming into your life. This is the way I coach leaders to look at it as well, but many at first have some unhealthy notions about money that hold them back from earning it.

Growing up as a young entrepreneur was my friend Ken H., a business to business salesman, always evangelizing negative opinions about others who had money and the material things money bought them. What Ken didn't want anyone to know was how hungry he was to be like them. Ken always wanted a Porsche, not because of the car itself and the appreciation for how it was made, but how others would perceive him in it. He walked around convincing people he was holier than "money," but it was phony. I classify Ken as a "phony holy." Phony holies attempt to justify their spirituality to offset their shame of being greedy.

After that experience, I encountered many more phony holies who attempted to hide their hunger for money because they hated this part of themselves---greed. They felt shallow and unacceptable in their love of having money to keep up with the rest of the world, so they outwardly behaved like it never mattered chanting, "*how much you don't need money to be happy.*" To them, the shame they assigned to money according to their view around it catalyzed the motivation to show others that they weren't of the same superficial cloth. They attempted to smoke-screen the opinion of themselves that they were superficial if they wanted money so badly to feel secure and competitive. After more examination in coaching people with these concepts today, it became clear they are afraid of money, even more, afraid of their attachment to money. They were afraid of their internal conversations with themselves about money.

300

I've seen leaders in business attempt to do the same. They fail to guard their profits, justify the value of the solutions, and miss out on market leadership. And when their identity is mixed with the money they earn, the pimp factor of having nice things threatens the sustainability of their business in the first place. *They seek impressive lifestyles instead of fulfilling lives.* They don't see the role profit has to play in creating the future they seek to create. I began to see inspiring changes in their leadership when they took their identity, more specifically their beliefs about money out of the creative process. When money was de-mystified this way and decoupled from concepts, all it became about was money--- a vehicle or resource that is produced when value is created for another person or company.

Earnings (profits) are warranted to oxygenate the desired outcomes they wanted to create---their mission, vision, values which almost always were made of service to others genuinely rather than as a cloak to hide from the shame of wanting more money. Once this mission and vision is more important than their need for adulation and flaunting status, they found that their business profits were made successfully. Bonding with this work became more filling and meaningful than any favorable approval of another person could give them. Status could never quench the thirst the way loving what they were creating could. This deeper satisfaction gave them new eyes, priority shifts, and values.

Conversely, if you see companies that are committed to meeting their mission and values while not profitable, the enterprise is a church, not a business. Let's realize that to oxygenate the purpose of the business; it must have the financial performance to sustain itself.

A coaching client was earning just above board, barely cracking a profit, not looking at financial statements with the motivation that by not looking it would have a positive valence. He was 100% committed to his mission as a business, but wishy washy about making money at it. I'll repeat here what I repeated to him over and over again: "nobody cares about profits as much as you do, and nobody ever will nor should care as much as you do. And if you don't care about earning profits, go get a job."

So, if you're not pigheaded about knowing your numbers, what you're earning, how much sales your team is generating, and how much operating cash flow you have in the checking account, you're placing your capacity to learn and create the future you desire at great risk. You need to be money motivated as a secondary choice (action) to support your primary choice (goal/vision/outcome). Because if you think you're somewhere else financially than you really are, your quality of decisions could be putting you into bankruptcy soon without knowing it. You write checks you can't afford hoping with faith it'll all work out, but you don't have data you can live by. You don't own a business yet until you get this capability.

Financial visibility makes you resourceful. Good accounting, as scary as it can be, helps you see where you are compared to where you want to be, to carry out your company's purpose. The problem here with small business isn't a lack of structure; it's a lack of noble guiding ideas to rally a team around. Since they don't care about your profits, they care if the agenda is suitable to a meaningful course in life. Work today is defined as a place where I can self-actualize through the manifestation of a cause that is worthy of obedience.

Remember that earning power is the one asset you can control as a leader over your real estate, stocks, and other things. This is because you have unlimited talent to convert into value creation for your marketplace. You get paid to be creative, and deeply understand your market. Your earnings are commensurate with how essential you are in the eyes of your buyer. What makes you essential? You can measure this by 1) how much leadership and direction you give them, how much confidence and trust you provide, and how much capability you give them to create what they want (your customer). The man who knows the most about his/her client's wants, needs, and conditions wins, because these data points are what drive innovation and market value. This is the true essence of entrepreneurship.

So, if you focus on money as a sign of success, you're missing the point. Money is a vehicle for creating what makes you essential to your market---direction, confidence, and capability. All of these come from converting a conversation with your ideal customer into a solution they can't live without. The more essential you are, the less you must market and sell to produce business. Instead, the business comes to you. Money is time. Time is space. Space is the place out of which creations come. Creations come from the reflection out of connections through conversations. Listening is leaning into conversations until they change you. And if they change you, then the inspiration you inherit will reveal the creations that your market needs or is going to need, to make you essential and get paid nicely for it. But money isn't a measure of success. Success is measured by how much you organize your life around what matters most to you. Who you are isn't significant, what you create in the world that others value is.

Key points to remember:

1. Money is trust. You must trust that your earning power is in direct influence by your ability to focus your talents. And, when you focus on value and creating it for the joy of it, you set up a level of trust that others are being served from your heart, not your head. This goes a long way. When you focus your habits behind this decision, you keep your word, finish things you say you'll do, and respect others' time and tend to appreciate others for who they are and how they impact you. These habits are what make you continuously a great reference and resource for someone they care about. When you invest your talent, great value for others, and amplify your dependability, you are positioned for opportunities in trust, such that you can relax during downtime knowing that things are in motion to bring you near the wealth you want and relationships you influence.

2. Money is time. I know this to be true because in sales you don't get paid for time, you get paid for results. Your economy of means is via opportunities that reward you for value you create for them. Time isn't money because you can spend more or less time and still get the same result. It's the quality of the time getting ready for the result that shapes it. As you earn money,

you buy time with it. You hire people who perform tasks to help you leverage your abilities and grow and invest in rest and relaxation to enjoy life outside your business.

3. Money is a function of generating discretionary decision-making that is creative in orientation. You choose who to be with, where to be, and which activities you choose to be doing when money is available.

4. Money doesn't define your identity. It doesn't make you a better or worse person, and if you're falling into money as a measure of who you are as a person, you will probably disown yourself when you don't have it. And when you do have it, your spending decisions will be motivated either by your ideal or your values. When you forget or remain unclear as to what matters to you (your values), money is an unhealthy source to replace it. You probably have ideals or false standards of who or what you must live up to, so you can offset your opinion of yourself.

5. Don't link your worth to your desire. When you link these two, you organize your efforts around deserving what you desire. In fact, you might add many more steps to creating what you want just to satisfy this earn out you place on yourself. It is simply living up to your ideals, not creating. When a music artist makes great music, they don't have on fame. Instead they focus on the music they create, and use fame as a tool to strengthen their reach to build demand for their music. But the focus is on the music not on themselves. When you let go of deserving from desiring, you no

longer bring your identity as a participant in the process. You leave what you think of yourself outside, as if it's not at issue. Creating doesn't require you to have a positive or negative relationship with yourself anyway. Artists don't bemoan their relationship with themselves; they focus on their art. This way, they gain more range to experiment, succeed, fail, and learn, to increase their capacity to create what they have in mind.

6. Being happy you can be at any time. You don't need conditions to change to be happy. So, organizing your life to be happy isn't the same as creating what matters to you, and bringing it to life.

7. When you realize that you're separate from your car, your house, your profession, your circle of friends, your neighborhood, your image, all of these are aspects that are not married to your identity. You might keep score on them when your negative opinions of yourself or sense of inadequacy motivates these to symbolically convey a position to the world to offset your negative belief. But when you're separate from all this---it is just content for what you create or not create. You're probably understand now that there's nothing to be. It's about what you create.

8. Money is used for letting others help you. When you invest in help, you get freed up to live enjoyable, and meaningfully. You can conceive of all this without money but bringing it to occur requires money. People are investments. When you see someone with God-given talent, invest! One day this may save your life.

LEARNING TO HELP A STRANGER

Chester was hungry as he rang the doorbell of a gated estate looking for help. As she peered through the curtains, Gayle saw a young man thin as a stick with a tin cup clanging on the metal to raise attention. At first, she thought how germs and danger could be lurking around such a dirty fellow, but Gayle's heart had a different intention. It wasn't sympathy she felt, but a deep empathy for a person so young looking and torn up. As she gingerly approached the gate, Chester spoke. He was in tears because his father had just died of pancreatic cancer a month ago leaving their foreclosure with the bank and Chester without a place to live. He was broke and broken, with an empty heart and empty pockets. She gave him $300.

Chester was so thrilled he couldn't stop bawling. He promised her that this money would take him far ahead and he'd show her how much. Gayle felt great about it and wished Chester the best in the world and to put his gifts toward his aims.

Years went by, even decades and Gayle had lost her job of 20 years as an executive. The company was downsizing and gave her a severance to last 12 months, and then Gayle was to live on her own savings. She lost her house and moved to an apartment and was making far less than before to make ends meet. Today, she just came back from her primary care doctor with a note. It was an appointment for a biopsy because the x-rays found a lump in her breast. She fainted on the spot. After 20 minutes, she got herself back up and lonely and scared, she booked the appointment.

Gayle's test results were positive, she had an incurable stage 3 cancer that only 302 people in the country had, and only one survived. Her health insurance had run out of room, and she had no way to pay for the road ahead. Her only alternative was to play it out and die.

But the story doesn't end here. That afternoon, Gayle found an envelope in her mailbox with a handwritten note in it. Behind the note was a copy of her insurance certificate she had sent in to fund her medical help.

Dear Gayle,

> *"Your primary care doctor phoned me at my office at Johns Hopkins Medical Center telling me about your situation. From the time I left your gate with $300, your reaching out launched me into a massive initiative. To make a long story short, I graduated in medical school top of my class, and today I'm the leading breast cancer specialist in the top hospital in the nation, and I'm going to do all I can to save your life because you saved mine."*

> *Love, Chester*

As the tears rolled down her face with black mascara trails, she noticed a giant zero on the invoice Chester sent back with a post it note saying "this is free of cost."

Gayle survived.

When you can reach out to someone, remember this, because you don't know how much good you do in the world with your heart's intention. What you appreciate appreciates!

LEARNING TO SEE

Being seen is a vital part of defining what is true about us. To love is to see. How we see something, a game, an industry, an opportunity, a thing, a person is where another person is definable. The word intimacy can be taken as "in to me see." We each exist within a network of relationships from which we are seeable. Properties are defined by patterns of interaction with others. Relationship is the organizing unit of the universe. No properties of ourselves are retrievable or whole until we are seen.

LEARNING TO LOVE

Love is the intentional act of accepting another human being as a legitimate other. To see where to help, you must generously listen. This requires you make a place of rest in the middle of things, retreat, and reflect on what is significant. Therefore, hard work will never substitute for intelligence. If you don't notice what is taking place around you and in you, you're out of touch with where you are. Therefore, cultivating great listening is generous and full of potential for high value activity. High value activity is both entrancing, pleasurable and involving for you at a high level of intensity, but also powerful and valuable for others involved, too. It serves two purposes: personal involvement and value creation for others. Making music is a great example.

Start your day with silence and end your day with silence. Make a place of rest in the middle of things during the day too. Schedule days throughout the year for three purposes: Relax your mind, reduce your stress, and rejuvenate your energy. Nothing stimulates all three of these better than going out in nature.

Forming your intentions start with wise attention. Wise attention leaves out the certainty and makes room from the mystery. You can act from an intention and commit yourself to create what matters, yet parallel to this aim, you apply an attention that fosters wise innocence. You combine what matters with what the universe is asking you to do. Over time turning the direction of wisdom tempts you into a "method" from which you take your directives in the future.

OPERATING FROM BEYOND THE DIRECTIVE

When you get good at something, people depend on you for it. Yet when the romance, the fun of it, and the energizing quality of it flees, you're left with obligations and requirements. It feels forced on you in some way what you're doing. You're trapped within your own excellence. You wish you hadn't gotten so good at what you do because it put a big roof over your year and put your kids into the best schools which you're now obligated to keep up. It's scary to let go and do the things that matter more than this. You're tethered to being responsible while breaking out of your core and meeting an edge. The edge is what's new, like a runway waiting for take-off. Conversations with the edge are like Captain Kirk going where no man is gone before. You want to dare yourself to leap into the uncertainty; into what has heart and meaning for you, and leave your excellence where it is to go there. Being paid for time limits this transition.

When you own a job, not a business, the risks are high to give up your payment for your expertise to payment to your organization or team. But risk is equally or higher to remain owning a job that you can't get out from under. After all, people buy *you*, not your business. What do you do? You multiply yourself through systems. Yes, there are certain activities you will never delegate because nobody is you! But if you look at successful entertainers like Frank Sinatra, all he did was sing. He didn't tune the piano, open the curtain, adjust the sound, move the props, or set the lighting up. All of this was done by people with extraordinary abilities and uncommon skill that he could rely upon. He'd fly in, get off the helicopter, sing, and get back on. He kept his unique talent central to what made him essential to his audience, but dropped everything else except just that. The less he did, the more successful he became. So, the answer is you first realize that to level up, you depend on specialists who have voluntary energy for what you do not, and second, that you develop their abilities in those areas by defining superior performance expected, giving good direction, taking fear out of learning new things, and always reinforcing great performance by applying why they happened. Frank had not only to be a great singer but develop people around him that could love what he depended on him for and always level up their abilities and strengths to great impact on the crowds he entertained. Frank loved to acknowledge his back-stage for all the great front-stage impact created by preparation, orchestration, personal responsibility, diligence, and curiosity.

Business ownership is a different economy of means than time for money. You're paid by the value you create for someone else, and it results in a favorable exchange. You get paid by others carrying out business tasks. Take a closer look: do you own a business; an asset, or do you own a job? Does your job serve your best life or consume it? Are you working hours or goals? Is your money serving your best life and self, or consuming these?

As you read this, you begin to see that any increase in your growth or production isn't because of working more and being more. It is how you structure your personal life and bring yourself into a fulfilling life, not an impressive lifestyle. Do not live an unlived life. This is the point.

To me, selling is a manner of living. When you go out into the world and sell, it must be abundance-based, not scarcity based. If you operate from the notion that you are not enough, then people will be objects for you to affirm how special you attempt to be. You are deep down preoccupied with power, out of your sense of inadequacy. "I am not ok. I am not enough," you say to yourself. When you come from this place, you seek to control and manipulate others rather than help and serve them. Your selling becomes diluted by your over-arching need to be important and to look good. This is ego-based selling.

REFUTE NOTHING, BE OPEN TO EVERYTHING

There are two manners of living. The first is to go with the flow----just react and respond to the prevailing circumstances. The second is to create. Creating means living life in terms of a creative orientation. Selling characterizes the manner of living creatively. Selling is probably one of the fastest ways to know how to influence people in positive and helpful ways.

Learning starts with philosophy, as a lover of wisdom. You come at life as your teacher. Everything is practice, like a lifetime boot camp. Learning starts with time. You come at life with activity, but also reflection, downtime, pulling back, seeing what is going on, composing where you want to be, and how you're doing to get there. And learning requires a framework—a learning laboratory for learning and reflection as you create the outcomes you seek to create.

CHAPTER 12

NAVIGATING THE HELPING PROCESS

Fixing someone represents the way of seeing life as broken. Rescuing someone describes the idea of seeing life as weak. When you help someone, with help that is helpful, you see life as whole. Fixing and rescuing are work of the ego, while serving with helpful help is work of the soul.

The verb lives in the noun, and hides there. If you fix others, they are losers, if you reduce others, they are victims, if you criticize others, they are dummies. Turn your eyes around. What do you disown in yourself that preempted you to change others by acting out? In other words, your noun is an unwanted belief that you use to find fault in others to offset your shame. "I need you to be dumb, so I can justify how smart I am." "I need you to lose so I can gain attention." Perhaps this an opportunity to look a bit deeper within yourself, and realize what you hate about yourself, and register it, instead of projecting it outward in your judgment. Others will probably respond differently when you shift your internal reference point to service, not judgement.

Serving involves two parts: A need to serve, and help that is helpful. Both are necessary to bring a helping process into fullness. This requires both passion and listening. The desire is outbound, while listening is inbound.

Let's examine the difference between helpful help and helpless help. Helpful help is help that adds value by giving something to another person they cannot give themselves. Value is always in the eye of the beholder. The one receiving help ultimately determines if value was or was not created from the help. When value is not created, the help is not helpful. This may even occur when the one giving help thinks what she is doing is helpful, yet the person receiving help is seeing what they're receiving differently. For example, what I viewed was significant for the persona I'm helping in one area may not be consistent with the actual help the person receiving it is receiving. Verifying help is helpful can ensure that the actual help is valuable for the other person. Checking in at various progress points to verify this creates a powerful alignment between the helper and one needing help.

The helping process involves two participants: the one needing help (receiving) and the other who is helping (giving). There are two kinds of help - visible help, and invisible help. Visible help is when the one needing help appears to yield to their own wants and needs and has advanced to selecting a solution to meet their needs and pursuing it. Visible help is a person who knows they have a problem and then envisions a solution to that problem. This all sounds normal until a built-in limitation arises. If you know you have a problem with your blood pressure being high, and you pursue a vision of a solution for yourself, you play the doctor. The only acceptable help would be consistent with your vision. Wanting help, in this case, is different from the real help that is needed. What goes unseen is an alternative which offers real or better help than the expected solution. This blind spot of not entirely knowing one's needs is often too vulnerable to put into the hands of another person, especially in today's marketplace, where finding information and getting free help is abundant. We are all inclined to consider ourselves experts, determining our needs on our own. And yet our preconceived notions omit better help because we under-serve our true needs. Experts lack the ability to see possibilities, while beginners' minds see far more.

Isolation is the dream-killer. Too many social rules have discouraged asking for help. We float the belief that we are one down; inferior somehow, when we ask for help. This isn't true. When our sense of inferiority rules us, we become isolated, shut down and turn off the valve for getting help. This why changing our attitude isn't the answer to creating what we want, and getting help is truly what it takes. Each of us has a thorn on the rose-bush. We are a moody, unpredictable, emotional, immediate-gratification-seeking species.

We accumulate memories from the past that we over-use and over-trust. This doesn't mean we're disqualified to create what we want; it requires a self-honesty about our true limitations. Our ability to relate is the key to creating what we want. And to do this we must clarify for ourselves and others what interests us and matters to us the most, so we can get the right kind of help for what we want. This means marrying the outcomes but leaving room for a different approach. We can't see everything there is to see in ourselves, in others, and in the world, and with the help of others, we can more fully see the periphery from where we stand. We can see larger systems in which we enact and operate.

The point is we need each other to know what is going on and deepen our capacity for comprehension as a fuller human being. We must attain our humanity over our ambition. We can help each other to refine our understanding.

Within the context of a sale, this means you enter with the open-minded curiosity in order to get the full picture. Structural thinking is different than situational thinking. To see structurally, you first know that you don't know. Dominance and submission make you dumber. If you construe an impression that you know, you're creating a folly obedience to affirm your importance and draw attention to yourself, not what is outside you.

Unfortunately, sales people fall back into dominance and submission when they take a position of being a hero. They negate the part of selling that is so critical to value creation---and that is to understand their own myth, and create a space where discernment and collective intelligence can flourish.

You use your capacity wherein intelligence can truly flourish by seeing so much more than just a situation or two. You as the helper put together a deeper understanding of the buyer. If this concerns you that's a good thing, you have a sincere heart. You're probably wondering how you can do this given the goals you have, and the amount of time this might involve in knowing your client on a structural level.

First, to dispel your fear, you would probably do this over time through a more gradual intentional process of discovery and exploration. You might find on the way that nothing is more helpful than seeking to understand your client and his current situation. This is because they don't understand themselves, in fact, they can't without your help. Nobody can understand themselves without the observation and presence of another person. We each live in ourselves in combination with the interactive process with others. We are living beings by this collective influence.

Invisible help isn't a one-way street, in fact, it's cultivated by another person, the helper, making it safe to explore what isn't recognized yet. The safety dynamic arises when the one needing help places great trust in the connection with the helper. But the helper is not being depended on to have all the answers. Invisible help is when both the helping person and the one needing help illuminate a real need to together, and yield to it. This is a fundamental type of relationship of co-creation. I'd like to suggest an approach to inspire this yielding process. Before I do, you may be thinking that invisible help is tough empathy. They are not the same. Invisible help is a bilateral process of cultivation while tough empathy is unilateral. A lot of low value and unnecessary help is forced when tough empathy is the visible help the giver's expertise or answers are motivating. But again, this is not invisible help.

The top 1% of entrepreneurs I've coached embrace invisible help while others don't. They're highly comfortable with their own ignorance, full of curiosity, and willing to unlearn their skilled incompetency. Their ability to depend on others for help and be helped is an unusual skill that brings them to the top of the food chain economically. They simply can't complete themselves and their theories alone. They instinctively invite shared intelligence. This is possible because they regulate their habitual ways of thinking before they limit their options.

Alternatively, people typically operate most of the time upon their conditioned thinking for making decisions and responding to situations. These habitual thoughts are concepts, beliefs, and generalizations which act as filters through which reality has assigned meaning. They are cognitive reflexes when left on automatic mode, which lead to strategies and behaviors (actions) often give rise to negative consequences. Skilled incompetencies are habits that inadvertently create unintended consequences. Human beings will default to conditioned thinking during conversations where the things they say and want contradict the inner thoughts and feelings they have. When these are contradictory, what is said and done aren't the same, we experience a great dishonesty when our actions and our words are not aligned.

HONEST HELP

Givers of help must find the line between honest and dishonest help. Dishonest help is when the helper jumps to judgment rapidly and draws forth a solution. If the doctor prescribes medicine without first diagnosing, is that honest? No. If a consultant gives advice out of his experience without gathering data from different sectors in the organization, is that honest?

Honesty requires validity. Sudden certainty without validation is dishonesty. The tendency to validate the data from which value is created begins with a shift of awareness. Whereas judgment arises from the head, honest help originates from the wisdom of the heart. The boundaries between the past and present are transgressed when there's a sincere interest to help.

This brings up an important point about value creation---that true value is about reciprocity and partnerships where there is equitable contribution, not entitlement. Honest help isn't giving help where someone doesn't need it, rather honest help is giving the *right* help, in a way that aligns with the true capacity of the other person. The helper must be able to see this capacity without exaggeration or minimization. To do this, again it requires an open-hearted listening. Rather than one down, one up, the interactive conduct is about lowering overconfidence and seeing actual capability in the one whose needing help. And simultaneously seeing capability in the helper too. This means that honest help is help that the other cannot offer to himself.

If honest help were to originate from the head instead the heart, expertise would wander out before understanding. Mark, the insurance advisor, came to terms with this after insuring thousands of customers to make this commission and earn out his bonuses for a Hawaii vacation. But all of this came crashing down because he wasn't providing honest help. He realized he had a short-term outlook with clients, and an orientation to them of selling them into the best opportunity to gain new sales heights, yet he had over-insured people more than they really needed.

320

Mark's humanity had lost to his ambition, and over time his customers begin to seek competitors. Before Mark wasn't interested in building their confidence in his level of understanding them, instead he took their money after the first call. Years later clients like Nellie lost their most cherished asset---her home after an auto accident on the freeway that killed a family after dropping her coffee on her lap and hitting the center divider. Nellie's policy didn't cover the hospital bills of the dying, and all of them lost their lives. Had Mark spent the time to understand her needs, he would have refused her business until she was insured properly.

Today, people like Mark who help: leaders, professionals, advisors, service people, anyone who others depend on are faced with so much speed and complexity that getting quality information is a necessity. The trap for a helper is having all the answers too fast. Our love affair with speed and our consumption of things we don't need has us overlooking honest help.

Today, our dependencies on others have strengthened the need for inquiry. Our society brainwashes us to be competent, self-sufficient and independent people. We lose sight of our vulnerabilities as we settle into the patterns of our social ideology. We fall asleep to choose. This demands that the helper seek a clearer understanding of what is going on before moving forward. Helpers must learn how to slow down before speeding up. Slow is the new fast. Yet still, many leaders lose to past success that have left bad lessons. They walk with over-confidence, certain of the answers. Listening goes out the door.

Honest help for the receiver is value. The trap for the receiver of help, the customer, the client, the patient, the one standing in need of something they depend on, is when they ask for the wrong thing and stick to thinking they're right. Self-righteous needs for help get the helper in trouble if he jumps in too soon. If the receiver is unaware of their real need for help, this becomes the opportunity for the helper, but first, the helper must confirm that the person needing help has no pre-conceived solutions. And if the helper thinks she knows the answer (has a vision of a solution), both have offset each others' capability for valid value to emerge. People seeking help think they know what they need. Buyers of products and services actively seek the kind of help they needs and seek to maintain a sense of control. They become tainted over time not to put themselves into the hands of someone with power. They find their own evaluation matrix of products and services. They base their comparisons on their own findings or those that a past helper has taught them. Helpers have a head full of rules about needing help and being weak. Being too needy or telling truth is assumed to bear a high cost. The more dependent I am, the more expensive my bill. This need for telling accurate information is then suppressed to protect risks and restrain runaway cost.

Sometimes the helper will see where someone is needing help, but the person needing help doesn't see it at all. Either they're too narrow minded to confront a problem, or they're naive, and it's off the radar screen. The helper then can find gentle ways to help the person come to terms with something in the background that must come to the foreground. This is what we call "latent help." Latent help gives the helper an advantage over competing help, in that he's the first to enlighten the need for help. Once the person sees there is a need, the helper can diagnose, explore the impact, and then propose a solution. Finding latent help is often what helpers in the sales profession miss because they're too busy smelling the perfume of people that recognize they have a problem or have reached the psychological stage of knowing how to solve it and have actively begun getting help. This latter advanced form of need development is confronting for both parties because the helper may think the person needing help is plain stupid and has taken on a silly idea. What does the helper do when the person is hard headed?

He changes the rules of the game. He can't challenge what the person has in mind. Instead he can augment it by widening other alternatives and exploring what's possible. When the helper asks questions about this, such as whether the person would also consider an alternative, the helper is inferring a gap between the current reality and the possibility her or she is laying into the mind of the person needing help. This gap---between perceived solution and an alternative compared to what they have now---is an activation button to make the person needing help change their point of view in a gentle way, without losing control or confidence. The helper is 1) knowing the person has a problem, 2) showing the person their actual problem, 3) expanding the person's awareness of what else is possible, and 4) confronting the person with the choice to move toward an alternative solution, one that is biased to the helper's best help and resources.

This shift from righteous, closed off person to an open and newly enlightened one is almost as helpful as the help they're about to get.

The conversation just prompting them to think about this more carefully is in front the greatest help of all.

Therefore, the helper must take responsibility for creating an atmosphere of confidence and safety. By asking questions with humility (knowing zero at the start), and following curiosity, the helper can come into understanding better the reasons for the need for help, the impact, and discover potential solutions with the helpers help in the picture.

Take these ideas out of the business atmosphere and put them in a household. Consider how parents help their children. They both have strong ideas about the patriarchal quality of a superior and a subordinate. That one who is dependent is weak, and one who governs a house has superiority and is entitled to having all the answers, solutions, and knowledge. The relationship operates on a deficiency-based model---one person; the helped is a project while the helper is the fixer.

Alternatively, what happens when each is treated as partners? What if each were to understand they have equal stature. They both mutually care about the outcome, or wellbeing of what they're occupying—their house, their company, their setting. They both confront their dependencies on one another. They commit to telling the truth; and being frank because it's safe, and second, they learn by what works and doesn't work. The truth is believed to be a resourceful tool. Just imagine how the quality of conversation would play out if these tenets became the dominant narrative within the mode of interaction. There'd be listening and confronting each other with their own freedom to choose. Obligation and control would be replaced by personal responsibility and common caring. What could become possible with these elements at play? Each could become committed to thinking about their thinking---following their choice to be true to each other, and themselves.

Find the cause of your ignorance, to generate other responses that only arise from the honest expression of yourself.

> *"Our way of being that conducts our manner of living*
> *Our way of being starts from nothingness*
> *Nothingness is not the opposite of something*
> *It is the beginning of being, the source from which all things*
> *ignite."*

As leaders, we can access the finest quality of expression we can occupy at any moment. We can lead down the middle between the co-existence of spirituality and commerce.

And when intention is born from our quality of attention, we can deepen our understanding to imbue our deepest source, to encounter our emerging future self and true purpose in the world, to a destiny that stands in need of each of us.

That what is present in our life and the building blocks to an emerging future which shares a common source of creative acts that feed into our destiny standing in need of us.

Leading down the middle is cast into us when our intention and attention are communing perfectly, such that everything the future needs is what is needed this moment. The place between the will inside of us signals where goodness is ready to expand imbues the larger will that possesses our best expression.

When we let go of standing in its way, letting go of judgment, fear, and cynicism to mobilize every ounce of effort from what has meaning, service, and a mystery unfolding only by walking contented with infinite patience, ready for anything, expecting nothing. Conserving legitimacy and acceptance is to grant significance and give equal consideration to the wildcard of life that comes knocking to find me where I'm asked to be.

You listen your way to create what stands in need of you. If you trust what has heart and meaning and stand with a foot into that territory where your intentions are placed, mysterious, almost predictable miracles begin to be summoned unforeseen life forces which come to your aid.

Current reality compared to a desired manifestation is a three-dimensional space where the invisible becomes possible when listening is so open that from nothingness comes the generative order that was embedded there long before you arrived here only to witness it for the first time. To really take this in, remember that it's about reflection. What do you want to build upon what is here? Creating is about constructing from what you have and utilizing it actively as you construct what you're moving towards.

Just stating facts about current reality is one aspect, but constructing from what is emerging, this is when life gets useful and interesting. I call this "harnessing surprise." What struck you is taken from a sea of possibility, which is the future emerging within the present moment.

The flow patterns of energy and information are no longer what you demand from the world but shifting to what need you can be in service to filling when life surprises you. All the out-bound struggle and confusion yields the internal rewards of being in soul service to a sacred project, one that is very pregnant from day one to be put where it belongs in the world through your opening of eyes to the necessity of this outer purpose informing your inner purpose.

All things petty, all things too small for you are outgrown and not at issue when the choice to create from this place is the centerpiece of directing your life spirit toward this. Only some of what is to be created is yours, and what is left to be filled in will reveal itself by doing.

You can bring this into third person where a connection between you and other, self and team, self and client can bring you into a compassionate course of action. The quality of leadership in action is brought forth by how the other is changing you at a deeper level. This sense of being changed by the other is the quality you listen from as the source of inspiration and collective action. It's a soulful sense of service to do what is called for and serves the other based on what your felt internal sense is telling you.

So, what animates you in this third person perspective is honoring differences and becoming constructive with them. The walls come down. And something is allowed into you that might not have appeared before. Yet because of your empathic awareness to understand the other in their world, you connect with kindness as a core property of motivation. You can do this by joining them where they are, not where you want others to be. And your quality of relating and trust validates their sense of importance to as your curiosity and sincere interest to understand where they really are coming from.

RECONNECTION

Let's say you have a great business or sales career going. You're selling like a champion, it's all going right for you, but... your sense of contentment isn't there. What's missing motivates you begin to compulsively seek to achieve higher pay at work to fund the material possessions. Despite the earnings, the new house doesn't fill the emptiness. You find yourself being ungrateful for what you already have.

This explains why most unwise sales people motivate their careers in poor or inadequate ways. They attempt to resolve the discontentment they have through superficial means---power, status, and money. But this is like trying to quench your thirst with saltwater. It doesn't do it for you. And second, anything that your money can buy isn't enjoyable unless it's meant to make others look upon you favorably.

Then one day your pimp factor gets so high that you're slaving to the shiny objects you own while paying your debts to keep them up. You have attempted to replace your discontentment with more stuff to impress others and to offset a deeper sense of emptiness inside. Advertisers love you because you're easy prey for the lost souls who don't know what matters to them.

Then friends begin to hang around you for your stuff. You pay for everyone's dinner to impress, but that credit card bill keeps getting bigger and bigger. Your reputation for buying everyone drinks is alluring, but you're slaved to their approval of you. When you depend on people seeing you differently than your negative self-image, you reduce the other person to an object netted in your need to affirm your importance. This is the internal motivation of the "taker."

When I was in my 20's, I went around wounded by my belief that I was an inconsiderate jerk. To offset this, I composed an ideal of myself to be a nice guy. Everywhere I went, my mission was to convey a nice guy image. Over time this made me so superficially generous in my attempts to twist people's opinions of me that I starved myself of my own needs. I'd give people money who shouldn't have gotten it, buy them meals I could not afford, and try to impress people I didn't like - any way I could to delete myself of my perception that I was a jerk. The irony was that it was stressful knowing inside that I probably didn't care for others, but my belief system couldn't live with that truth because I felt inadequate. I tried to be nice. Unfortunately, careful observers with shit detectors on could smell my BS a mile away. It was all just pretense.

Then a mentor of mine cut me with his words one day that I could "give a rat's ass about anybody." I was so upset because I so feared that he'd find out my little secret that nobody should know: That I don't care about anyone. Honestly, I was so afraid to be vulnerable, so I turned the other cheek and suffered because it closed my heart off. I numbed myself by reverting to a safe distance. But this conflicted with an intense need to belong and connect with others. I didn't think I deserved love. And since nobody could convince me enough to deserve it, I was bound to being right.

I became self-absorbed, in fact so much that I hid this underneath as the catalyst for "being overly nice to everyone." I was a closet jerk unable to expose my truth, until one day this mentor showed me that I wasn't alone, in fact, everyone has what I had composed. At some level, we all have ideals of ourselves that our negative beliefs negate. This is a bad job we assign our ego---to keep a lie for the world to see us by.

You wake up one day to the fact that none of the façade you've been projecting is making you any better of a person, and all you're doing is killing the pain with toys, status, power, and approval. In fact, your identity has become just that: someone you must become to get outside yourself to feel ok. You're a fragile, hollow person in a costume that looks better than you think you are.

Early in life we learn and store our experiences into a database of concepts, beliefs, generalizations, knowledge, and models of the way things should look. Our education system inserts a covert belief in our psyche that having knowledge is power, as if we become better people by what we know. Education is pointed to avoid a sense of inadequacy by knowing something other people do not. This marries our identity to a collection we keep from the past.

What's the problem with this? Creating. When we create something new, relying on our database limits the creative process by what we already know. A key aspect in the creative process is seeing current reality just as it is, not through our concepts. Our collection edits what we see through our biases, and we compare it to what we know and lean toward consistencies rather than differences. After a while, seeing what we know dulls our experience rather than making life interesting and honoring these differences. There's a sterility and staleness to operating from our collection. In fact, a few years ago, I heard an entrepreneur attempt to convince me of the nobility of lifelong learning. As if to collect action figures or trading cards, his pride was identifying his worth by how long and far his learning could carry him. To him, unlearning threatened his belief that his collection symbolized a superiority over others with less learning. Anyone who questioned his level would offend him because he took it personally.

Unlearning can also become linked to one's identity. People who convince others and themselves that knowing nothing is the way to be better people by annihilating everything they know. In attempts to convey, they purge the closet of all, they know their opinion of themselves as better people is justified in their model as one who suffers less when judgment is missing. Their self-propaganda is the clean-sweeper of anything they think is true to subscribe to a person with higher mind. By comparing themselves to others, their ideal of a don't know mind confirms their belief about themselves that knowing too much is dangerous and they must do mental house cleaning to affirm their ideal is real.

Perhaps the underlying concept they're attempting to bypass is that of people disagreeing with what they know. What's often interesting is pretending not to know something - which is based on the premise of knowing nothing - they know will make them a better person. They still know something by trying to appear they don't know anything.

My mentor told me about the guy who his whole life tried not to be a fool...everywhere he went he made sure than nobody knew what a fool he was. After preserving and pretending it all his life finally one day he asked a guru who he was. "Who am I?" he asked the guru on the mountain top, and the guru responded, "Who wants to know?" The man accepted from this point on that he was indeed irrevocably a fool, and that everyone around him is a bozo on the same bus just like him---with incomplete-able pasts, personal flaws, and broken pieces. He became less preoccupied with his broken pieces when his mentor asked: "So what do you seek to create?" The man got that his being a fool didn't disqualify him in any way for loving a creation he was longing to bring into the world. And that man's life began with him being the creative force in his life, oriented by what matters to him. His identity wasn't at issue anymore. Instead it was like an old friend that came along for the ride to his dreams with him.

When you remember what does matter most to you, everything shifts in your behavior. You no longer find refuge in looking good or need to distinguish yourself through exterior materialism. This all sheds like old skin when you place what matters to you as the predominant feature to organizing your life. You look upon the past with knowing what mattered *then* versus what may matter *now*. You appreciate what brought you this moment.

Knowing what you have is a major element of contentment. This includes what you have and do not have.

Gratitude is meeting life as if unexpected perfection was in everything. This is because everything the future needs is given to you this moment. Trust this, because when you look to your past, nothing was unnecessary. Everything was waiting for you where you are now. What brought you here is a compelling journey of endings, beginnings, losses, wins, positives, negatives, pleasure, pain, difficulties, ease, arrivals, disappearances, forgetting, remembering, successes, mistakes, violations, trials, errors, and compromises. Nothing is solid; everything is in a state of flux. Context is always in motion. Disruptive change is the only constant just as true ground is knowing there isn't any ground. It's not that we fear not knowing, rather we fear being afraid of it all because of what that fear does.

The wake behind the boat never disappears. The past is the past, and you will never complete it. The past is inevitably incomplete, in fact knowing this is the only way to complete it. It is history.

ALASKA BY DAY, BAJA BY NIGHT

As Brian took his seat across from me, I could tell he was in the mood to talk openly about his life. "What's your backstory?" I asked.

He took a long pause, folded his hands as if to prey as he uttered his next words. His sigh was followed by a big breath. Back in Michigan, his construction sales job was so taxing that he had a heart attack at 42 years old. His heart attack had also come just after a nasty divorce with his now ex-wife.

His doctor told him that if he kept working at this stress level, he would most certainly die. Brian decided to change his life. He sold everything, bought a bike and rode to California without any expectations. At Venice beach, he setup his tent and lived on the beach for 30 days. Brian said this time of contemplation, doing nothing, meditating, and living on the beach was a liminal period to slow down everything and pull himself together toward a direction.

Venice beach is one of the most popular beach destinations for bicycling in the world. Brian's new affinity for long range riding gave him the know-how he needed to attract the interest of a bike shop owner, Bill. Selling bikes is now Brian's passion.

But we were meeting in a café in La Paz Baja California where I have a second home. What was Brian doing there? He explained that his colleagues had encouraged him to ride up to San Francisco that October, but Brian didn't care to see more city, he wanted to see something new, so he decided to ride south into Mexico down to the tip of Baja to Cabo San Lucas.

This was Brian's first time in Mexico, and he said he felt more alive than ever before and loved the kind treatment of the cheerful and loving people. Riding down Baja presented him with the desert vistas and passages for deep contemplation and revelation. The wide-open space offered him access to a wiser attention and more open engagement with the natural energies of desert habitats. And doing this alone had brought him into contact with a true sense of himself, with just him, his transportation, nature, and the road to guide him on his journey south.

To Brain, going South meant going deep into oneself. Going down meant reaching ground in his being that touched his soul. He told me that this sense of himself was so solid that it was a joy he hadn't felt ever before. He loved to walk deep into the desert at night to track the stars from every side of the night sky.

He dreamed of learning Spanish, staying in Mexico and loving more of his life with a bike shop of his own. He said that to sell something successfully, you owe the world your happiness.

TRUST AND ACCEPTANCE

The word "courage" is fascinating to me because "Coeur" in French means "core" or "heart." I have taught active listening to leaders for years, but I often wondered if the one actively listening cared sincerely about what the other person was saying.

For years people would say a thoughtful goodbye in person or emails to me with the word "Namaste." I just figured that for them it must mean to "wish you well." My curiosity was piqued, so I asked what it really meant. A client of mine answered with, "I see the divinity in you." As I walked out to my car after lunch with him, I asked myself how a person would see the divinity in another or all things. What interior place from within them would open such eyes? Perhaps to see one's own divinity would incline one to see it in others. To be divinely originated is quite a beautiful view. I also wondered that is a person is seen this way, and they don't see it in themselves as others do, what could be possible?

Benny was a construction worker hired by my general contractor to help us build our restaurant business, "Zen." He was 38 years old, ,dark skinned of Mexican origin and had an infectious smile.. His work was so good that we asked if he would spend the night at our location during the building phase to lower the propensity of theft. He agreed willingly, and we adjusted his pay accordingly. After two months, Benny was just as excited as my wife and I were to get the restaurant open. He offered design ideas and referrals to furniture makers to help us with our theme. As things progressed, I began to see a Benny beyond the construction worker as someone who was great with people. So, we invited him one afternoon for a talk about his future.

Benny was hired as our first waiter and from the first day he was so delighted to help that customers that often people would mistake him as the owner. He knew nothing about serving, but his passion for our vision and his willingness to do-good on our investment in his talent brought out his very best. We often recognized Benny for his customer service ability, his passion, and his effect on other employees. After 6 months, Benny had become a team leader and was supervising the outdoor dining team with excellence. One month later, to our surprise, Benny suddenly didn't show up to work on Monday morning. After three days of trying to reach him, he showed up telling us that he had been kidnapped, beaten up and robbed and had lost all his money.

We lended him $500 to get back on his feet and get back to work. But the incidents didn't stop there. More and more these strange experiences and excuses kept occurring. The terminal point was Benny breaking in one night, taking all the money in our drawer, and running off with the music system for the venue. We never saw Benny again. Four months later, some women who ate at our venue asked if we had seen or heard from Benny. "NO," we replied. She told us that Benny was a bad person in trouble with the law, and that he was a thief was a record of bad situations. She said she found out about this through his family, and work he'd done in the past for her friends.

Benny was abused as a child with parents who burned his feet and constantly tortured him. Now I understood why he would never take off his shoes or wear thongs. I suppose his aggression toward us came from his own wounding. Benny couldn't overcome his original conditioning, despite our fair and loving treatment. What astonished me was how much our seeing the good in him brought forth good contributions. If we give attention to a trouble-maker, we change their behavior. Based on Benny's track record, my wife and I could have been badly harmed. We were so naive, but no matter how hard we attempt to know someone, in the final analysis, we do not.

It wasn't safe for Benny to be in the presence of love. To come up from the darkness and allow it wasn't possible for him because of his preoccupation with his worth and shame. Whatever concepts of himself that he was clinging to become the short circuits to his passage to greatness. His residual unworthiness came to the surface.

How close could I get to the negativity in Benny? The more I acknowledge it and investigated it without identifying with who I am, the more I was brought closer to the divinity in him and me.

THE TEACHER WHO SAVED MY LIFE

Standing at the copy machine at Ivan's house, I removed the staple from Margaret's report. The eleventh-grade paper was the main event to pass the grade to twelfth. After removing her cover page with a few kind words written there from Mrs. Farnworth and an "A+," her report was the perfect way for me to avoid failing my English class. I always tried to find easy ways out of undesired assignments and tasks during high school. Cheating on exams, copying others' work, and buying reports from past students was a work-around that got me by until the day Mrs. Farnsworth called me into her office after class one day. I had turned in my report (Margaret's report copied) and put my name on the page cover to fool the teacher.

There we were, sitting in two desks among an empty set of 40, as Mrs. Farnsworth gazed into me in disbelief. I knew she was asking about my report because nothing I'd every turned in or delivered had this quality of work product. And I could sense she remembered

338

reading Margaret's report a few years ago. Mrs. Farnsworth had an earthy manner of dress and laid-back teaching style. Students liked her because of her ability to be approachable.

Mrs. Farnsworth put the report down in front of my eyes and pointed at the front page and topic. "This is not your work John!" I didn't deny her but didn't agree with her, yet. "Whatever you tell me otherwise, I know this is not your work." She was not interested in my story. "If you deny it, I'll walk you down to Bob's office (the principal), and you'll be expelled for this. We'll contact your parents and give them the news, and you're out." As she said these words with conviction, I could feel my nerves in my stomach poking at me. I had images of being cast out from my father. This would have been the final blow after he barged into the school administration office one morning and called me in to yell and scream for failing three classes.

As I sat there semi-hearing her and hearing the internal bomb scare inside me, she said she had another idea to present me. "John, I'll give you a second chance. If you redo this assignment and give me "A" level work, I'll forget this incident, but you will not be able to score higher than a "C" on the paper. In that moment, I wanted to prove to her that I was capable. Somehow, she knew that expelling me wasn't going to serve any good purpose and that her concern was to teach me a life lesson. She reached out to a lazy cheater with another chance, because she believed in me more than I did.

She gave me one week to produce the work, and I busted my ass more than any other time in my life to show her what I could do. I selected a topic I cared about, and did the research. I was at the library daily, reading up on the topic. I wrote the first draft, then second draft. Then I typed out my final draft and presented it to her the following Monday at the beginning of class. The sensation I had of turning in my work to someone knowing I had something special in me was so satisfying.

A few days later Mrs. Farnsworth took me aside after class. She told me what she liked about my report and give me an "A" but wrote a "C" on my paper. That moment of completion, recognition, and receiving the effect of my own creation changed me forever. Cheating meant denying myself this growth and joy.

When you give help, remember the actions are different than the person. I didn't have the best actions, but Mrs. Farnsworth knew who I was. And this shaped who I was from there on out.

LETTING OTHERS TAKE POWER

A man once approached me leaving my house in the city. He asked me for a good place to eat steak. After 5 minutes trying to explain how to get there, I decided just to invite him and have a meal together. There are no accidents. After our conversation, his keen way of seeing me helped me shape what I do in my truest work. He said, "I help environmental humanity people think and act upon a profit by becoming business people, but you JD help business people who are making big profit reclaim their wholeness and restore their heart-felt involvement in what they're doing as a means to repair the world." I felt like I was given new eyes on my path forward. This stranger had it in him to help me see what I am. All I had to do was walk outside my door.

Everything and everyone is equal to you, no more, no less. We're all hanging around the playground, playing the game of life, and all of us are connected to each other as equal characters in our journey.

Help that harms oneself comes from an inner place of fear or worth. Sandra, an upholstery entrepreneur, found herself bitter and burnt out after the second year of her business. She feared that if she didn't give her most demanding customers what they wanted, they'd go to the competition right away. She lowered her prices, worked longer hours, and devoted herself to maintaining her client's loyalty and making them affair-proof. Over time, clients developed entitlement attitudes, and requested immediate responses for minor issues. Sandy's resentment grew until she was showing disdain for customers as enemy who consume her. To affirm her importance and value, access became her brand. The referrals continued to flood in as customers touted her quick action and attention to detail. Sandy's hopes withered, and all her enthusiasm faded into crying behind the scenes about her business becoming a living hell.

Sandy's predicament was martyrdom, taking her own life in the service of others, numb to the harm it caused her. Approval and appreciation had trapped her in a deep hole. Acting from the space of a small self (inadequate), her desire to be seen as a good person and a belief that if she took a day off or projected her preferences would lead to despair, Sandra was operating from fear and control to avoid loss and humiliation. The outcome of her actions pointed to a pathological form of altruism. She had gained a false sense of power through self-sacrifice and service martyrdom.

As we worked through her deeper motives, Sandy could see she could be helpful, grounded in a healthier form of altruism. Taking a long-term view, her endurance could be governed by choosing the right clients, taking free time, and focusing habits to source her creativity and energy. She began to shift her inner dialog away from social approval to the identity of a good person who helps in ways that are helpful to both giver and receiver. And that the helping process doesn't need to involvev working to exhaustion and disempowering her team. Instead, she began seeing a bigger picture about serving others and bringing her team together in skill sets that could deliver the help without her killing herself.

Many of us are biased toward acting altruistically because we believe it is our role or spiritual duty to do so. We rescue others in our attempts to save ourselves from feeling like bad people. Mothers continue providing for their adult children and disempowering them. It is human to be altruistic, yet it creates unconscious tendencies to undermine what truly serves others. The heart of the matter is our levels of awareness and capacity for reflection, to interrupt self-deception. We can review the concepts and mental models from which we make rules for ourselves, the ones that give unhealthy help. Harmful help is not helpful help. The difference is in who gains. The helpful help model is when both giver and receiver are gaining value through the helpful process in ways that are sustainable.

When we see and regard the autonomy of our children, of others, and our relationships, we give them the capacity to be resourceful rather than take it away via our own affirmation of power. If our notion of power shifts to seeing and allowing others to be whole, we become

342

less controlling and instead observe and bear witness to the wholeness in others.

It was June 1991, and at 21 years old I was spending a week at a dude ranch in Arizona at a meditation retreat. The instructor gave me a vision quest, saying to take a walk out in the desert for hours and see what I observe and notice with my heart and mind wide open, ready for everything, expecting nothing. He said, "Just go and see John!" He said what I come back with will be significant. Two cactuses stood together side by side in perfect union, a little one and large one. As I debriefed my quest with the instructor it quickly came to me this was my father and me. The mythology of the reflection was to "be a good cactus." Little did the teacher know that thirty years later that cactus is the metaphor for my way of life and for the one reading this book - *you*.

The Cactus can survive in harsh environments, and when the rains come down, the plant takes in all it can absorb for the long haul. This is like you in a transformative conversation helping someone. Help no matter what, because you choose to in any situation. Operate from a higher value. Be kind anyway, be loving anyway, give anyway, because in the end, it's just between you and your Creator. The lesson of the cactus is patience. The wisdom is in letting life be just how it is, and letting others be just how they are, and meeting these with welcome arms. You don't have to see the world as you are, rather, see the world in its own conversation.

DON'T BE IN SOMEONE ELSE'S BOX OR YOUR OWN

We all have assumptions, generalizations, mental models, concepts that we use to make sense of the world and to remain safe. These mental constructs fall into three types: me, them, and the world.

- This is who I am (I see myself as)
- This is who they are (see them as)
- This is how the world is (see things as)

As we develop through our experiences, our hunches, impressions, and observations climb a ladder of more and more certainty, where what we believe dictates our reactions and responses to what is happening around us. Unfortunately, about 80% of these constructs are hidden beneath our normal levels of awareness.

This dynamic becomes very complex in human relationships, whereas our database of constructs from which we download to interpret or add meaning to what is going on. We assume the intentions of our significant other or bring expectations about what is supposed to be done. Patterns then develop, which lead to negative consequences that we assign to other people as blame, instead of seeing the source of the patterns arising from the constructs that govern what we say, think, hear, and do. Our internal database is like a reflex loop in that we use our constructs again to edit life. We tolerate our certainties to unhealthy levels.

You could say we all have a "box" from which we self-deceive ourselves. If I believe I'm stupid and need a strategy to not appear stupid. If I believe I'm greedy, I need a strategy to look humble. If I'm not considerate or generous, I need to a strategy to show how nice and kind I am. You've seen these types who, when they smile, it looks like they're gritting their teeth with vicious anger behind it.

How about the belief that I am inadequate and need a strategy to appear important or powerful? We sell ourselves on an ideal to offset the negative beliefs we hold of ourselves. Then we seek ways to galvanize our image to the world to offset the shame we assign to our belief. We tuck this part of ourselves way down deep to hide from the world because we fear isolation and humiliation.

In relationships, our tendency is to use pretense (project an outside image different than inside reality) to hide that secret self with a false one that's like a costume. The smoke screen is like a neural net that loads up other people into it to offset negative belief. So, if I'm preoccupied with power, I feel inadequate and must have people admire me or affirm my existence by my created heroism.

If I'm someone who is stupid, then I need someone else to be dumb, so I can be smart. This explains why the qualities that we dislike in other people are the ones we disown in ourselves. And this makes us judgmental and fragile. We get offended easily when others criticize us. Or when others contradict our judgement, we take it personally. And when we pick our opposite of our costume, we end up losing interest in them later once we're successful. If I'm someone that is unlovable, then I need you to admire me to avoid being threatened by you leaving me. Fear of isolation and fear of humiliation are borne from the seeds of the concept that something is wrong with me, and I can't accept it. This is often why a therapist encourages you to love yourself first before you can be loved. They encourage clients to work on self-acceptance, boosting self-love to deserve better. But after many cases of attempting this, I've found this doesn't lead to positive change; it makes lousy creators out of couples seeking to create a better relationship.

One of the problems with this approach is that you put what you deserve into what you desire. It suggests a better relationship with yourself is possible---that you must accept you as you are, no matter what. This is dishonest. Positive thinking is positive lying. Affirming yourself to be something you're not says to your mind: "Who, but someone that is not this would need to try to be." Being someone or something you're not is not only stressful and phony, but it's also a lot of hard work.

Learning to be helpful help is learning to be you, with every imperfection and attribute as a whole person. Your nature is to be loving, caring, kind, generous, and compassionate, and for this, you have basic goodness just like you did when you were born. Like me, be a good little cactus.

As you grew older you learned what not to do, what to fear, and you formed an opinion of yourself. Some qualities about you are great; some are not.

You can't love what is not lovable. That is superficial. When we attempt to love parts of us we don't like, we begin to trace everything back to the same rooted place we started from----something is wrong with me. Alternatively, you can get to know what you like or hate about yourself and just sit with this without taking issue with it. Like old friends, some people just don't change---exactly---you are the way you are. This doesn't disqualify you from creating what matters to you. What matters to you is created for its own sake.

So please rid yourself the *deserve to desire belief system*, and just stay with what you desire, but take your identity and your concepts out of it. Now, the primary thrust is creating a relationship that matters or creating a connection that matters, but the focus is on the creation, not you. It's a shift from a 1st person orientation to a 3rd person one. You aren't preoccupied with your self-opinions, they are just there--- all of it...your self-doubt, constructs, etc. Choose to create what matters to you anyway. You are in touch with your mental content but giving your attention to bigger desires that will replace what you were preoccupied with before.

Please remember, what matters to you doesn't originate from your concepts, what matters to you is a heart question of what you love enough to bring into existence. This is a fundamental shift to a different source from which you bring creative action toward a specific outcome. The orientation is toward the creation, not toward the removal, manipulation or fixing of the internal construct. This is why human potential backfires. People are so drawn to fixing and helping themselves instead of creating what matters.

Once outside of your own constructs, you're able to observe them like an eye behind an eye. You can detect when others attempt to net you into their "box" of constructs to play into their strategy. You don't have to sign-up for their game or insert them into yours, but instead, you can relate with what is true. This will probably lead you into new territory and nuances that disconfirm old thinking and outdated constructs. But they transcend indirectly through the creative process.

Make working on your issues a hobby; instead, put your attention into creating what matters to you. When you begin to organize your life this way, selling is having a role in helping others create what matters for them too.

How much is enough, as much as you want it to be? The key is to stay true to what matters to you. This is not referring to what you need to be happy, or what you want to make a better place in the world. This is wanting what you want without justification just because it matters enough to bring it into the world as you picture it.

A consumer is the one who waits to fill something missing that is not enough. Creating doesn't originate from lack, it originates from love for something before you create it. When you help others identify this as their primary motivation, your help is motivated by outcomes they desire rather than problems these seek to remove. In business you don't learn this. Instead you begin with the problem the consumer is having. The problem with this problem-solving approach is duration. Once the problem is solved the dependence on your solution is gone, and opportunities are lost for both.

Wanting and *expecting* are very different dynamics regarding the future. Expecting the future involves anticipation. You predict upcoming events based on the past. Wanting is desiring something for its own sake. With expectation comes fear. When fear is anticipated, actions are taken to prevent the expectation.

When wanting is wanted, the outcome is separate from what you know; you disconnect from the past. Wanting brings you close to your true desires while expecting uses the same approaches as the past.

348

Expectations don't generate the growth and learning that desires do. This is why creating is not problem-solving. Removing unwanted problems don't require the new approaches that a creation would evoke.

Expectations often come from external motivation when a role, rule, or another person or group expect something of you. When these expectations aren't wanted within, there's a disconnect. There's a sense of empty or hollow meaning in the action. We do what should matter rather than what *does* matter.

It is a bit unusual to treat a relationship as a third person, but it's smart to do so. What is to arise out of a relationship is not just one person or the other but *what is possible from the relationship as a whole system.*

SHATTERING THE CERTAINTY

To illustrate this, just remember a time when a buyer of yours bottom-lined you. They had a mental map at play that "It works this way or that way." You were feeling pressure to follow their criterion. To avoid insulting them, you attempt to be nice, you lower your price. You figure you'll let this one gets through and hit them up later with an upsell or add-on. They've boxed you into their evaluation matrix of how to buy what you do. Now you have become commoditized, type-casted as giving in easily to please, and you're referred to the next person the same way. Both you and the buyer have skilled incompetencies at play. The end result is zero value creation for either of you. Instead, both are trapped by their own certainties and assumptions as if one assumption fuels the other. Assuming you won't make the sale makes you an easy catch, and you lose respect and give away power and control of the helping process. The buyer is blind-sided, unable to see how they see and defaulting to what they deem as right. What a sad ending.

What would you do to counter the previous scenario? *Change the rules of the game*. Reengineer the pre-existing paradigm the buyer is operating from, and bias the new one to your helping approach. And also let go of your fear. Instead, pay close attention to what is true for the buyer and get inside his conversation with himself. You ask questions to help the person visualize what lies beyond the limits of their expected buying vision. "What if you also could…?" "What if you also had a way to…?" You expand their evaluation matrix and crack the door to invisible help they didn't know they needed until you asked them these questions. These capability questions inspire a picture of a different future that includes your solutions. Before doing this, find out what the person was seeking to accomplish originally and how they see themselves using the solution they have in mind. Do not make the one needing help feel stupid or under attack for their righteous way of thinking. Just embrace it as a starting point.

Another way to cultivate invisible help is to share a powerful reference story. Stories are game-changers because, like the story arc of a well-made film, there's a setting, a struggle, a breakthrough, and a resolve. Telling a story of someone they can relate to, who is like them, who started at point A and got to B, can help reshape a paradigm with hope. The pros make invisible help safe because the story will open up possibilities beyond what seems real. It generates believe-ability in another passage, one that if selected transcends the invisible help they didn't know they wanted but needed.

Like magic, I've seen people yield to invisible help when they express their desired future. As they're asked where they truly want to be, the subject matter is so different than their current reality that the challenges and opportunities involved in closing the gap create room for invisible help. Aggressive goals unearth people's incapacities. Often the truth telling of where someone wants to be versus where they are can open them to the willingness to learn and grow, where invisible help is welcomed.

The helping process is a complicated system. Giving help also has its built-in challenges. Cultivating invisible help requires the helper to suspend having all the answers. Reshaping needs for help involves humble inquiry, by following curiosity instead of following expertise. It's often the expertise that causes great business people to jump ahead too quickly and forget which phase to stay in. They advocate instead of inquiring, playing an answer-full expert, not an honest helper. They advise too early during the sale, instead of selling their advice first by positioning invisible help.

The first phase is diagnosis, and then afterwards is the prescription. The diagnosis begins when the one wanting help has a pre-existing vision of a solution directing their decisions, actions, and communications. Expand the evaluation matrix by asking the questions that allow the one needing help to think beyond what they expected before. First ask how they see themselves getting help, and then add on your additional capabilities through which they picture life with your help.

Next, have the one needing help compare their current way of doing things to the way you're helping them re-envision their methods. Exploring the impact of this contrast is where motivation is strongest to shift their loyalty to invisible help. By stating the capabilities you'll add and comparing it to what they had been doing before, this gap will motivate a shift of mind.

Real help starts with humble inquiry. This requires that you the helper suspend all your certainties and start with nothing; in other words, a blank slate. As you begin from this, you seek to understand the buyer by picturing what they're describing to you as their current reality. You begin without using your database to know what is going on. This way you will ask questions to help see a picture, a story, a pattern that isn't easy to miss. There are four types of questions for you to gain an understanding with the buyer of this picture of current reality:

1. Information
2. Clarity
3. Discrepancy
4. Implication

Asking for more information can be closed or open ended.

Clarity is taking a part of what you hear and expanding upon it.

Discrepancy is inquiry into an inconsistency between two pieces of data that contradict each other.

An implication question is asking if what they're saying is implying something that appears to be suggested.

Here's a set of questions you can keep in your hip pocket to help:
1. Tell me about it, what's causing you to be concerned about XX? Help me understand what you're thinking and feeling about it?
2. I sense frustration - what bothers you most about the situation?
3. What is causing what appears to be going on?
4. What have you tried to solve it or change it?
5. What is the immediate impact of the current situation?
6. Have you considered XX or YY, as an alternative?
7. What's it going to take to get you from A to B?
8. What obstacles stand in the way?
9. What must be started, stopped, or continued to mobilize the change?
10. When and where is your first action step ahead?

The helping process involves your capacity to hold space for the person to dive into the questions, and allow them to surface with reflection, and compose plans. Products, answers, and services don't sell, they prove what the help implies that you give them. The conversation is more important than the product or service. The better you can understand and help the person understand what is going on, and clarify what is important, the better decisions they can make. The big challenge for you here is to ask ten questions to one statement. And the second part of the challenge is to listen with your open mind and heart, like a good little cactus, to translate the information into helpful "what if" questions with the intention of transforming confusion and complexity into clarity and understanding. Again, you create the space for creativity and discernment to arise, as they clarify their needs and wants via your sincere inquiry. This is partnering, not parenting; this is adult to adult. Invite, don't tell anyone what to do.

CHAPTER 13

AUTHENTICATION

You've been mundane and interchangeable when looking from your customer's perspective. For them, buying from you means comparing apples to apples; it all looks the same. You've just entered the commoditization trap!

Discouragement sets in motion. Your customers want the price they want, they know what they need, and you have few options but to play their game. Margins are slim despite your intent to remain profitable. What's the offset? Value Creation.

All value creation starts with self-knowledge. If you asked your 10 best clients why they work with you and refer you, it's because you have a personal gift. You have unique skills that, as business became demanding and complex, were relegated to the back seat. You started spending your time on everything other than activities commensurate with this domain. This results in a loss of energy, enthusiasm, and creativity. You're too busy with innovation-killing time traps that suck you dry like a vampire. It's time to come back home to yourself and be who you are.

The weirdo in you needs salvation! It's time to get real! Bringing yourself to the front of the room is like showing up in person with your imperfections. Letting go of the fear of others seeing your nuances and taking advantage of you is a great thing because it puts respect and trust back into the other, and in their basic goodness. Each of us are basically good at the core because we came into the world pure and innocent. We just a get a bit "de-geniused" when the scars of difficulty and pain, loss and grief, and rejection spook us into cynicism. We put a shield in defense of a negation of love.

All industries have a lifecycle that moves decaying business forms and models out, and emerging and innovative businesses forms in. A new means of production or organization replaces an old one. This process of creative destruction is a term coined by Joseph Schumpeter, an enlightened economist in the early 20th century. Innovations cause old inventories, ideas, technologies, skills, and equipment to become obsolete. The question is not "how capitalism administers existing structures ... [but] how it creates and destroys them." This creative destruction, he believed, causes continuous progress and improves the standards of living for everyone.

Schumpeter was among the first to lay out a clear concept of entrepreneurship. He distinguished inventions from the entrepreneur's innovations. Schumpeter pointed out that entrepreneurs innovate not just by figuring out how to use inventions, but also by introducing new means of production, new products, and new forms of organization. These innovations, he argued, take just as much skill and daring as does the process of invention.

Invention is going through a radical transformation. Today, innovation is not without the reverence for the whole. Sustainability has become a primary force in "going green," as consumers now favor commerce that is combined with spirituality and global responsibility. The new goal is to build a "prosperous enterprise" which suggests that the two can co-exist and maximize prosperity by respecting planet Earth as business growth increases.

To become true to this sensitivity, entrepreneurs are seeking self-knowledge and mindfulness as vehicles to help them become more of who they truly are while remaining competitive. The collective process of competition and collaboration starts with letting go of judgment, cynicism, and fear, like old skin regenerating. What's involved is an authenticity, courage, and boldness to move from the head (left hemisphere of the brain) to the heart (the right side of the brain).

The right side of the brain is associated with all the creative aspects—design, big-picture, connecting separate parts together, and dimensional thinking. Context, space, texture, tones, frequencies, and patterns all give rise to a new use of human intelligence from which the wholeness is reclaimed by the individual. The entrepreneurs who thrive are the ones who are focusing on their own humanity while tapping into incredible potential.

They can pre-sense emerging future possibilities on the way in, and then operate by taking meaningful leaps into uncertainty until their creations come into life. It is with this obedience to that which has heart and meaning that replaces individualism with a sense of coherence and community consciousness.

Weirdoes are those who choose to foster the honesty of their self-expression. They hold space for themselves, others, and the world in its own conversation. They see method and system, something they already know as a potential limitation. They see the present moment, listening generously, and showing up as the source from which they're touched by a readying future. Authentication isn't self-made, rather, the power of self lies in the collective voice by which the entrepreneur senses what stands in need of him and doing what he absolutely must do.

The leader begins to walk with a sacred project in his step, one that is unfolding the path out of the mystery ahead. As he walks, volatility yields vision, uncertainty yields understanding, complexity yields clarity, and ambiguity yields agility. He walks the mystery path with practical feet, knowing that everything he needs for the future is given to him at this moment. He creates the future, instead of predicting it.

Being more of yourself takes courage. There may be disapproval, but selling your soul to avoid isolation isn't worth the invitation. The weirdo learns to bring his entire self to life, the good, bad, and ugly. He knows not to wait, that acting instantly gives him information faster, from which he can better see the future emerging, rising, and assembling as he walks into it, openly.

All the data around him is a source of defining features from which his leadership is composed. The truth is his ally, as it makes him resourceful. The reason why he does his work is the reason why others want to be led by him. It is the center of his brand to become more of himself. The point of all that he does shapes the behaviors in his business travels, decisions, actions, and communications, from which an essential story is narrated, and that replaces what was trending in the past. The past is something he cannot complete, yet he completes it by accepting its incompleteness.

So, the salvation of the weirdo is a process of letting go, and letting come, a quality in your awareness that is reverent to your cause. You are creating a cause, not a company. You are born out of a community with dangers, opportunities, and strengths from which your truest work and best self are called forward.

It's not hard to find this path, in fact, it's been right where you are—you are not living an unlived life! Everything is up for grabs right now, if you to rethink what really does matter to you, not what should. Take stock of what has heart and meaning for you right now, and you'll bring the weirdo to the surface. Then voice what matters. This voice is your homecoming back to your own heart.

 I am not sure of a better way to start or end the day than watching the sunrise or sunset in the peace and tranquility of nature! Nature has three qualities to offer you: 1) it moves medium-slow, not fast. 2) it heals you, and 3) you can access deep reflection via internal stillness. Humberto Maturana, the philosopher, said, "The only way to change your history is via reflection."

It's the day before Thanksgiving, and I'm sitting on a high bluff looking at the distance to the horizon, after a trek up the hill on my mountain bike by myself. I can contemplate this as a high-altitude point overlooking my entire life building process, and the landscape are all the aspects in my life that compose it.

I say to myself, "Now, remember that anything you want to create is up for grabs. This is the moment to rethink everything." Starting with nothing, you connect with your horizon; your future self for personal cultivation. Turn to the East where the sun rises represents what is ready to begin in my life. I remind myself that life is temporary, and all things must end, at some point. Then I connect with the West, where the sun sets, and what is ready to die in me. North is my spirit, and south is my soul down deep into my ground of being.

When you confront that you're not immortal, the brevity of life suddenly awakens your heart's desires. What matters to you isn't conditional anymore. Dreams and aspirations begin to visit you like a piece of music you faintly hear from inside your heart. You fundamentally choose to become the predominant creative force in your life. You're on the way to something you deeply desire for its own sake, and your love for it is generating the effort.

REGISTER

The office was so busy you could hear a buzz running through it. Things were moving and shaking, patients coming and going, money billed, money paid. It all seemed so productive...until one day she looked up and looked around her. Like an ostrich with its head in the sand, she'd gotten so in the game that she lost touch with being on the game. Being in the game is like looking down at your feet for so long and far that you look up and don't know where you are.

When you fail to register where you are compared to where you want to be, you're a hopeless doer. Knocking out a to-do list is an addiction when it feels good to appear productive. But the short-term actions are well aligned with the long-term intention.

Alignment

Are you bringing your actions true to your intentions? Take a snapshot of your current pipeline of opportunities. Is it positioned to create your goal? Do the current ways in which you organize your work align with your goal? Do your current habits align with your intention?

A FOOT HAS NO NOSE

There's a great tale of African wisdom about just how dependent we all are with regards what lies ahead in our lives. As I read it, I'm warmed in my heart of so many beautiful souls that have supplied grace to my journey. I am so grateful with a full heart for their contributions.

On Thanksgiving Day write down the 10 souls who supplied strength on your journey and brought you into who you are today. Then reach out to each with a full-hearted thank you and how and when they enriched you. Their love and support for you originated from seeing potential in you.

Of the many interactions I had with my mother those many years ago, one stands out with clarity. I remember the occasion when mother sent me to the main road, about twenty yards away from the homestead, to invite a passing group of seasonal work-seekers home for a meal. She instructed me to take a container along and collect dry cow dung for making a fire. I was then to prepare the meal for the group of work-seekers.

The thought of making an open fire outside at midday, cooking in a large three-legged pot in that intense heat, was sufficient to upset even an angel. I did not manage to conceal my feelings from my mother and, after serving the group, she called me to the veranda where she usually sat to attend to her sewing and knitting.

Looking straight into my eyes, she said "Tsholofelo, why did you sulk when I requested you to prepare a meal for those poor destitute people?" Despite my attempt to deny her allegation and using the heat of the fire and the sun as an excuse for my alleged behavior, mother, giving me a firm look, said "Lonao ga lo na nko" — "A foot has no nose." It means: you cannot detect what trouble may lie ahead of you.

Had I denied this group of people a meal, it may have happened that, in my travels sometime in the future, I found myself at the mercy of those very individuals. As if that was not enough to shame me, mother continued: "Motho ke motho ka motho yo mongwe." The literal meaning: "A person is a person because of another person."

You cannot understand the actuality of another person without seeing their relationship to other people who influence. Without an observer, you don't exist. It's been said that bosses are created. Brian Billick, winning coach of the Baltimore Ravens, said, "If you behave like an idiot, I'll treat you like one." This suggests that the way he coaches mirrors the position of the athlete. His coaching emits information and energy given to him in emotional patterns and field connections imprinted on his treatment of that person. The word "relationship"

362

means to "repeatedly elate." Our own true selves depends on the mode of interaction with have with other people like a social field bound by a rhythmic, retentive pattern of circularity. We are not independent of these patterns.

As you gather your heartfelt gratefulness of your special contributors in your past and their impact on you, begin to identify the creative movements that are queuing up right now in your life story. Just remember that whatever you appreciate, appreciates! What you notice expands. What you ignore is reduced. When you acknowledge someone's gifts or contributions to your life, it expands. You help them see their place to take in the ecosystem.

Leadership is your place to continuously express the highest quality of being you can occupy at any moment. The word in Japanese "ba" means "place." A genius loci is an intelligent spirit or magical power that resides in a place. Very few genius loci of this form are able to move from their native area, either because they are "part of the land" or because they are bound to it. Your rightful place in the ecosystem is a place made for you. To know your place, you must know your deepest intention (source), the way others around you move or touch the sacred in you, and through these, your best self and truest work is available to create value for others.

When you're intentionally silent and still, reflect on this: What is expanding or contracting in your life? What is gathering and rising? What is flowing in, and what is flowing out? What is settling or releasing? What is wanting to emerge? What story are you telling through your life? You're in a conversation with creation, and the world is coming to find and confirm you!

WISE INNOCENCE

"And what does it involve being consciously in conversation with creation?" I ask myself. It is to be available and open to receiving it. You set an intention and then look to "wise innocence." Wise innocence is the part of you that knows you don't know how you know what you know. The cultivated "don't know mind" yields that everything the future needs is given to you in this moment. It is the source of letting go, to let that which is emerging, come. You're open to the outcome, yet not attached to it. "Is this God?" I ask myself. It is the force that is behind God.

It's like clearing the decks for action or passing through the eye of the needle. Something is ready to die, while something else, still indistinct, is waiting to be born. It is the point where endings give rise to beginnings, and beginnings become endings. All things must change. Even you will change your mind, and everything will be there for you when it is supposed to be there.

In the scriptures, the camel had too much to carry on its back to pass through the doors of a village. All the non-essentials needed to be left behind to grant passage and set forth into the village. When a singular intention becomes clear, you give your mind big business to attend to and ignore the petty stuff. You take meaningful leaps into uncertainty, organizing your decisions in service to a calling. Life is constantly renewing your understanding as you live forward into the mystery of what it is unfolding.

We're all just walking in the dark; stepping down with each new stop on the mystery path with practical feet each moment, only knowing what is implied next by walking. We can see to the edge of our headlamps' field of visibility like a car driving on the highway in the dark. The enemy is in us—fear, resentment, cynicism, and judgment. All three cloud our window of the world ready to relate with us just as it is coming toward us, not what we make up about it.

There is an old Chinese tale about a woman whose only son died. In her grief, she went to the holy man and asked, "What prayers, what magical incantations do you have to bring my son back to life?"

Instead of sending her away or reasoning with her, he said to her, "Fetch me a mustard seed from a home that has never known sorrow. We will use it to drive the sorrow out of your life." The woman went off at once in search of that magical mustard seed.

She came first to a splendid mansion, knocked at the door, and said, "I am looking for a home that has never known sorrow. Is this such a place? It is very important to me."

They told her, "You've certainly come to the wrong place," and began to describe all the tragic things that recently had befallen them.

The woman said to herself, "Who is better able to help these poor, unfortunate people than I, who have had misfortune of my own?"

She stayed to comfort them, then went on in search of a home that had never known sorrow. But wherever she turned, in hotels and in other places, she found one tale after another of sadness and misfortune.

The woman became so involved in helping others cope with their sorrows that she eventually let go of her own. She would later come to understand that it was the quest to find the magical mustard seed that drove away her suffering.

As Carl Jung said, "all the problems you have are insoluble, you can only outgrow them in the pursuit of bigger urges through the creative process."

Even volatility, uncertainty, complexity, and ambiguity, all bring you vision, clarity, understanding, and agility, as the dream becomes the catalyst for assimilating and learning as you live forward. You learn what is emerging and embody it because you make life up as you go along. There is no cure for uncertainty. Do not pathologize your fear or hurt. You can only truly reflect, while in action, attending and befriending it all. This explains why there really are no experts. All that can be given are direction and connection (the vertical and horizontal connection), and an open will to live into the mystery forward, with willingness and alacrity.

The universe is a wildcard with very little cooperation most of the time. Can you trust betrayal? Can you work with the negative and positive aspects that life surfaces? Can you welcome everything, and expect nothing? In your life as a creator, you make room for the present moment just the way it actually is. The present moment is an acquired taste and learning ally. It is the beholder of truly being grateful for all that life presents you.

NEGATIVE EMOTIONS

One of the reasons we do not face our goals is because when we are faced with an unexpected barrier that we are unsure how to deal with, we shut down. Creating any goal requires first a strong focus, especially when emotions run high. We need to stay flexible and attentive to what is going on within us without losing sight of what we're creating.

Current reality is not always nice to observe, but in the creative process bearing witness to what is going on is essential to learning. Creating is learning. This is true because when you create a goal, you begin separate from what you know. You have to know where you are compared to where you're going like an artist paints a painting in stages. As a leader, you depend on visibility. If you're the blind leading the blind that's not good. As doers, we move through moments to get to the next moment. We miss the available comprehension in the present moment that brings insight, helps us see differences, and incorporate emerging opportunities and pathways which pull us through. Our visibility and comprehension are possible by understanding ourselves and what is going on by stopping and being present.

Self-aggression is when you believe everything you think. If you don't see your voice of judgement, you violate your ability to see what is different than what you think. And yet the difficult feelings we experience about the future we think of, or the past we hurt from, these all originate from our stories WE HOLD TO BE TRUE. Stories are the concepts we hold rigidly of who we are, what others are, generalizations and persevering beliefs that make understanding things lopsided.

It disturbs us to live up to ideals of ourselves and to offset our unwanted beliefs. Positive thinking the future hurts us when we lie to ourselves as a survival skill that sets us up to be under-prepared and over-confident when things don't turn out the way we expected. Our attempts to hoist super powers and human potential to dominate our deep sense of powerlessness or go with the flow---all of these are compensating structures that outlaw our ability to be flexible to learning to create a desired goal. Perhaps we can let go of predicting the future, and instead, create one.

A significant loss of heart is easy to fall into during key moments in creating your goal, especially during setbacks that frustrate you with emotional tension. Creating is often called a love/hate relationship. Laziness is just a loss of heart, giving up because striving and exertion wears you thin when victory hasn't come yet. When you feel dragged down, unable to move, complacent, the tendency is to compromise the goal and question it. Lowering it makes the goal seem more workable to avoid discouragement. We may remove discouragement but still not create what we want.

Emotional tension is such a difficult inner enemy to work with because comfort and calmer waters are our survival instinct. Creating goals causes an imbalance. Anxiety is the sense of fearing the worst of the future you want. The sales person is anxious about rejection toward a creating a big sales goal. To preemptively strike on the fear, the person pulls back, gets timid and brings themselves further away instead of progress toward the stated goal. They externalize the fear by staying out of situations and avoiding them before it happens.

A struggle with one's own fear becomes more consuming than what has to be done to meet the goal. Aggression is in the form of telling oneself a belief of what will happen. Psyching oneself out, the person is prevented from looking at the source of aggression more directly, and instead steps away from it. If they could stay, even though it is uncertain what will happen, the truth of the hurdle is it is only a hurdle. Constraints and creating go together. Staying true to fear's presence actually brings the person to more creativity. Getting to know the whole picture is what the discipline of "staying present" involves. You learn not to hold back and give awareness intimately to whatever is going on. You learn how to remain self-objective during tough times.

Depression arises from the refusal to follow inspiration to create a desired outcome when the individual neglects to act upon it. You basically don't give what you've been given. A deeper belief of powerlessness or worthlessness predominates their behavior. Staying present to depression is about not acting out nor aggressing up it by attempting to be significantly powerful. Who else but a person who must portray and convey their sense of power and control is someone

369

who thinks they do not have it? Self-help and human potential is drawn from the belief that one has little power. Turning on mind powers is like a new drug...unlock the powers of the mind, and you can be a no-limit person. These ideals attempt to awaken the giant within, affirm themselves with self-propaganda slogans of grandiosity and confidence.

The person attempting to affirm their importance is caught and trapped by ideals of themselves to be seen as important by others. Heroes love to be the lifeguards wanting to be called to rescue, except some heroes push people in first. And when their identity (opinion of themselves) drives them, failure cannot be used as an asset. Everything present is taken personal, especially the opinions of others. They become heroes to rescue others to avoid the unwanted belief they are cowards. Or they become nasty dictators to dominate and control others out of the unwanted belief they are less adequate than others, or insignificant.

Fear is a concept of danger that suggests a need to control the outcome in some way. Dwelling in the present is outlawed by the threat of what could go wrong. When we act from the place of what scares us, we neglect the chance to stay in tune with fear itself and see that fear is our way of lookout for the regard we have ourselves. Like a big bear, our fear warns us to find a refuge from what we predict will happen.

What would happen if you befriended the obstacles of fear, depression, and anxiety? You don't have to like what is there, but you can meet it. In May of this year, one of my best lifelong friends took his life. It was the most different emotional passage of my life of 48 years. Every interior blast of emotions ebbed and flowed like turbulence on a flight that seems endless, and yet, I could bare it. Practicing the principle of separation.

I began to see my ability to hold space for the rawness of the emotions as well as other tender parts of my heart that felt crushed and squeezed. Over days and weeks, I contacted other parts of my heart that truly felt compassion for my friend's suffering. Like steps and stages, I went from guilt and powerlessness to a wiser, relaxed sense of attention to the event. Everything I learned in being flexible, patient and present was tested. I learned that I could stay with an experience like this.

I remember it's like getting my wife pregnant. The exertion of controlling when this will happen pushed away the possibilities, while just staying present and enjoying our intimacy when it arose resulted in pregnancy when I least expected it. Trying to force a pregnancy undermined it, while letting go and being present to our intimacy naturally organized forced to set the seeds for my wife's pregnancy, which always came as an astonishing surprise, making it magical and meaningful. Creating is about first building an unforced space for new potential to live there. I often wonder whether our biggest danger is failure, or is it not understanding the reasons why something was successful.

The exertion in that moment gave me a sense of not giving up on my ability to be present right now. Here's what grabbed me about this: *As you stay with what is happening you find yourself in different spaces and energies. Moments of despair, discouragement, rage, anger, resentment---these seem like a signpost to moving away from these places because of the bee sting like discomfort.* But in the creative orientation, you practice the capacity of "separation." Rather than being the emotions, you observe your emotions. You stand in a different place in the room with what you've experienced and live next to it like a roommate living in a guesthouse. You vow to stay with the limitless quality of being aware such that you push away nothing, and welcome everything. And this is how I was able to work through the ebb and flow of the loss, the confusion, intensity, and pain.

My conclusion: Your experience of these difficult states become more interesting when you remember separation. In fact, the feelings capable of being experienced instead of grinning and bearing them. They are not enemies, but just a current reality absorbing what is happening. There is nothing to push though, overcome, and the kind of striving we often hear. I think these efforts are used by people who lack the skill of separation. It is their default way of pushing themselves around to deaden the pain or run through the mud with everything you've got.

Exertion gone wrong sets you up for a dramatic turn to giving up--- unable to move or do anything. Exertion gone well softens your edges to stay present no matter whatever arises. The insight of what to learn or do isn't possible without the emotional currents brought on by the concepts and beliefs. The notion of turning this around is letting go of the ideals and concept I held and starting where I actually am. *Life is what really brings the insights.* Integrity (right exertion) is determined by how long you can stay with the ambiguity until something new, fresh arises to greet you. Time is the advocate, not the adversary.

Bad emotions, negative experiences, shitty moments don't need to be seen as a problem story. They can be an opportunity story, or story-free, with no place for use. The learning is in not having to squeezing learning from everything, but to instead to accept things as they are without control or expectations. Any experience can be a basis for learning and seeing insights. Not every obstacle results in an oyster with a pearl. But it is possible to survive the ups and downs and still remain in a creative, receptive, flexible, and focused orientation on what you want to create. The thread in all reform is in choice and orientation. Influencing ourselves can open new doors by exceptions to control everything. When you look far outside what you're conditioned to see, what you see changes.

How to Apply: Start taking a sacred pause decisively in the middle of things. Take a full blown free days to stay away from business, to build attentive openness and relaxed attention to whatever might arise. Schedule 30 minutes of intentional silence at the start of every day and build in 15 minutes the late morn and late evening to keep the stance of relaxed attention. Be ready for anything and expect nothing. Sit, walk, listen, and live with as much openness, internal space and vacancy for bringing forth our highest intelligence. If you stand like a hard tree, you will break in the wind, but if you're flexible, you're still standing when the storm blows over. No feeling is final. When you start to lose your flexibility of mind, take a time out for 30 minutes and stay calm, take 10 deep breaths.

And ask, "Can I stay with what is happening?" State to yourself: "It's like this…" Then describe with full loyalty to report the truth to yourself the facts of what is going on. There is nothing wrong with feeling fear, having emotional difficulties, in fact, it is the first step to be a leader: to be a human being. You don't have to centralize back into a "self", in fact there isn't one. You will never really know who you are or hold any model of yourself that lasts. Forget it. Let go, let come. Place your trust in everything the future needs is given to you this moment. Don't look in any other place for comfort than this.

The mystery is your greatest source of hope. The ego is trying to stop the directness of our experience. If you choose to play life from mystery, then you learn from an emerging future possibility as you walk, taking meaningful leaps into uncertainty. Like a freight train with conviction and faith, you lay the tracks down as you go. And it makes the scenery more interesting, inspiring, surprising, challenging, and amazing for you to meet and learn from. Everything, everything, everything…*is waiting for you*. Push away nothing, stay ready for anything.

LIVING CONCEPT-FREE

In the hardest or most negative moments, you can use the energy and information at play to awaken and learn. To really assimilate the most from it, *leave your concepts at the door.* Perceptions, interpretations, and expectations are downloaded from the past.

Instead, mindfully position yourself to accept the present moment as your invited guest at the dinner table. Make room in yourself for disconfirming qualities in reality that fall outside what is familiar. You don't have to bring your hard-handed preconceived judgments to everything. After all, isn't life just a giant boot camp anyway?

Just consider what life makes available to you if you entered this moment with no anticipation. Your past is history. Right now, none of your conclusions of who you should be or not be are necessary. Let go of your expectations of yourself, of everything, and stay open. And that whatever others are doing or thinking isn't at issue. What's left? NOW! All you need to bring is your intention, and wise innocence and the best is yet to come into place.

Have you forgotten that life is beautiful? The field of possibilities is revealed right now. Every step along the way be grateful for the brevity of life!

Bobby

Your ideals of yourself tell you to be this or that. You use these ideals to compare what you have and do. These ideals are shaped from your negative opinions of yourself. When you attempt to live by your ideals, you are rarely able to live up to them. One example of this is a level of commitment that is out of touch with your goals.

When Bobby, a wealth advisor in New York, went into his biggest case opportunities, he learned that with his narrow focusing ability and tremendous energy, he could make it all happen. His goal was to be #1. Nothing less was acceptable to him. He prided himself on his ability to always come through for his clients, especially when a wall was hit. He'd use the wall as a way to get steam and wield extra force to slay the dragon. Over time into this 40's, he hit a level of exhaustion that could not sustain. An energy crisis started to neutralize his need to think things through. After losing several 8 figure deals tragically, Bobby began to feel ill. All his hard work was getting much traction and instead had taken its toll on his health. During downtimes, he'd watch his phone like a tenacious mosquito. He'd hover over his work all the time. He felt he constantly needed to apply himself, bring his will power, and do whatever it takes. After his first heart attack at age 43, his doctor sat on the side of his hospital bed with a piece of wisdom to share: "Hard work will never substitute intelligence."

Bobby learned that his over-commitment level was actually diminishing his returns. His 70-hour week wasn't producing any more than a 40-hour week; he was just attempting to meet his ideal of deserving what he desired.

As you consider how much commitment is required, consider the time to value math. It's simply how much time to put in for the return you receive. There is an intrinsic and extrinsic return. Both count.

Trusting your decisions involves a choice to be a learner, not just a performer. The choice to occupy a learning orientation makes life your teacher. Whether it works or doesn't work, you treat both of these results with equal value. To learn, you must give yourself second chances. When you take your identity and ideal of the process of creation, you open the opportunity to use failure as an asset. You go out into the world and collect checks for the value you create. As a sales shaman, you learn in both scenarios. As you grow in your habits and experience the total sum of your capabilities is locked into a certain size check that you always know how to get. But if you go for a new size check, you must take your thinking, habits, and capabilities to an entirely different level. You can get very bored at the size check you have now. But a new size check may require a rethink of the method, rules, and rituals that got you here. But it won't get you there.

INTEGRITY AND MYSTERY

What the fuck am I doing? You might be asking yourself this question all the time and you should. You will change your mind. As things continue in life, new subject matter enters that picture that adds or subtracts from the way you intend things to be. One of the most humbling truths is just how little in control you are of everything. The only time you have any control over is the present moment, but the future is still a mystery. So, you live forward into it. How do you relate with the unknown? What is inside the unknown? What will you inherit or be revealed?

If you've ever lived through a natural disaster or hurricane, you probably realized nothing you had imagined could have ever come close to the experience of it. Living through hurricane Odille in Baja California meant a category 4 hurricane that wasn't on my radar the week before it arrived. Nothing could have prepared my family or me for what was required to live through it. At 1am. the eye passed over our home, bringing 145 mile an hour winds, flying debris, and a shrieking sound that made your stomach sick and your heart race. Thank God we made it through the night safe. We cannot predict the future; we can only create one.

As the hurricane approached, our only survival asset was telling the truth of its potential. This thing can kill us. Negative preparation is what you do when you tell yourself all sides of reality, good and bad, and worst without exaggeration or minimization. Weather people speculate a lot, but the present moment you can't fake yourself out of when a storm this size is pouncing on your roof and trying to blow you off the earth. If God and I do have a post-life conversation to report on my findings, I'll request he remove two things: hurricanes and taxes!

The space between where we were, and the hurricane coming com is state of emerging properties like unfolding yarn. What was to come meant a mystery would be revealed. Integrity is how long you can stay in the ambiguity without editing or making up what is unknowable. We can only verify what is going by observing what is actually going on. That space between 8pm and 1am was my test of integrity. Living without certainty is the only certainty.

Ground is found in groundlessness. It is a commitment to honesty like no other. And honesty offers you the chance to be nowhere but right here. Honesty brings you right into direct collision with the present moment. That day Odille filled it. There was no escaping its path, we accepted our confinement and turned toward the storm without any particular anticipation. We let go, let the storm come as if it was knowing us for the first time, living us, as we lived it. It was as if we

378

had to forget its name for a while until it could be named. Any mental model of it was just a mirage---expecting, anticipating, worrying...none of these were of any use. That day I found myself so open, so empty, that I was free to relate to the experience in its own conversation, not mine, like an out of body moment.

After the hurricane passed, we were not the same people as before. We had been visited by a natural phenomenon that reminded us just how powerless we truly are, and how to live without a false sense of power. Mystery is full of surprises.

Everything the future needs is given to you this moment. The underlying question is "do you trust life?" The nature of life is a mystery; a wildcard. Life isn't always in cooperation with your expectations or intentions. Life is messy therapy with its own agenda.

If everything the future needs is given to you this moment, then what about what goes around comes around? Is the future listening to your past output? Is the future listening to your optimism or pessimism? Your sins? Your badness or goodness? Do good things tend to happen to good-mannered people? Does your thinking become a resource that the future depends on to deliver what is present? What is essential for the emerging future to be responsive to your desires, intentions, and beliefs? Does the natural order enfold into your interior condition? Does your behavior determine your future?

I propose that good behavior and decisions that are goodness-based probably bring a more favorable future, but there is no guarantee. Good-ness based behavior can either be: driving to avoid negative consequences, or for the sake of doing good things as a creative process itself.

We experience the future as it is rather than how we expect it. Whether the future is in cooperation with what we expect or not, it is by nature a wildcard capable of going in any direction. Nothing stays the same despite what we believe and predict. No weather forecast is accurate; it is only speculation. Speculation is overused when we attempt to predict the future instead of creating one. Creating the future doesn't need us to expect anything. We create the future as it emerges.

Where we assume where power originates determines the response to how much control we assign to ourselves in having the future come our way. We seek to control the future, rather than experience it as a movement independent of our behavior.

Where does the power come from that moves your life? Or what are the sources of creativity? The artist would say the power is in the painting. Picasso said the true power is in the painting, not himself. The vision of the final state of the painting is what draws forth devotion to creating the work of art.

The future is out there, a mystery, unable to be seen until we walk, like laying down the tracks as the train is moving. The track-laying is moved by the forward motion of the train. Action creates the clear path.

Jordan reads a book about narcissistic personality disorder, and three months later her closest client, Kaela, drops the bomb about her abusive marital relationship and the cruel and unfair treatment by her husband. Jordan is a marital and family therapist helping people deal with serious emotional traumas, but didn't see Kaela's challenge coming at all. Did the book know where to put itself in the timeline? Is the future awaiting Jordan's picking up of the book so that Kaela gets help and support?

VALUE CREATION STARTS HERE

It starts with your insistence to be whole. To be blessed is to be whole. The one thing your helping depends on is for you to be well. The word health is "whole." That means all your bottom lines have high margins, not bankruptcy. People love people who glow. You glow when you're walking true in your faith!

The deepest part of you requires reflection and silence to be able to come in. Every human being has a story to tell. Their lives are journeys of the most unique kind.

Start conversations with a blank canvas. When you go into your conversations, leave what you know behind. Replace your presentations with consultations. This requires you to bring nothing--- what you know, how you appear, what you do. This might seem more like a threat than an asset, yet to really listen generatively, you have to empty yourself as if you are cleaning a closet to make space for something new.

A MEETING OF MINDS

Martin was returning to work in his London office after spending two weeks with his brother in New York. He was coming back with a heavy heart. It was not just that it was the end of a wonderful holiday; it was not just that he invariably suffered badly from jet lag; it was that Monday mornings always began with a team meeting and, over the months, he had grown to hate them.

Martin was aware that colleagues approached these meetings with hidden agendas; they indulged in game-playing, and he knew that people were not being honest and open. The meetings themselves were bad enough — but then there was all the moaning afterwards. *"The usual people saying the usual things." "I could have improved on that idea, but I wasn't going to say." "I was thinking of making a suggestion — but I couldn't be bothered."*

As this morning's meeting began, Martin braced himself for the usual moroseness and monotony. But, as the meeting progressed, he became aware of a strange background noise. At first, he thought that he was still hearing the engine noise from the aircraft that had brought him back to London — he had had to sit over the wing, and the droning was terrible. But, as he concentrated on the noise, it became a little clearer.

He realized — to his amazement — that he could hear what his colleagues were **thinking** as well as what they were **saying**. As he concentrated still harder, he found that he could actually hear what they were thinking at the same time as they were speaking. What surprised him, even more than the acquisition of this strange power, was that he discovered that what people were saying was not really what they were thinking. They were not making clear their reservations. They were not supporting views which they thought might be unpopular. They were not contributing their new insights. They were not volunteering their new ideas.

Martin found it impossible not to respond to his new knowledge. So, he started to make gentle interventions, based more on what he could hear his colleagues **thinking** than on what he could hear them **saying**. *"So, John are you really saying ..."* *"Susan, do you really think that ..."* *"Tom, have you got an idea on how we could take this forward?"* He was aware that his colleagues were unsettled by how insightful these interventions were. They looked at him mystified. In truth, he felt rather proud of his newly-acquired talent.

Emboldened now, Martin forgot his usual misery at participating in such meetings and began making comments of his own. However, he became aware that some of his colleagues were looking at him quizzically. One or two even had a gentle smile playing on their lips. Only gradually did it dawn on him — they could hear **his** thoughts, and **he** was not really saying what he was thinking.

As the meeting progressed, Martin became aware of changes to the tone and style of the event. It was clear to him now that, one by one, each member of the meeting was learning how to hear the thoughts of all the others, and this was subtly changing how they interacted with one another. The game-playing started to fall away; people started to speak more directly; views became better understood; the atmosphere became more open and trusting.

The meeting ended. As people left the room, Martin found that he could still hear what they were thinking. *"That was the best meeting we've ever had." "All meetings should be like that." "In future, I'm going to say what I think."*

The first part to meeting of the minds is to empty yourself of what you're appearing to be. You probably have lots of ideals, such as being professional, being creative, being this, or being that. This is all about your identity. What you see and do will be preoccupied with this piece. You lose the essence of serving the other person when your ideals get in the way. It's like clouding the water. Real value creation starts with deep listening, and leaning in helps change something in your heart. You come to understanding the other in a way that calls the caring part of you to the surface. You upset the normal ways of seeing things in the past. Setting your thoughts aside, your entire way of looking at something is like hanging your clothes on the line.

The second part to empty yourself of is the discomfort you have with opening your heart. You have to remember that you have an organ of perception inside you that is naturally inclined to reduce the suffering of the other. You probably want to go deeper and connect with the other person's most important values and desires, but to get there, it takes conviction.

KNOWING YOUR STUFF

By the way, suspending what you know doesn't mean dispensing of your strengths, talents, capabilities, and deliveries. You must know these to create value for others. If you didn't know what you have, how could you help people create what they want? They depend on you for what you love and do best, and yet you must keep all of this in your hip pocket until the time is right.

Your most important ability to develop is creating an atmosphere of trust. If the person feels safe, you can access the truth of where they are and where they want to go.

Steps:

1. Suspend all your existing assumptions, perceptions, and interpretations by collecting important information from your client's situation (their story), to see a clear picture.
2. Open the conversation about their 3-5 year picture they envision. Eliminate ambiguities like more, less, higher, or lower. Concretize the content of their vision together by asking for more information, getting more clarity, bringing up ambiguities and discrepancies, and what certain things imply.
3. Determine why the content matters. Ask why, why, and why this or that matters. You may begin to see when the motivation is to remove an unwanted problem versus create a desired outcome.
4. Respect the current view of a solution your buyer or client has in mind. Draw it out. Ask them how they see themselves utilizing a resource like you or your company.

From these steps, you will position yourself for three capabilities:

9. Capture insights (separate what you knew)
10. Honor differences (legitimize and accept everything)
11. Integrate (see possibilities and bring them into a creative process)

With a flexible, open mind, heart, and will, your comprehension will be drawn from balanced intelligence.

JOE'S INSIGHT

Joe showed up 15 minutes early to his appointment and reviewed his notes from the last meeting with Paul. Paul was an electrical contractor and entrepreneur in the construction industry who depended on Joe for safety management standards to keep in compliance with requirements. Five minutes past the hour and Paul wasn't there. Then 15 minutes past and no sign of Paul.

Joe began to feel angry because it seemed like Paul was disrespecting his time and implying that the meeting began when Paul was ready, not Joe. A low-grade anger started to well up inside Joe, and by 20 minutes after the hour, Joe put a call into Paul's voicemail saying how disappointed he was, and how arrogant Paul was for showing up late and taking Joe's time for granted. Joe also told Paul that he owed him an apology for wasting his time and being such a jerk. Suddenly Larry walked into the room to let Joe know Paul's daughter had food poisoning and passed out suddenly. She was rushed to the emergency room.

Larry could see Joe's facial expressions shift from red in the face pissed to almost being in tears. Joe was completely under the spell of his assumption of Paul's intentions, which gave rise to the action to call Paul out. How was Paul going to take that message from Joe while dealing with his daughter's crisis? Joe felt like a buffoon and acted like one. Larry offered to add some food for thought. Joe agreed and listened.

"Joe, what if you had simply accepted the situation as if you invited it, and instead of reacting and getting worked up during that 20 minutes, you could configure something useful to do with the time, to stay in touch with the present moment?" "And what if you could simply get to know your assumption, and strategy, and behavior that could arise from it, and experience it, but not act from it?" Larry was implying that Joe could slow his habitual thinking down, observe his internal emotions, and interrupt his propensity to jump in when he assumed others' intentions. Larry assured Joe that staying with what was happening is accessible with patience and understanding.

Joe picked up the phone and left a heartfelt apology on Paul's voicemail asking for forgiveness and sharing his concerns for his daughter Jenny. Paul texted back, saying everything was ok and thanked Joe for coming around and saying what he said so truthfully.

That night Joe's wife Patty was getting ready to take him to a family friend's 40th birthday party that started at 8pm. It was 7:46, and Joe could feel the heat coming on that being late would cause others to disrespect him. As he walked with anger toward the bedroom, he stopped, took a deep breath, and asked himself: "What am I feeling? And what am I assuming?" He took a seat near the hallway and looked off into space. All he could hear was his next breath. It was as if a void had opened and space was made to reflect on his current moment of becoming aware of himself and what he was about to do next.

Every time he pushed Patty to rush, she would increase her latency because it put more pressure on her to be ready and she counteracted with resistance. Patty didn't have the same model of punctuality that Joe did, and Joe knew he could acknowledge this difference, and accept it, maybe even learn from it. So right there, he walked into the den, picked up his favorite bio book on Margaret Meade, and opened page 35. The page was full of great content, and Joe was immersed. As Patty walked into the kitchen saying she was ready, Joe ran to thank her for the time. While she got ready, he used the 20 minutes to fill his mind with great content in that book. Being late was like "an invited guest, like unexpected perfection," He said.

He also noticed that he could meet reality just as it is, without judgment, fear, or beliefs hijacking his feelings and giving rise to the anger to fuel his criticism. Joe then told Patty that by meeting life this way, he could forgive himself for being human too.

Later that night after getting back home, Joe noticed that his ideals had been making him terribly unhappy all his life. That always being punctual added a standard of himself that life would not always comply with. Page 35 said, "Life is a wildcard, expect nothing, and be ready for everything." He knew then that his intention to be on time was a great value centered habit, but without his ideal, he could live with the messiness of life, and meet it just as it is, in peace and harmony.

And that being late was not married to his identity of being a good or bad person.

From then on Joe found people being late a lot less for his meetings. He found that when he let go of his preoccupation with it, and expectations, that people chose to be on time instead of being netted in Joe's manipulation and requirements. People felt free to choose. Joe's anger was put to rest. Then it got even better; he stopped yelling at his son Corey to clean up his room. Corey's room started looking cleaner. The more he let go, the more things could move in ways that his controlling was limiting. He wrote a note to himself to read these bullets at the start of each day:

YOU DON'T HAVE TO LIKE LIFE ALL THE TIME, BUT YOU CAN MEET IT

EXPECT NOTHING, BE READY FOR ANYTHING

EVERYTHING THE FUTURE NEEDS IS GIVEN TO YOU THIS MOMENT

YOU CAN STAY WITH WHAT IS HAPPENING BY TAKING A REST IN THE MIDDLE OF THINGS

SHOW UP AS A WHOLE PERSON

YOU CANNOT PREDICT THE FUTURE

INSTEAD, CREATE THE FUTURE

DON'T WAIT

GIVE ALL YOU'VE BEEN GIVEN

(Joe's Napkin note)

CHAPTER 14

PERIPHERAL LISTENING

When was the last time you truly felt listened to? It is a basic human need to feel important and understood. Yet today our attention spans are so besieged that it's a rare occasion when someone is fully paying attention.

Each one of us participates in two conversations. The first is with ourselves, and the second is with others. We don't listen to people when the volume of our inner conversation neutralizes our outside one. How do we turn it off? The answer is that we don't.

One day in session, a client asked me why I thought his wife kept yelling and nagging at him. He said that before she was diplomatic, but today she yells with fury. I asked him what he thought his contributions were to her behavior. He had pattern of avoiding her. Rather than gathering a clear understanding, he'd just say "sure" to minimize the situation and move on. Later on, in other conversations and situations, it became clear that he didn't know what she said to him. It went "in one ear and right out the other."

We create our bosses just like we create our spouses. When we try to change unresponsive bosses, we make them nuisances. They stay on us because we don't give attention to what they ask for or say. Then we play the blame game, putting the onus on them for being the bad guy; convincing ourselves and others that we're right about the boss.

Unresponsive bosses help themselves out being important or needed. When the employee says what's going on, and the boss does nothing about it, the employee eventually stops giving timely and quality information. The boss creates her own ignorance. This gets worse when the boss delegates so much that runaway authority happens.

Our kids turn away from sharing information we depend on. We cut them off from truth telling when we try to conform them to our standards and ideals. We project our formula for adequacy on them and turn them into performers. This steals their humanity because they're not operating from a creative orientation where choice organizes behavior. Instead, they violate their own gifts and desires as a means of approval and to avoid isolation.

Overconfidence has a destructive way of expecting something to be what it's not. Rather than listen to what is going on, we see only the positive side of current reality and under-tell the negative aspects. This becomes especially true with our relationship with our self. We lose a level of preparation necessary to win the outcome we want because we're not telling the truth. Overconfidence is terrorism; incompetency, although annoying, is often a starting point from which we begin to build capacity.

We build up strong reasons NOT to listen over time. We attempt to substitute the vulnerability of releasing what we know with an attachment to what we know. Outside our peripheral vision, the world around us is responding and retaliating to our stance. Our needs to be confirmed, feel special and affirm our existence then dominates our humility. People stop telling us the quality information that we depend because we've shut them down through our own influence. We become prisoners of our own machine.

Listening deeply is not intended to turn a salesperson into a therapist. The intent here is to profoundly impact the other lives they touch, personal and professional. Peripheral listening can be described as listening from the total place. When you listen from total place, you open all your organs of perception: head, heart, and hand. You begin by listening into what the person you're speaking to has experienced to this point in a story or narrative. You are so where they are, rather than where you want them to be that you lean in such they change you. And that means accessing a quality in yourself that is animating by surprise, astonishment, and meaning that a quality of voluntary energy to help comes forth from your ground of being. You bring your inner knowing to the surface.

When this surfaces, you begin listening from inside yourself as to what has heart, meaning, and significance by not just listening to the words, but more importantly the *person* behind the words. As you hear the story, lean in so that something kicks up in you. Paying attention to what changes you is like staying present to the story they tell you without counter story-telling. The other person cannot not tell the story because it reveals what is going on deep inside if they feel safe in your presence to do so. It is your responsibility to cultivate this level of safety.

Story listening is listening to the unconscious. During story listening, language has themes in it. It is the unconscious speaking such that themes, images, places, and things keep repeating itself. As you take this in, nothing in you is countering it; you are so empty, open, such that nothing internal shuts you down. Whatever is going on your life isn't relevant. If you relate to the other as if you know the truth about them, you invalidate your tendency to jump ahead. You check out and then check back into their story. Do not browse your own experience to find a matching story; hold the polarity between the two. Honoring these differences makes room for something new to be understood.

One of the primary principles of these teachings is *whatever you make space for can move*. When we don't suspend our certainty and attach ourselves to what we know (the old self), we ignore what is real. At best, our downloads from the past are placed over reality like a veneer to reconfirm our suspicions based on outdated information. When we claim to know what is real, we forget that what we think is factual is at best a relative truth. You cultivate the remembrance to forget that you know anything. We call this "checking-out" and "checking-in" to the present moment, ready for anything, expecting nothing. You access your listening from nowhere, which means "now here."

As you "check-out" like this, you listen with your tummy, not your head. Your belly button is your ear. Your soul is being stimulated by the other person as emotion comes up like tidal changes in you. It is to lean in such that the other person changes you.

As the story listening changes your interior condition, your will for the other becomes stronger than your will for yourself. This summons a genuine, open-hearted urge to care for the other. The process is see, love, help. Seeing is the process of deep listening into the story. Love arises from the sensing perception from which empathy, understanding, and compassion seek to lessen the suffering of the other. And helping is giving the other something they cannot give to themselves.

WHOLE LIFE INTEGRATION

Signing off is hard for business people. They struggle to turn their minds off during non-work hours. Yet, they depend on this time to heal, reflect and integrate their experience, so everything else gets better. The ability to sign-off is a skill I call "unpluggability." You've probably experienced it when "going off the grid" when you're away from screens. Screens (cell phone, laptop, tv, etc.) are what turn your internal distractibility against you.

Given space, anything can move. This is a principle I learned from meditation practice.

You're not here to agree; you're here to shine. This is how you help the whole.

The ensemble of talent, style, and a unique way of seeing the world composes our genius. Most of us are on a different path and asleep to accessing this uniqueness. When a person begins to live into their genius, they become weird. Weird according to the Welch meaning is to "have one foot in each world."

The Greek word for genius was "daemo." We are happy when we make our genius happy. A person's worst demons is their genius turned off. Either you are growing or shrinking, you can't stay in a middle place very long because context is in motion. We must embrace the 50/50 relationship with life---that half the time it works, and the other half it doesn't, but we must treat both of these with equal value.

If you don't give the idea in your mind, it will rot and will rotten you. Either we step into our story and bring the beauty that we are, or join the hypocrites.

Balance is about being who you are in all that you do. Balance is presence. To be present, you must learn to control your attention. And you must also learn to be human. Bring culture back into alliance with nature. God never took our gifts away in our journey, they have always remained, and we just don't see them. And others don't either. Your identity is not your business; you have a Technicolor life. Service, meaning, and mystery are in everything you experience. Meaning is the language of the soul, service is the work of the soul, and mystery is the presence of the soul.

THE MOST IMPORTANT THING TO REMEMBER IS THE MOST IMPORTANT THING

THE MOST IMPORTANT THING: The most important thing is knowing the most important thing. Simplicity is acquired via a hierarchy of importance. Some things matter the most, while other aspects of your life are important and optional. If you made a list of the five most indispensable qualities that you cannot live without, how much do they cost? Most likely almost nothing. So I ask you: which path are you on? Are you creating an impressive lifestyle, or creating a fulfilling life? The most important thing is knowing the most important thing.

Choosing to organize your life around what matters to you is a fundamental choice. The motivation behind obligation is different than choice. Music is not made out of obligation; it's created out of generative love. It is made for its own sake, not obligation. I found that many people set up their own obligations as a way of avoiding the confrontation of their own freedom. The help creates conflicts to manipulate themselves into action because it's an easier alternative than the creative process of desiring and deciding to create something that matters.

When we remove our identities from the creative process, we let go of justifying what really does matter, and begin living fully. What matters either does or doesn't, it requires no further explanation. Many people walk through life not knowing what matters to them. They cloak a deep sense of powerlessness by remaining unclear as a preemptive strike to avoid failure. But suddenly they wake up one day with the capacity to end the hypnosis of their conceptual fear. Instead, they choose an alternative way to organize their actions: The most important thing! What matters most to them becomes a predominant creative force in organizing their decisions.

What matters to you right now in your life? To what do you want to devote your life spirit and energy? If you could live your life over again, what would you have done differently? And what's the first step toward moving this aim into being? This step will bring forth new information and learning, from which your creative process fosters new capacity. You will begin creating something separate from what you know.

Two things to keep in mind: 1) what is your vision? and...2) where are you now relative to it? Honesty and Love. You must keep this in view side by side: vision and current reality. These two forces are the catalysts for bringing new creations into the world through you, because between them tension naturally seeks to resolve the discrepancy between what you have and what you want. It's like stacking nature's laws in your favor by positioning the path of least resistance where energy is easiest to flow.

What is the most important thing? That's a very personal question. It is that which you deeply to desire to create most. And that can be the one thing that your focus serves. What is the most important thing? What aspect of your career life motivates or fascinates you the most? What could become possible if this becomes the centerpiece of your creative process? It's just one choice away from you.

REFLECTION AND NATURE

Beth, a top sales producer in Southern California, writes: "I am not sure of a better way to start or end the day than watching the sunrise or sunset in the peace and tranquility of nature! Nature has three qualities to offer you: 1) it moves medium-slow, not fast. 2) It heals you, and 3) you can access deep reflection via internal stillness."

Beth continues: "I'm sitting on a high bluff looking at the distance to the horizon, after a trek up the hill on my mountain bike by myself. I can contemplate this as a high altitude point overlooking my entire life building process, and the landscape are all the aspects in my life that compose it."

I say to myself, "Now, remember that anything you want to create is up for grabs. This is the moment to rethink everything." Starting with nothing, you connect with your horizon; your future self for personal cultivation. Turn to the East where the sun rises represents what is ready to begin in my life. I remind myself that life is temporary, and all things must end, at some point. Then I connect with the West, where the sun sets, and what is ready to die in me. North is my spirit, and South is my soul down deep into my ground of being.

> *"When you confront that you're not immortal, the brevity of life suddenly awakens your heart's desires. What matters to you isn't conditional anymore. Dreams and aspirations begin to visit you like a piece of music you faintly hear from inside your heart. You fundamentally choose to become the predominant creative force in your life. You're on the way to something you deeply desire for its own sake, and your love for it is generating the effort."*

CONNECTION

Beth continues: "As I sit quietly on the bluff, I then start to connect with something pregnant seeking me to come into reality—a sacred project. My inner knowing has come to the surface to meet what is true for me right now. This connection is what is called "the vertical connection" to your deepest intention. From within you is a guiding light or idea that you care deeply about. This idea that has yet to become true orients you at the deepest levels. And it presents you with unforeseen possibilities that come into the now. My relationship with the unknown is a friendly invitation."

Your deepest intention, when originated from the source of being, characterizes your place to take in the ecosystem. When you see the true nature of your work, you develop a love and appreciation for it. And it is organized by your deep curiosity and wonder for what life has in store for you. It is all just an adventure! Your first step is to offer yourself an invitation to organize your life around what matters most to you. This is the invitation to the open heart.

Beth continues: "I'd take an empty pocket over an empty heart any day. I'm reminded of the moment when a philanthropist offered Mother Teresa a very large sum of money to donate to her cause. After refusing it, she exclaimed with open heartedness and conviction, "Thank you and I'll say no for the third time, but after this, do something for me instead. If you could today find someone alone and impoverished, and marginalized, and tell him that he is never alone, this would make all the difference."

To open your heart, you'd turn to journal, and remember the souls who brought you to where you are now. That a vast treasure of unique abilities and figures shaped what you learned, like rich supply lines to fuel your journey. You're reminded to make everything and everyone your teacher. Even those who insulted you, these are your teachers too. So, you write down their names and next to each human being they brought you a gift. What did they tell you? What did they bring you? How did they change you? When you see the qualities in others around you that amaze or inspire you, you develop a deep love and gratitude for their gifts.

The capacity to witness the magic in others is distinguished from yourself. You live in a gift economy now. Nothing becomes what it is without the advent of relationship. Patterns between us give rise to properties we can define in ourselves. We all are just being done by the influence of relationships. Cynicism must be let go as vulnerability, intimacy, and depth come forth.

As you gather your heartfelt gratefulness of your special contributors in your past, what you notice expands. What you ignore is reduced. When you acknowledge someone's gifts or contributions to your life, it expands. You help them see their place to take in the ecosystem. The word in Japanese "ba" means "place."

A genius loci is an intelligent spirit or magical power that resides in a place. Very few genius loci of this form are able to move from their native area, either because they are "part of the land" or because they are bound to it. Your place to take in the ecosystem is a place made for you. To know your place, you must know your deepest intention (source), the way others around you move or touch the sacred in you, and through these, your best self and truest work is brought into creating value for others.

When you're intentionally silent and still, reflect on this: What is expanding or contracting in your life? What is gathering and rising? What is flowing in, and what is flowing out? What is settling or releasing? What is wanting to emerge? What story are you telling through your life? You're in a conversation with creation, and the world is coming to find and confirm you!

THE COLLECTIVE UNFOLDING

Ken, an executive for a Fortune 100 IT company on the west coast is at a two-day retreat program to develop managing leaders in the company.

The trainer conducts an exercise to take the leaders down into their bodies to open their sensing perceptions into empathic listening. The exercises involve listening from the entire body until the other person, the words they say, and the person saying them, changes you. The trainer then stops, and asks, "Does this makes sense?" Suddenly Ken pops back up into his head. He's outlawed from the deep dive journey of the exercise each time the trainer says this sentence to be in rapport with the group.

During a break, Ken tells the trainer that when this is heard, it short circuits his ability to stay connected to his open heart. During the next session, the trainer then demonstrates that he received the feedback and made a shift in his question, "Do you feel it?" Ken said the whole room clapped at that point as if he had been the point person to represent a collective voice. In our 1 on 1 coaching session, Ken mentioned that he must trust this voice and bring it out in an instant. He mentioned that his voices of fear, cynicism, pride, status, and judgment all covet the open access to this communal voice.

I explained to Ken that when he opens his sensing perception, he taps into a social field from which energy and information flow patterns can shift and members of a group change their interior condition and see in new ways. These new ways are new levels of understanding from which they "feel" a certain pattern of creative order brewing that must be brought into realization. I said that he could use a jazz trio as a model for this connective energy field to compare his experience of it. Each participant in the jazz ensemble plays from the others' interdependent influence.

The properties unfolding through each are linked from a larger whole that appears to be revealing itself as the improvisations are trusted and come forth. Like a canvas super-imposed on them, each surrender to play from the whole, like a channel. I heard one musician describe it as "losing oneself and finding oneself" within a field of possibilities from which the song plays the group." He called it playing the "macro-saxophone" as if to capture every available creative ingredient ready to be blown into that horn through him. Ken began to understand this field of power and to access its flow patterns of creative energy and information; one must develop the capacity for "pre-sensing" emerging possibilities pregnant with movement.

What staggered Ken was comparing his past to what was becoming clear now. In the past, the force behind his creative process was his own intention and goals, while this source was of a larger field of order from which his empathic listening could become generative in creating something seeking him. As he opened up more to these

402

dynamics, he found that it followed him everywhere and began to surface in every conversation when he could feel the inner shift of letting go as something ready to be born, would come into his open heart. He found that the moment he noticed it, reflected on its significance, and expressed it, others in contact with him would deepen their level of trust and intimacy to share what was true for them too. I mentioned Carl Rogers quote, "That which is personal is always universal."

If I'm given beauty even after I haven't been beautiful, I am honored and seen as beautiful anyway, to remind me of my true self. Why not join the seer in seeing me truly? I'm not always at my best, but the grace I'm given by the love around me is everlasting, and there because what I see isn't what he sees. I want to see as he sees. It begins with the most basic question.

RESTORING THE MIRACULOUS

Frank Ostaseski, Founder of Zen Hospice says, "Seeing miracles isn't seeing something new, it's seeing what is new in the ordinary." Fran, an OBGYN thirty years into her career, was like calcified wood. Her work had become so routine, 7 deliveries per day, 28 per week, 1,100 per year. The grind was getting old and dull. Baby after baby, Fran reduced herself to just the method of her work and was experiencing a sense of soul-loss.

The biggest challenge was her popularity. She was the most gifted and skilled practitioner within 300 miles and trapped in her excellence, feeling fraudulent. Her inner world was turmoil, life-less, and sterile, while her communities' perception of her was animated, passionate, and endearing to her work. All the spiritual punch and no substantive sense of fulfillment inside got to her. She became exhausted, emotionally sick, and checked-out.

It was April, 2 days after Easter Sunday and little Susie was minutes away from leaving the womb, only this time was to be the moment Fran would return to her wholeness and be the blessing to the world that she'd forgotten. As the little baby was held in her hands the sparkle in Susie's eye was as if to hypnotize Fran. Something unlike had happened before connected between them - Susie was altering Fran's interior condition. The glimmer in her eye brought tears to Fran's eyes as the baby had touched her soul as if it were the first time. Fran said it was like stepping out of time, touched by the timeless. She vowed to maintain her inexperience and stopped refusing influence. Going forward, she conserved what she called "making life appear." And when she did this from her heart, she appeared too.

Two hours later Fran sat down and re-wrote her Hippocratic Oath as a healer. She renewed her sense of conviction for her work and found again what is remarkable in bringing life to the world. "It is in every one of us," says Fran now on her 35th year as gifted healer. She retired from the thought of retiring. And what had struck Fran so profoundly was the direct connection between her and Susie. Like a gift sent from the Heavens, Susie had packed the spiritual punch in a look Fran will never forget all her life.

When we refuse influence---from others, from what takes our breath away, from what life expresses, we lose our wholeness, joy, and happiness. We can choose to maintain a sense of wonder, and curiosity starting today from what emerges in different ways. Our experiences can integrate such that our larger, essential selves come to the surface. Life is a journey, not a trip.

IS THE UNIVERSE A FRIENDLY PLACE?

What do you think now? Remember, I lived 50 years of my own life under the assumption that the universe is a dangerous place. The pain I couldn't get away from as a teenager during my parents' divorce ripped away my sense of trust for others and all things. This is a dangerous worldview to carry with you.

Now reflecting back, I can see that when everything and everyone is made out to be dangerous, you cannot access yourself safely either. I wasn't at home in my being; my heart; my world. I couldn't relax, enjoy moments, and give myself to others. I lost touch with my basic goodness and shut down and used my technologies and other defense mechanisms to keep out all that was unfriendly. I distracted myself in things as form of protection. I couldn't surpass the grip of fear armoring my heart. I shunned any chance to receive love around me, to preemptively strike at incoming hurts I made up like phantoms. Making the world out to be dangerous camouflaged my sense of feeling unlovable.

Later in life, I came to see everything and everyone as a friendly place instead of phantoms, and when I saw it like this, I found myself seeking to reach out, understand better, and show up. I saw how I saw things as just a model of the world from which I was living.

WISDOM WITHOUT AND WITHIN

"And what does it involve being consciously in conversation with creation?" I ask myself. It is to be available and open to receiving it. You set an intention and then look to "wise innocence." Wise innocence is the part of you that knows you don't know how you know what you know. You're open to the outcome, yet not attached to it. "Is this God?" I ask myself. It is the force that is behind God.

It's like clearing the decks for action or passing through the eye of the needle. Something is ready to die, while something else, still indistinct is waiting to be born. It is the point where endings give rise to beginnings, and beginnings become endings. All things must change. Even you will change your mind, and everything will be there for you when it is supposed to be there.

In the scriptures, the camel had too much to carry on its back to pass through the doors of a village. All the non-essentials needed to be left behind to grant passage and set forth into the village. When a singular intention becomes clear, you give your mind big business to attend to and ignore the petty stuff. You take meaningful leaps into uncertainty, organizing your decisions in service to a calling. Life is constantly renewing your understanding as you live forward into the mystery of what it is unfolding.

We're all just walking in the dark; stepping down with each new stop on the mystery path with practical feet each moment, only knowing what is implied next by walking. We can see to the edge of our headlamps' field of visibility like a car driving on the highway in the dark. The enemy is in us—fear, resentment, cynicism, and judgment. All three cloud our window of the world ready to relate with us just as it is coming toward us, not what we make up about it.

Even volatility, uncertainty, complexity, and ambiguity, all bring you vision, clarity, understanding, and agility, as the dream becomes the catalyst for assimilating and learning as you live forward. That you learn what is emerging and embody it because you make life up as you go along. There is no cure for uncertainty. You can only truly reflect, while in action. This explains why there really are no experts. All that can be given are direction and connection (the vertical and horizontal connection), and an open will to live into the mystery forward, with willingness and alacrity.

The universe is a wildcard with very little cooperation most of the time. Can you trust betrayal? Can you work with the negative and positive aspects that life surfaces? Can you welcome everything, and expect nothing? In your life as a creator, you make room for the present moment just the way it actually is. The present moment is an acquired taste and learning ally. It is the beholder of truly being grateful for all that life presents you, even as life is a game of hide and seek. Nothing stays the same.

The word ecstasy means "to step aside." To be unavailable to the present is like cutting off the rhythm of life in a creative pattern of order, frequency, and tone.

LISTEN TO YOUR HEART THEN ACT

Hesitation inhibits the velocity of learning. That faster you begin a new business venture, the faster mistakes you eat for breakfast afford you a real business education. The greatest risk is not taking them. If you want to learn how to create business, start one.

If you desire something, decide to create or not create it. It's a choice you make. You don't predict a future; you create one. Action creates clarity. Clarity doesn't create action.

So, trust your decisions. Stop getting ready to get ready to get ready to get ready. You're not ready until you're ready to stop making things safe. Leveling up requires you leave your security, status, and comfort behind.

Jump in. You're never prepared for what's coming next. Set an intention. Then be wisely innocent to learn as you go along. There are no experts. You don't know what you don't know until you try.

Act in an instant, and you will learn faster. After all, every moment is one you're making up as you go along. There isn't anything truly made to be consistent with what you know, despite your brain circuits wanting to pretend you know. If you don't stay away, your brain will project things from the past like a projector instead of seeing what is actually going on.

Editing ourselves, life, and others is the signpost of no vacancy for the new future possibility to come forth. Yes, even you at times are fooled by what looks familiar, but you have to maintain your inexperience to stumble upon what is ready to emerge, to operate from your wholeness.

Going astray is a bold approach because what we encounter or challenge ourselves to do may not follow the familiar. We cling to old ideas, expectations, concepts, knowledge that holds us hostage to repeating what we want to see as the same.

21st CENTURY EDUCATION

The future is uncertain. You can't have it your way, ever. Half of life is coming to terms with just how powerless we all really are to manipulating life. We are on its own terms. And yet we have choices to make about how we intend, attend, and connect within the present moment moments in which we live. What we fear the most is just how free we all are to choose. We can rethink our lives at any time without any reference to the past. What matters to us comes and goes from one thing mattering before to not mattering now. We are in constant flux with this question.

We don't want to be controlled by life despite having no control. The education system today is geared to predict, not learn from it. So, we mentally construct something called "time" to avoid being controlled by it. We use our model of time to protect ourselves from the uncertainty of the future. Yet the mystery is alive and full of virtual possibilities that await us when we let go of having control over it. What presents itself is just at the perfect moment, as if the future needed it right now.

One of the key skills of the 21st century is learning to hold space. Holding space is having the integrity to tolerate ambiguity, volatility, uncertainty, and complexity until grey becomes a clear path. The clear path is born of yielding vision, clarity, understanding, and an agility like staccato steps over sharp rocks. We press long enough to feel the sharpness but light enough to move toward another stepping point.

Holding space starts with opening yourself to something you don't know. In fact, you don't know how you know what you know. The only verification to knowing anything is what presents itself to be true right now. Holding space isn't automatic for you because your brain is wired to make sense of things, even if it lies to you. You see what you perceive. Your thoughts distort, contaminate, and fill in gaps with theories and non-facts to make it look like it knows, and yet there's another companion hanging out in the same place called awareness.

410

If you ever wonder what the scientists say about using our full brain power, it's about turning your levels of awareness into a highly tuned vigilance watchdog on the brain's tendencies to get mechanical.

The fundamental ingredient to holding space is trust. Trusting the unknown isn't friendly to the brain since it suggests something that threatens survival. Uncertainty breathes danger. The brain alerts the nervous system to prepare for attack by drawing adrenaline from the glands and responding with a stress response.

The body is preparing for something around the corner to fight with, flight from, or freeze when it arises. Holding space is the room to let this go. It isn't that fear is the constraint, it's not touching the fear itself. Fear itself is good. You wouldn't be scared if you didn't care about you and didn't want you to get hurt. Fear is out of respect for your survival. It's a good alert. But relating with it is a whole other story. Receiving fear as it is requiring steadiness, stillness, centering, and breathing right. The nature of fear isn't permanent, it comes and then goes away. The knee jerk reaction feels discomforting.

Holding space requires letting go of comparisons to ideals. Ideals steal relaxation by comparison thinking. We fill in what we'd rather be doing by "should's" and "ought to's." Downtime makes us panicked, anxious, and nervous because we feel out of sorts with our ideals to be producing, working, fighting, and being responsible. We define standards of perfection and attempt to live by them such that downtime is negated. This is often why slow time, reflection, and meditation get side-lined to the frenetic pace of life. We consume and clog our time up with staying busy instead of holding space for rejuvenation, reflection, to become a lot less busy. Hard work never substitutes intelligence.

WELCOME EVERYTHING

Even in the hardest or most negative moments, you can use the energy and information at play to awaken and learn. To really assimilate the most of it, leave your concepts at the door. Perceptions, interpretations, and expectations are downloaded from the past.

Instead, mindfully position yourself to accept the present moment as your invited guest at the dinner table. Make room in yourself for disconfirming qualities in reality that fall outside what is familiar. You don't have to bring your hard-handed preconceived judgments to everything. After all, isn't life just a giant boot camp anyway?

Just consider what life make available to you if you entered this moment with no anticipation. Nothing is be reduced, everything is significant here and now, as you unblock reception to what is emerging.

Your past is history. Right now, none of your conclusions of who you should be or not be are necessary. And that whatever others are doing or thinking isn't at issue. What's left? NOW! All you need to bring is your intention, and wise innocence and the best is yet to come into place.

Have you forgotten that life is beautiful? The field of possibilities is revealed right now. Every step along the way be grateful for the brevity of life!

Traci's Selling Stones

"Born of the Earth to Sell for the Earth." This is Traci's revelation during a walking meditation through the trees where the Chichara bugs harmonize from tree to tree to attract a mate deep in Oaxaca, Southern Mexico next to the state of Chiapas. *"I sat in the field of trees as if they could speak to each other in rich tones and sound blends."*

> *"Standing outside Susan's office I could hear her voice among the cacophony of sounds all around me as if my walk in the fields outside Oaxaca City were speaking inside me. The gentle mother at El Tule tree placed the St. Judas card in my hand. Placing my fingers over him my pocket, my best was yet to come. Everything must change, except the soul. Every experience is a selling stone to reset what is yet to come, and what the future needs to come into reality."*

As she toggled between her memories from Oaxaca, the dots connected...

"The old world of selling brings with it outdated thinking about what a seller is supposed to do, and how to get buyers to do things as of the sales person were some manipulative magician. Unlearning old habitual patterns and ways of thinking starts by learning to relate. Selling is a helping process of giving and receiving help from a fundamental connection. The helping process rests upon the quality of relating with self, life, and whole, integrated in one essential, timeless place, that gives rise to an atmosphere of trust—to trust what life is organizing and cooking up. This atmosphere regulates the flow of information upon which real help can begin, and my basic goodness is told where to put itself when I follow its emerging signal from far in the distance. My selling stones show me the way to help, and when I listen to the grand array, the tone and frequency is like an invisible hand guiding my instincts."

KENT'S INTEGRATION

Kent found the bridge between two worlds that are interdependently connected. During a trip through Oaxaca City Mexico with his wife Jen, Kent finds himself (on day two) visiting one of many beautiful Catholic churches around the plaza in the center of town. In the entry way, the light coming through the door beamed on one block on the cement floor as Kent looked up to find a large statue of Mary of Guadalupe.

A skinny seventy-year-old man was seen on his knees with his palms clinched in a fist out in front. His bags full of fruit, vegetables, and

414

grain were set to his sides as this little man looked up to the Virgin's face. As Kent looked through the view finder of his camera, tears welled up as this old man's devotion to this the spirit of the Virgin was filling every ounce of his attention.

As the man lifted his palms in the air as if to imbue a spiritual installation, Kent broke down from crying out of control. His wife Jen entered, as she saw the man, she turned to Kent to see he was in deep sorrow and very touched emotionally by the old man's connection to this figure and receptivity for divine intervention. Kent had never encountered this level of vulnerability, as if the old man's faith was the life-giving nutrition needed to stabilize his being.

Sharing power with the Virgin spirit meant to give permission to the reception of potential energies and that animate life. To grant such power to a mythological figure made real regressed Kent back to his infancy when everything was looked upon magically. He saw just how tender and dependent he was on worthy caregivers to bring him safely into the next stage of development. He had forgotten this mythical, magical part of himself and this situation was helping him reclaim a lost or hidden part of his being that he forgot to connect with fully.

As Kent slowly backed away and back outside where the sun was shining on his face, he connected that moment with who he is, and what his work in the world might be if it were made true. Kent had an experience that connected different parts of his life spectrum as if each was linking them together from past to present. When Kent found himself in a client appointment the following week, he was looser, less preoccupied with the outcome and more interested in helping instead of getting the deal.

Kent's assistant Coleen was struck by Kent's warmth and contagious way of listening that she commented to him that something was different. To add to this, the client sent Kent a heartfelt note letting him know how understood they felt and that Kent was a great listener. In fact, what struck Kent most was that the client pre-ordered two years of product in advance and elected to do all their business through Kent's company going forward. The account upgrade was a 350% increase.

DEBUNKING THE HYPE

Salespeople are prone to human potential dogma. They are allured by the magic powers that gurus tell them is within them and have yet to use it.

Many performers organize their lives around drawing attention to what makes them unique and special, making every attempt to look and appear noticed and different. Somewhere along their lifeline, they feared that if they looked and appeared the same, losses would occur.

Then the materialism fetishes and pimp factor are added to the need to look unique and special, like a tattoo or nose ring makes someone stand out. The nice car, home, dress code, way of acting, where to eat, and the type of gym—all the style is like a costume party to allure the person they want to sell to. It's amazing that some of these people can't come close to affording any of it, and yet think they can camouflage this by looking like a big shot. Plastic surgery gets expensive when you pay the price of appearing made up to be a phony, to control the world in some way. Meanwhile, all the bills from fixing yourself up like an expensive Ferrari becomes so consuming that the kids are raised by baby-sitters, not you.

Perhaps the next seminar can give them the super-powers they need to lower the kryptonite and level up. Maybe the positive thinking and affirmations that they are legendary to fake it until you make it will one day land the lottery. Selling has been a profession of misrepresentation and fakery, instead of being real and authentic. Looking the part without the substance is like counterfeit money. And looking like a top gun sales legend is a lot different than creating value for people. The focus gets diluted in "I'm not enough," therefore "I need to look and be seen a certain way" to get what I want. It's fakery over personal values.

That being said, ask yourself why you the salesperson needs to work on your deficiencies? You have so many beautiful gifts and strengths to take aim with, so why do you attempt to plug up the holes in yourself? Why can't you come by your weaknesses honestly, know them, and either overwhelm them with a hyper focus on your strengths and/or manage them by finding others to offload? If you focus on your deficiencies, over time, you'll have a lot of strong ones, but then miss out on the glory of your strengths.

People who work on their deficiencies make their creative process about overcoming themselves, their obstacles, and their quirks. This is not what professional creators talk about in bringing their creations into life. If you sit down with an artist, they don't look inward, clean up their negative thinking and/or self-doubt, work on themselves, none of it. They are involved in creating their creations. Working on themselves would be at best a hobby, but more of a distraction.

You are incomplete and do not need to fix yourself, your quirks, your attitudes unless some behavior is directly in the way of what you seek to create. But be mindful, the focus should not be on you. Creating as a habit is by nature focused on creations, not yourself. And that is where your focus is best, 3rd person, not 1st person. The more you attempt to focus on yourself---self-improvement, the lousier creator you will be. And the less you'll be present to things going on your life. Being pre-occupied with inadequacies is like putting a wall between yourself and living the life that is here this moment. Everything and everyone as you view them gets compared to your opinion of yourself.

If you try to lie to yourself---pretend to be what you are not, you lose a certain level of respect for yourself. Chanting affirmations to yourself is like fooling yourself into a false reality. Who but a person that would need to affirm this so intensely would be someone who didn't have it? Who but a person what would need to chant how successful they are would be someone who was not? The affirmation begets the underlying belief that one is not enough.

Like most of us, you are afraid to let it all hang out. We all love to belong; in fact, it is part of nature, but approval-seeking doesn't have to be all-or-nothing. It is liberating to let yourself be, and leave fixing yourself in the bleachers, to become the predominant, preeminent creative force in your life. In fact, you've probably noticed that when you focus in such a way you are separate from the outcomes that occur. Whether you fail or succeed, without your identify infused in the process, you can use failures as powerful assets for learning and strategic adjustment. Yet too often you think what happens defines you in some way---which you are a good or bad person. You're the only one keeping score on this.

You don't need to believe in what you're going after, in fact, you can't until what you want comes to fruition. You cannot predict the future; you can create a future.

To create it, you must have a place to go---a vision or goal from which you organize actions today. Second, you must report the truth to yourself. This isn't easy, but it is an acquired skill. Self-honesty is the capacity to show up and remain present to what is going on without editorial. You come to terms with your expectations, perceptions, and interpretations to ensure they aren't in use when unchecked for validity. As a value creator for others, to help, you first commit yourself to truth-telling just like it is---the facts!

This capacity is important because it gives you a leap off point; a point "A" from which to begin the creative process. And creating value for another person or business is at its most basic level---a creative process. You begin with a desired state that is wanted for its own sake, and then establish a current state by contrast. This purports the needs for actions, not just any action, but "informed action" that do service to the desired state. Sounds simple? Almost so simple that it is hard.

We don't need to make creating value for others a process driven by a psychological view. When we make it about this, the process becomes about you instead of bringing value to the other. Listening as act of articulating what is valuable to another person is listening into their world.

POSSESSION

There is a form of possession that I like to talk about, and it isn't demonic or weird. It is the topic of possessing ourselves. Letting go is, to me, the process of letting something other than ourselves possess us, inspire us, touch or move us, astonish us, pull us outside the familiar and challenge us. It is the generous permission for what is not us to change us.

We spend most of our adult life attempting to possess---ourselves, others, and life. We attempt to control things to go our way instead of the alternative. We are violated by differences. Disruptive change isn't friendly to our nervous systems.

So, if we aren't operating from our agendas to possess like this, what is left beneath or beyond it? We enter a world, a dimension of life that isn't explainable and doesn't have to be. Words possess us because they don't have the same meaning for each of us. Yet in the world I'm describing lives a field of possibility, flow, and energy that doesn't hide in words. It is not able to be named. The minute we name something, we fixate it in time; we make it static. When we claim we know something it commands obedience. What is not this loses its place to be there; it is disconfirming. We then confirm to habits born from what we can explain; what we know.

Nothing stays the same. You can see this as you walk, moment to moment, through your life experiences. Some are consistent with what you can know or explain, while other moments aren't in compliance with or consistent with what you know. What if you realize that you don't know how you know what you know? What if after all this you know nothing? If certainty were suspended, what then would be left? Asking this question, I've noticed things I haven't before now. Life gets more interesting looking at from nothing. After all, being alive starts with nothingness. Our brains fill up our thinking with knowns which seek to maintain our experience instead of our inexperience.

To maintain our inexperience, we must look at our brain from another place----mind! The mind is our awareness, the place from which we see through the brain. When the brain is quiet, we can see without the distortion of our habitual judgment. Judgement isn't the enemy per se, we need it to discern what is going on, but pre-meditated judgment can be very disturbing to see what is really going on. To be aware is to observe something else---an object or thing that is separate from the observer. This would imply that the mind is the regulator of thoughts produced by the brain, which is the mechanism.

The mind is the browser, while the Brain stores concepts from which at attempt to reuse as a source of sense-making of what is going on. Unchecked, the sense-making can be treated as fact, when the concept is non-fact. Hence, when we construe our concepts to be facts, we see what we perceive rather than perceive what we see. Learning to see is to see our own seeing, which is suggesting that we see our automatic mind stuff from another place—the observer. Who is doing the observing? Nothingness.

START WITH NOTHING

Nothing isn't the opposite of something. It is the space behind, around, and in, and outside everything and everyone. Nothingness is what brings being into being. It is your ground of being in groundlessness. Therefore, it is not empty, but the place from which all things begin; the source; the fundamental space from which creation comes.

If creativity moves through you like a vessel or channel, you access these sources of creation from previous chapters. These capacities are suspension, redirection, and letting go. Shame, fear, and judgment are no longer primary to what is experienced, instead, nothingness is met with alacrity. Will and willingness come together to enact from a grand will, one that supplements your individual will. This is the fundamental reality that is awareness seeking the unpossessed awareness in you.

If you touch down to this space and backup enough behind what you're doing right now, you can connect with places of potential like a matchstick lit by a spark. Selling without nothingness is disturbed by what you already know. Since you're full of knowns, you have no vacancy for something new to come. Seeing anew is outlawed by seeing what you already know. 90% of selling begins from downloading this way instead of coming freshly.

What if you sell separate from what you know? What then, by coming from this space could move? What intention might make itself appear for you to imbue it? This intention isn't coming from what you know; it is coming from the potentiality of pure space made conscious. What is not there becomes there. But if you drift away, wandering off to reconfirm what you already know, the experience is less interesting. You are under the possession of habituated thought. Concepts replace nothingness as to block the reception from letting go into pure space. Concepts keep pure space from seizing you, like the way one is captured by attraction, or astonished by the stars on a clear night sky.

As a seller, we are told that to have a method, a process we'll have more potency in our ability to create value for easy buyers as well as the tougher ones who are more conservative, the laggards. The challenge with over-reliance on a method is that you cling to it when moments of opportunity require difference response than what stays in compliance with the method.

There's certainly merit in having a system but be careful not to believe that it'll make your success happen for you. The most important aspect of selling is connecting with the deepest sources of your most honest expression. Often times getting there requires a stronger determination early on to master the fundamentals, such that you know these so well that it goes automatic.

Beyond the technical dedication is a level of trust and adaptability that begins with such a high level of skill that determination is no longer necessary. Usually, people that need so much determination to create what they want aren't very good yet at what they do. But through the school of transactions, you go into the marketplace and by getting the check time after time you develop a wisdom from which you increase your adaptation from instincts that become available.

If you watch great athletes or entertainers, football quarterbacks reach such a high level of skill that this takes over. This has an interesting impact on the motivation to train, develop and work on their game. At first, their motivation was full of the determination to prove themselves and get to a desired level of playing the game. After this phase, they begin to integration their own self-expression and manner of looking at the game and playing from their own wisdom. They have a philosophic framework to orient them, a set of guiding ideas that are based on deeper values, and the tools that keep them playing at their highest possible levels of the game.

Bruce Lee's personal philosophy of life was based on freight-train dedication to the method to get to a place where the reliance on the method is replaced by using one's honest self-expression to adapt to the challenge presented in each fighting environment. Technical mastery led to an organic process of fighting. Bruce became so skilled at this art that he could invent different responses which instinctively interrupted his opponent's readiness and expectations.

Bruce said that "martial arts" at its essence is honest self-expression. Every fight would require him to start with nothing and trust his instincts by letting the method fall away and be like "water to fit the cup." His concept, "mind like water", meant to be soft and powerful like water to adapt to the opponent as the source of how to intercept the fighter to defeat him. This flexibility is what Bruce taught his students to know themselves so well internally and their method such that they were able to meet the challenge of the emerging fight and draw forth the capacity like a warrior would be so open, to do whatever is necessary.

DRAWING INTO OURSELVES AND BACK OUT

As we grow up, our parents and others around us often bring us into core beliefs from which we compose our manner of living. Early on, Tom's parents' divorce had him questioning if it was his fault. The myth he made true and the one he began to live by was that he wasn't enough to keep his parents together. He believed that to control fallouts like these, especially ones where your heart is left out to dry, they must be protected by only himself and nobody else. Tom's generalization was that the "world is an unfriendly place with takers housed in the people around him." To defend this threat, Tom elected to live self-enclosed with himself as his best friend. He found that self-sex gave him a way to sooth his own needs. It was his way of preemptively avoiding the fallout of someone else pleasing or delighting himself, so he literally delivered on demand his own delight.

Later on, Tom turned to short term sexual relationships with women and earning lots of money with which to pay women to please him. Again, all of this was under Tom's self-enclosed control system to regulate outsiders from hurting or fooling him. Tom didn't trust anyone. After years of going into isolation to negate the phantoms he saw around him in others, Tom became a cynical critic of the world as if nothing was ever good enough for him.

Dana, Tom's latest hot sex partner, was Tom's best entertainment yet, except Dana dropped Tom like a hot potato. After days of tracking her down, Tom found Dana in a bar making a list of all her boyfriends. Dana took Tom to a table away from everyone and started crying. She longed to have a long term committed relationship in her life, but said Tom was another one of many short term temporary hits that made her feel wanted for her sexual talents, not her whole self.

Dana's manipulation of Tom was to get in and get out fast enough before the ceiling came down and she'd be trapped in dependencies. Dana had made it her primary focus to depend on nobody, because to her, Tom was full of danger and mistrust just like everyone in the world. It was if Tom had looked in the mirror and saw his own face for the first time. Dana was just as afraid as he was about people. The universe was, according to both of them, an unfriendly, scary place. Tom felt like an object to Dana, not a person. Being reduced to a source of entertainment was so small that it made Tom open his eyes to see what he was creating. That night Tom called the help hotline of a family therapist, Judy. Judy mentioned that Tom had kept himself safe, locked inside, and away from his model of a dangerous world.

"What would you be if you didn't believe the world was dangerous and untrustworthy, Tom?" Judy asked in a grounding voice. "What would be possible if you cut loose your model of the world, Tom?" Tom broke down because all the pain he'd held inside was never expressed in grief and loss. Tom had sealed off the world, his shame went toxic, and the pain was kept down deep. Tom saw his own blind-spot when Judy said, "What you see is what you get, Tom." He could see how the world he thought was the world he continuously created because of a "cognitive reflex." The reflex meant that Tom's belief possessed his attention such that all he was inclined to see confirmed his suspicions. When Tom's belief went live, his behavior kept anything counter to his belief outside, off the radar. And when Tom keep people at bay in superficial ways, he made them so invisible that literally no one would love him. Everything continued to appear to be mean and vicious to Tom, consistent with his belief.

Judy went on to explain that we see what we perceive rather than perceive what we see." Tom started to see the motivation that made the story of his life clear. He'd isolated people because he deep down had a belief that he wasn't worthy of love. In fact, Tom learned that he had become fluent in understanding his unwanted belief of himself. Then Judy said something very disturbing: "Whatever you think of yourself, Tom, doesn't have anything to do with what you long to create—in your dreams and aspirations. You can choose to be true to yourself and reconnect to that inner voice that talks to you about what you want most."

Tom Davis had setup his life to avoid being hurt again, but his preemptive strike to throttle back from being loving or caring toward the world and his future was blocked by his deeper belief system that he relied on for protection. Tom was like a porcupine with quills that ran others off because Tom deemed himself an unlovable creature. And to work around the pain, he setup a self-enclosed system to lubricate his pain with self sex, using women as pawns, and other ways to offset his discomfort.

Judy encouraged Tom to turn toward his unwanted belief, and access the underlying hurt and pain that fueled this obedience, and made himself impenetrable by the world. Tom buried his pain every time he looked for the quick fix to feel ok. Tom found out later that Dana was a heroin addict and three months after her recovery she said the heroin was like getting a warm hug from a mother who she could depend on without loss. The pretend hug felt safe, but today Dana sees it was superficially imposed through a faux thriller, heroin. Now it was Dana's step on her journey to meet life again and to meet herself as a loving being and know a world full of loving beings.

Dana had replaced her fear of depending on people because she saw them as enemies, not loving beings. But after opening her eyes to this model of the world she had held so tightly, she elected to let it go to see what else the world could be...what she saw were beings just as afraid and timid as she was. And that by knowing we are all on the same bus, she could bare her wounds safely as a way to connect with others and their quality of love deep inside. She had let go of her certainties about the world and opened her heart to other possibilities.

Dana took Tom out of lunch after starting her second life. She told him that she was learning to "stay fluent" and in tune with what was going on---with her, with her current reality. She explained that the heroin was her way of leaving herself instead of staying in touch with what she was experiencing. Dana learned that staying with her experience was a great choice because she was separate from whatever was going. She was not her emotions, her moods, and her pain, in fact, she could backup and stay aware of anything despite what was happening in the present---good, bad, hard, easy, ugly, or soft. She said she could live again because she checked back into life and everything suddenly got more interesting. Then she said that when you learn to stay like this, and not escape what is going on right now, you can choose what to focus on. When she sold the IT cloud systems with her employer, the next sales appointment brought this aspect with her.

Before going into the meeting, she was preoccupied with her shame. Her opinion of herself as someone recovering from addiction made her think poorly of herself. Her coach/boss mentioned that it's ok to have that; in fact, it can be treated as an invited guest, and by staying in touch with it, Dana could shift her focus on what she chooses. "I choose...," Dana said inside herself. Then she filled in the sentence with what outcome she wanted from the consultation she was leading. During the meeting, she worried about the prospect finding out about her recovery process. She stayed fluent with that, and yet brought her attention back to what was most important. After several pivots from self-talking about her opinion of herself back to creating the outcome, it got easier to command her attention where it mattered most. After she got the check, and a new happy prospect became a customer, she reflected that her opinion of herself didn't matter when it came to create a new relationship—or creating anything. She cut loose her old opinion of herself and focused on her creation. Her boss reminded her that she already knew how to do this, and she just needed to remember how. It was like the time she made her first child. The entire focus was on the child, not her mother. With the new-found shift to a more creative orientation, Dana became more and more skilled at her creative process, and whether it be cooking, working out, building new accounts, creating a new relationship, she was integrating the discipline of personal mastery into her manner of living. Everything she was creating made her feel more involved in life. And after creating several wins, she used these as a platform upon which further creations were generated.

Dana Miller learned that creating isn't concerned with identity. What she thought of herself wasn't relevant to the creative process. She didn't need to hide from her unwanted beliefs. Instead she stayed fluent with what she actually thought, and focused on other matters---

ideas, desires, and outcomes she chose to create. While creating, she was unsure of herself, full of doubt, second-guessing herself, and yet stayed focus on creating. This shocked Tom, because he was certain positive thinking, will-power manipulation, and conflict manipulation was central to her creating, but none of it was. She didn't need positive thinking or affirmation to hide her unwanted belief, which would have been positive lying. She didn't need will-power manipulation because the focus wasn't on herself. Instead, the love for her outcomes became her primary catalyst for creating. And conflict manipulation would have motivated her to remove unwanted circumstances or bad parts she deemed in herself, which wouldn't have had any lasting motivation, just problem-solving with short term energy. Instead, Dana learned that creating at its best is about love. She learned that the generative side of love is what motivates outcomes she created for their own sake. Like creating music, Dana brought into focus what mattered most to her and created it as the centerpiece of organizing all of her choices.

Tom discovered that people in the recovery movement who subscribe to a lot of popular self-help techniques are lousy creators. Those who work on themselves invite an unwanted belief they are the problem and must fix what is blocking their potential---their confidence, will, all that. Dana explained that Tom could go down that road, but why bother? Tom could fix his quirks and still not create what wants!

After joining Dana's team, they defined a shared vision of an outcome and modified their strengths to weaknesses to be a dependable team to each other. Soon after they went onto creating the #1 sales position in the company's ranks, adding three hundred new accounts to the business in their first 18 months. And, soon after, Tom created a marriage with the love of his life and found that creating what mattered to him drew forth his best energy for the future, enthusiasm for life, and motivation to learn and build uncommon skill levels. As he created new business his new-found skills were so clear that he didn't need any determination because he became so good at what he does.

Dana and Tom meet for 1 hour every week to reflection on what they're creating and see all sides of current reality to get a clear, constructive picture together with shared understanding. They look at numbers, their sales opportunities, their process, their personal habits, their supporting team, and their current customers as an entire system. Constantly refining their vision of current reality, Tom and Dana use failures as assets. They keep their opinions of themselves and each other out of the picture, because none of their beliefs are valid. They tell the truth of what is presenting itself just as it actually is appearing, and continue to suspend their old models of reality to see the data more deeply and, as if was speaking to them in picturing it.

Every quarter Dana and Tom consolidate their gains by listing their goals, accomplishments, exploring the reasons why they achieved them or didn't, and what to strategically adjust on in order to make further progress toward their desired outcome. They called this process "consolidating their gains" or as Tom would say, "The Completion Process" by accepting their creations and living with them. Tom would say that the most fascinating part of creating something is you get to live in the universe of your creation.

What makes Dana and Tom consistently at the top of their game is structural tension. They establish this all the time as the primary organizing force of their sales efforts to create and maintain clients. This means constantly knowing where they want to be compared to where they actually are now, and setting an informed foot into actions required to create the desired outcome. They see creating and learning as the same. By proposing new actions different from what they conventionally know, Dana and Tom are always pulled by new ways of creating business to suit the next goal they have in mind. Because goals change behavior, Tom and Dana set goals that matter to them most, and when they do this, it brings them into a higher quality of expression and action in service to the goals. They embody what they create.

Drawing ourselves inward and then back out is a process of shifting from internal focus to an external one. We find ourselves inside ourselves all too often, attempting to shape the outside to offset what we don't like inside. Instead, going back out is leaving our identities out the door and focusing on what we choose to create. Tom, a guy from a hurtful past, closed his heart off by believing the world was unfriendly, and learned how to use the creative process to tap into his desire to create a working relationship with Dana, one with an atmosphere of trust that brings shared vision and shared understanding to a whole new level.

Tom didn't need self-improvement for this; he changed the underlying structure to structural tension. Dana Miller recovered from using substances like heroin in an attempt to leave herself. After recovery, Dana learned how to use the creative process to organize her life and build great value with Tom's help. The genius of structural tension is that we can change our lives and behavior by changing the structural dynamics that govern us. By leaving our identity out, and starting creations from what we don't know, we can bring our hearts' desires to life by staying with current reality as we go and keeping true to what we aspire to bring into world. When we create from love, we become it. We embody what we create.

CHAPTER 15

DISPLACEMENT

When you sell, you probably prepare your process, anticipate objections, and rehearse your presentation. You attempt to know what will be required when you get there. That's like a singer knowing how the concert will go. You probably know where I'm going with this. No situation is ever the same.

I've taught selling skills to coaching clients for over two decades. And what I'm always staggered by is about 70% of it is never used. For example, Jason goes in to present a powerful of his online web services to a large OEM manufacturer. After the meeting, we debriefed and found that there was the "real meeting" and the "expected meeting." He said that in the real meeting the two executives were intimidated by Jason because it exposed their vulnerabilities. In fact, selling this up to their boss meant looking stupid. Where is Jason's hard-prepped presentation in all of this? Nowhere!

As you get more experienced, you come into situations starting at zeroes. You are ready for anything and expecting nothing. It's as if you're unconditionally in a constructive state no matter shows up. What can you do to be ready in such a way? Stillness. When you let go of thinking and anticipating, you come into the situation with peace. You aren't attempting to control something you are assuming you need to control. This brings you into a powerful ability to listen. You aren't listening from what you know; rather you are listening to what emerges from the whole---the situation, the energy, and the stories of those there, the collective field in the space. You actually participate in a collective dream. The stillness helps an exclusion occur, such that you're so empty, that you're able to be with everyone you meet in new and available ways of paying attention. The exclusion can bring about what you desire. You see from all eyes in the collective field. I call this "social design sourcing" or "social presencing." Connection first, content second.

CONNECTION FIRST, CONTENT SECOND

So where are you in all of this? What will you do with your new voice to establish expertise and be someone worthy of respect? You don't even go there. You displace yourself by re-calibrating your attention to highlighting the presence of other people there. You look for and emphasize, notice, and take in the movement happening between you in the space. Giving power to empty space to give rise to collective social presencing is an amazing field of power you can occupy. This may sound weird, but collective intelligence is when you are nobody granting power to the collective. "Us" in this sense is shifting from I to We. This social fiend has genesis in its origins. Empowerment to the other (the field, them, we) is very generous; it is self-decentralized. Sales persons describe this shift as an uplifting feeling because they claim there's a less contracted, wiser and relaxed attention they can give to the space.

The flow patterns of energy/information from which this space has permission to flow is like convection current running between players in a jazz trio improvising together. Each one feeds off the pattern of interaction with the other. They learn it is ok to be generous and build it into their performing. The stream in between is coming and going like a 2-lane highway going both ways. There is circularity of generosity and reception as sharing is acted up with major consequences. We the audience are moved by the music that arises from this connection. You cultivate those qualities in the mind that serve others but make you happy simultaneously. It is a clever way to enjoy life, and I recommend you help yourself to it.

You can see that how you are isn't fixed, and that the creative process of your life is a creative process. The brain can change through what you do, by applying mindfulness to selling and seeding the actions and behaviors that arise from generosity in value creation. You are witnessing how things are arising and passing in momentary experience. The transformative power of it is when you're seeing it. The body is a field of its energy that is in constant flow, and when linked with others', the collective combination makes for service to another human a natural force. It brings the best out of you.

There is a place in communicating where your conversation appears to be original. It is not yours, nor theirs, but it is carrying emerging information you are becoming familiar with as you deepen your understanding and listening together. The conversation itself replaces any self-ownership with a shared collective social field that changes by the participation of its parts, just as it informs the manner of participation. Touch a finger to the water, and water touches the finger. The finger is to know it and be known.

Any experience in which expectations of it are assigned as valid is an illusion. This is because oncoming experiences which are different can and will invalidate what was once real. Explanations are for those that want to know things properly. Explanations that we accept are like pacifiers. We stop asking questions. We stop reflecting.

The conversion has its own creative process, as if it were the third person in the room. What is this interconnected field? Is it unity consciousness becoming known through open minds? It is the one that goes into the two back into the one? Like a jazz trio, it is the internal correlations inbound and outbound from and to this collective field. It is transformative by way of aesthetic presence.

This best way of relating to the field is to show up with all senses open to receiving what is ready to emerge. When certain activity in the connectivity of the whole, an interconnected nerve system informs its parts. The parts related via the arising configuration of the whole which are inextricably linked to the branches. This organic process of sharing and doing things together from this place is what I call "conversation animation."

A superordinate force from which everything is bound informs the basic goodness in each fractal to imbue its flow patterns of energy and information in an operative flow. A fractal is an uncompromised representation of the whole in one aspect of it. What is inbound is an emotional choice to accept as valid input. The jazz players unblock the inbound stream to inform their activity in this manner. They receive the transmissions via a trust in the coherences of living without independence from the whole.

A musician in an orchestra brings is his own niche. He integrates himself into the whole, who are depending on him. Yet the sound originating from the whole orchestra doesn't point to or distinguish the independent voice. Niche is significantly configured by the whole, and the whole is integrated to imbue the dynamics of the niche. The operation of the niche is breathed into by the operational coherence with the unbroken whole.

What is to know? If you are saying that what another is doing is right, you are giving them their knowledge. You define, in your listening, what you accept as valid as to what he or she knows. We accept as valid as to what confirms with what we think and construct our world to be. What you know seeks to be satisfied in reinforcing certainty.

A different level of understanding can come when paying attention and a profound truth emerges. An essential quality from you is transferred to another human being. When you attempt to predict things, you are gripped by fear. And when things don't play out how you modeled it, you are angered. Fear and anger cause us to cling to things staying a certain way. Both are ways of saying no to the moment as it is now. We look for things to repeat a certain way as we expect them to be. Yet, when you're mindful you can live with experience without grasping, holding, or keeping it, contrary to the truth that everything is changing. When you open your heart, you are available to this flow of experience without holding on.

Exercise: Stillness Meditation before the Sales Appointment: After closing your eyes, sitting quietly and taking ten deep breathes, ask yourself these questions:

What do I want to create?
How can I serve?
What do I hear?
What am I paid for?

The question of what you seek to create is a question taking you into a creative orientation. It's the intention question. Where am I aiming to go? You don't expect this; you want this. It is an end you deeply desire. It is what your heart wants.

The question about how you can serve is a question of the spirit of the intention. This might connect you to a large sense of purpose, conviction or calling that is sitting in your heart's intention. This is like asking the timeless eye looking through your eyes (the big mind), what stands in need of you.

The question is a scanning and browsing question asking your current state what is ready to climb out or emerge. You hear a story in motion.

The question about what you are paid for is about your truest asset in business, your gifts and talents and your application of knowledge. It

440

is the most valuable and unique quality that human beings seek when they seek a relationship with you and your team. It is the "magnet" question.

Arming yourself with these questions is like chalking the billiard stick to make a strong contact with the cue ball in pool. You have your best state of mind online, and your concentration is hot.

Buyers get frozen when a salesperson is needy---needing attention, agreement, control, an answer, a yes, a sale, a win in the sales contest, a trip to Hawaii incentive; whatever is centered on the sales person's field of influence. The energy is divided and minimized by individualism. But what if the potential for value creation emerged from a collective space? It isn't just about oneself, or about the other, the buyer in this case. But it's about you and them, the space itself, as if this was the dominant, governing feature supplying the opportunity and allowing trust to surface. Turning people away from you is an interesting alternative to helping others find something interesting inside themselves. Turning people toward you denies them of this internal experience.

Most traditional selling is about getting attention, get people to notice you, and trust you. But what cultivates trust isn't this, it's about how interested you are in taking their attention off you and onto the space itself. How can you create the context for this to happen?

The conversation itself is this container to begin diverting the attention from you to something else.

REDEFINITION

You understand that this sales gig you do is greater, larger, something more cosmic, cool, and made just for you to meet the greatest qualities that live deep within you. How neat is it that you get to help people get what they really want?

The people you help can't directly inherit this magical quality you have because they're certain about where they need help. This presents a serious challenge, because to help you have to participate in a powerful redefinition process. The journey into this redefinition is truly about letting go. The key to the door is how you create an atmosphere of trust to do this, and how the other (one needing help) is willing to unlearn their heavy certainties about what they're seeking and expecting.

At first, you'll begin moving in to look like the expert, but this keeps you prisoner of your own methods and certainties just like the buyer has you pegged as a "sales-person." In actuality, most sales consultations start with two video recorders talking to each other---both of you are organizing your perceptions from the past, not the present.

Redefinition starts with your perceptions. First, make a conscious choice to stop pushing, talking, saying, advocating, presenting---it's all unilateral bullshit. People don't care what you know until they know you care. Appearing you care isn't the same as actually caring. Getting interested begins with stopping all your thoughts, plans, and attempts to manipulate and control the buyer into obeying your command. If you claim you know something, automatically you're inserting a command for obedience.

Rid yourself of any need to affirm your importance. As much as you crave attention, it doesn't serve you or the buyer to organize power via looking like the hero. Stop being one. The buyer is not a victim; they are a creator capable of living, learning, and making things happen. So, you're not the answer to their problems, nor the fixture for their tragedies. You're a *success ally* who is able to bring your attention out from a humanity-centered place, such that the divine force within is able to cooperate with meeting emerging needs that help the buyer understand better.

You're not selling anything but a transformative conversation, which begins with getting the buyer a new sense of direction. You surrender to the possibility of this natural order and help the buyer yield to something new, and different from what their past tells them to evaluate. You exempt both you and the buyer from the jurisdiction of your own biases.

Taking ownership is overrated and out of touch with what is true for the human experience. You don't own what you say, do, feel, and think, it is shared by relationship. Authenticity isn't a singular game; it's a plural one

Taking ownership is a way of seeking protection from just how vulnerable you are to a world of incidents, others, and everything that can access and change you.

Half of you at best takes ownership, but the other half is receptive and open when you're true to your experiences. Properties in people are only known by the patterns of interaction in relationship with something other.

CHAPTER 16

PROFESSIONALLY UNCONVENTIONAL

The Art of Being Professionally Unconventional

Leaving a lasting impression is more difficult than it was ten to fifteen years ago. People's attention spans are distracted with the complexity of life. What can we do to respond to this growing epidemic and thrive in our business?

Answer: Be "professionally unconventional" in all aspects. I call this P.U. for short. That means stinking up the joint, leaving our mark. Here are five strategies to being PU:

PU #1: Make conversations the core imperative of what you sell
If you're focused on what you're selling, you may be falling into a dangerous trap that impedes your personal freedom and limits the level of value you create in the eyes of your buyers. Your buyer doesn't value what you do for the problems you solve for him, rather, he values your ability to make him think about and reflect on the challenges that he has before him.

One of my favorite coaching stories in the war chest was a remark I heard after asking my client Jim how he'd rate the quality of the session. He replied, "John this is the first time I've actually thought in three years." "Thought?" I asked. He was sincere. This was the first time he had a chance to think about his current reality and his desired future. He said he'd gotten too busy being busy to do something that could make him a lot less busy. Work had become so incessantly frenetic for him that any pause became hostile territory. This led him to a sense of chronic powerlessness, worthlessness, confusion, and disappointment.

Getting Jim to consider his three-year future, really see deeper into the roots of his challenges, recognize opportunities to harvest, and position his strengths toward his aims were the fundamental game-changers for him. At this point, it became clear to me that entrepreneurs who leave their mark have conversations that change lives, not products. And that business is a networked series of conversations strung together that position businesses for extraordinary value creation.

When we make conversations our top priority in what we sell, we find better questions to ask. Not presentations, I said "conversations!" These conversations return a sense of power and hope in our clients. We empower them to get on top of solutions through settings we create for them to think clearly. And when we get closer to our market on the inside like this—their future, challenges, opportunities, and strengths—we have a rich landscape of ingredients, to create powerful recipes through our business solutions. We can give clients what they really need in the 21st century world of complexity—power, confidence, creativity, and direction. And this makes us very difficult to commoditize.

PU #2: Conduct Random Acts of Appreciation That Are Sincere

It's been said that "what we appreciate, appreciates!" When we show others gratitude, we maintain their support and involvement as a key supply line to sustaining our success. Often times, brimming new opportunities turns our attention away from who got us here in the first place. The natural order of such neglect moves toward shortages, not abundance.

Think of how many people's unique and distinguished abilities contributed to your life to bring you to where you are now. I'll bet you could say five thank-you's a day from your heart to heroes in your life. They put their time, effort, money, and trust into you for a great value to them. They have helped you lead and help others and pay forward the dedication and devotion that helped get you to your place in life today.

So, don't forget what got you here. Don't cut the supply lines of support and fan ship that hold you up. Don't hold onto something because you're afraid others will take it away. Share it and make space for new and more to come. Being grateful involves giving away what you have. It's a principle of abundance and confidence.

Sixty-seven percent of all relationships, personal and professional, end because of lack of recognition. People have two needs you undeniably have to fill in your home and work relationships to keep them participating in your life. They need to feel heard and feel important. *Don't be interesting, get interested.* Really take a closer look at what you're doing to meet these two needs. You want to be priority to them, meet these needs first. And if you want to have your needs met, start by meeting others'. You want to be listened to, start listening. You want to feel important, be considerate of people's time, qualities, and gifts.

PU# 3: Focus on what you believe, not what you sell

Imagine going into any insurance agency to buy the lowest premium "the minimum insurance limits." Suddenly the salesperson asks you permission to make sure he's clear on your expectations. He begins his story by imagining it's…

> … "7am and you just picked up a cup of hot coffee from Starbucks and get on the 405 fwy at 70 mph. Suddenly your coffee spills all over your lap, and it's burning your leg. You look down to address the situation and seconds later KABOOM, you just slammed into the center divider, suddenly 4 Dodge 300's slam into you. Do you want to pay for the parts of those cars or their drivers' hospital bills as well?"

The salesperson gave me the sincerest look in his eyes and said, "I'll only insure you if it's right. Otherwise we can't work together." I respected his convictions. I believed in what he was believing, so I bought the "right" coverage. His belief and his story made me emotional. I didn't buy insurance that day, I bought the preventive cost of those people's hospital bills and did the right thing.
People don't buy what you sell; they buy *the way* you sell. And the way you sell is underscored by what you believe. They buy what you believe because this way they do it for their reasons, not yours.

PU #4: Listen from Heart and Soul, not the Head

The greatest gift you can give someone is a listening presence, not a listening person. A listening presence is a stance in a conversation where you've suspended all your judgment. You're poised as unconditionally constructive. Try to assume that the person is doing their very best despite the fact that what you're getting may not be.

Listening presently means detaching from the past. It means to let go of the control over any outcome in the future. Being present with someone brings out our highest capacity of being because we're not worrying over what they think of us, and what we think of ourselves. What's left is just presence, as if every fear, cynicism, and judgment were stripped away, and what's left is you as the source from which your attention arises. You must have the courage to step in this way. Be bold enough to face yourself; no impressions or projections.

But this takes some practice to lower the chatterbox in your head and attend fully with others. Create a space daily of 15-minute intentional silence to strengthen your levels of awareness. When you're standing in the presence of the open heart, and the open will, you're attending from the other person's world, not your own. The downloading of all the rules, dogma, and thoughts no longer drive your responses. You enter with alacrity, full embodiment, and openness as if the words were flowing through you like a deep channel. When you connect with this place, your inner knowing emerges, and you listen from a larger context.

You begin operating from the standpoint of being in the world, and the world being in you. Like the sculptor, Erik Lemke would say, "My hands are suddenly taken over by a natural order and would know what to adjust as if I was pulled by something more than my own doings."

When you attend to another human with such willingness and simply listening from them, you become a powerful sounding board to track what they say. They can see themselves through you in profound ways. You may find that as you open yourself and become vulnerable without all the answers, you find a strong sense of connection to the person you're with. They sense the tenderness in you, the kindness, and generosity that helps them seek a relationship with you. By letting your guard down, and being reachable, so are they.

This means being respectful of other people's time and keeping your agreements. Be polite and say thank you, and finish what they count on you for. When you do this, it compliments them so highly. In fact, they'll open any doors for you, because they know they can depend on you and you've gone beyond what they expected.

And never underestimate the power and reach of a small act of kindness. That smile you gave to someone crossing the road could be resurrection to a suicidal person who's just given himself a second chance at life because he looked into you and woke up. If each person is a carrier of a sacred project, honor people for the vast treasure-chest of something in them; they're bringing something to the world that no one else can. You're like a midwife to others' personal gifts. When you see this in them, you've outgrown all your shame and will see your own gifts too, shining outward in the fullness of your potential.

PU #5: Throw out best practices, do it your way

Best practices are at best, *a myth*. Many entrepreneurs in our coaching program the VIP Coach are seeking answers and looking for the "best methods." They argue they want short cuts, "don't reinvent the wheel." But what they don't realize is the practices they seek are from the past. Those served someone else's goals, not theirs. This is why so often best practices fail by falling short. What people really want is deep involvement, and having a sense of what matters helps engage you in this profound way with the life that's here.

We seek answers because we don't trust our own. Rather than enjoy the journey and experiment, we get locked into a series of shortcuts, seeking to lower failure. Figuring it out is true innovation. It involves rethinking things, throwing out the past, re-circuiting around existing constraints, acting instantly and working through the learning process to cause something desired to exist.

Geniuses are not copycats. They come by their work in an authentic way. They develop their own tempo and unique style as a function of how they create. Every creation, whether it be a relationship, art, or any subject matter they seek is its own universe, from which they take specific actions, and they live within it after it's created.

THE GENIUS OF CLOCK SPEED

"Fierce alertness and agility come from having flexible attention with an open mind and heart, to act in an instant. Being reactive is very different than being responsive."

This is the whole point for Jim, my colleague who manages a dynamic top-notch sales team at Xerox. All he coaches his team on is "clock speed." "It's the number one critical success factor to great sales performance," so he claims.

"What if?!?" you ask yourself when you go into new territory with your business. You are creating separate from what you know as you grow. This requires a certain paranoia.

Jim calls himself DOCTOR DOOM because he's found his paranoia to be the most productive approach to channeling his fear as a guardian against potential failures. It motivates such intense preparation such that the weather systems that prevail rarely rock the boat and cause concentration loss.

Each time they train together, the team prepares swift comebacks on their buyer's most common pushbacks. Each individual is equipped with a repertoire of fast-action rebounds that eloquently and gently reset the buyer into a different way of thinking. Each helper is aiming to upend misunderstandings with compassion, not aggression. It's the capacity to immediately U-turn the prospect gracefully that makes all the difference.

TRUSTING THE BEAUTIFUL QUESTION

Conversations have life within them. They animate new content when you realize that everything you need to know is not in your head yet, it is right in front of you waiting to enter with beautiful question holding information. You must trust this with faith, as if the question already knows where you are, and is ready to be heard, but not embodied yet.

Every sale has a beautiful question standing in the center of it waiting for you to gather it up and bring it forth. Like a gift sitting in the environment, the question knows it is coming to harvest. What composes the question is the entire system in which the question is held in context. You live in a web of relationships that compose this question to be asked. It is a courageous attempt to belong to the world in which this question characterizes its total voice. The question belongs to where it's trying to go and survived by what brings it into reality, through your sensitivity.

How do you step aside for the question to have a placeholder within you? You suspend your certainties, begin with a blank slate, and follow your curiosity and wonder. As you begin, you may not sense the question surging from within you to reach your lips. It's not coming up right away. Holding the space for this is vital to opening the aperture for the question to take hold in you. You are like a midwife for the question, and the willingness you have to pay generous attention to it kick-starts its presence.

As you listen within, you also listen without. You involve and extend your attention into the person saying words toward you. You hear the person speaking in addition to the words, such that you let them change your interior condition. This "permeation" is a vulnerability to give yourself fully to attending to the other without any cynicism or disconnection. These sources of resistance short circuits your capacity to empathically listen to the other and cut the divide between you and them. You may sense within you energies of love, appreciation, acceptance, and a natural urge to lessen the suffering of the other.

All of this understanding captivates your attention in a 3rd person orientation rather than 1st person. You aren't looking at what you project from your conditioned mind; rather, you move beyond your own bubble to arrive in their conversation outside yours. You aren't preoccupied with power. Instead you are filled with humble inquiry and loving curiosity to understand others' pains and pleasures, as they reveal them to you. I and I would be 1st person, while I in them would be 3rd person. The field structure of your awareness action shifts the space, such that different flow patterns of energy and information respond to your attentional depth. Your perception penetrates and deepens, as something new is ready to be born.

You have arrived at nowhere. Nowhere is the place where things come as things go. It is the presence you bring to the present moment. This generous listening is so open that your individual will is no longer driving the ship, and a grander will, one that is omni-present, wiser, and whole is animating your being and seeing itself through you. Suddenly your responses to the other appears to be new, and you have left the familiar. You have stepped into new territory, crossed a threshold, and arrived in what is ready to emerge. You can sense the sacred in you coming forth. It is like a natural gravity flow. It is an evolutionary drift to your future self as you're offering yourself in your true presence.

THE PU BUSINESS CALL

When you make a PU business call out, pay careful attention to your first question that you ask. I've audited thousands of sales pros over 15 years, and one thing that boggles me is fumbling into asking for time:

"Hey ya gotta minute?" Take a careful look at this question. Do you have a minute? Ask that to yourself. What's your answer, no? Most people don't have a minute. So, it's a question that either gets a NO or builds tension against someone who's afraid to say no and stays on the phone anyway waiting to dodge or bug out in subtler disinterested ways. You hear a sigh that says it all. The question makes both you and the receiver dishonest.

"Are you busy?" How often have you been asked that? In our techno-tragic life of rush and gush, driven by a love affair with speed, is anyone not busy? Nope. If you're NOT busy, basically something is "wrong" with you. When have you made a business call to someone and they answered, "I have all the time in the world for you, hit it, my feet are on my desk, and I'm all yours, thanks for interrupting my boredom." It's obvious they have no business or no goal or challenge to involve them. Why would they need you, let alone afford your help?

"Am I catching you at a bad time?" This one's worse than the previous one. Is it ever a good time to take an unexpected call when you don't know why someone's calling?

Here's what I suggest to my coaching clients. When they call, be honest. Ask them this:

"AM I INTERRUPTING ANYTHING PRESSING (or URGENT)?"

It's an honest question that gets an honest answer. If the receiver says "yes," Then you pivot to another time respectfully. If the receiver says, "no" then they can actually talk because they're not in the middle of something truly pressing and telling you they'll listen.

Often times I'll ask this question, and the answer is "oh I'm fine thank you." Or "Nice to hear from you..." These are obviously responses that are conditioned and automatic. When you ask my question it gets people's attention, it sounds different than the usual, and sets you apart. Most of all it begins with honesty.

Once you get the "yes," you can then ask for the time you need and gain an agreement, by letting them know why it's important to talk.

"The purpose of my call is..." Get right to the point, furnish your message (the one thing they should know above all else; the context).

Don't beat around the bush, get to the point up front, this goes for emails too. Once the context is clear, you have better entryway to request the time needed. If the call matters to the receiver, they'll give you the time. No one has the time until you furnish this. It's never about time; it's about meaning that affords you their time.

Here's a bonus: you could add a "promise" to the prompting of the call. "I promised to call you at 3pm today on the dot," or "I promised Larry Gerard I'd call you at exactly 3pm today, am I interrupting anything pressing?"

This way you're perceived as dependable right off the bat, polite and respectful. You'd make a lasting impression that gains credibility fast.

RESETTING THE BUYING CRITERIA TO FLIP THE SHOPPERS

Buyers are smarter than ever before and firm on their buying approach. They're far more convinced they know their needs and wants because they have the internet to do their homework. Either another seller has helped the buyer clarify a vision a solution or the buyer acquired this line of thinking on his own.

Today, there are far more options available to the buyer in the marketplace than ever before, making their attention span less than before, and your uniqueness less visible. The last thing you want to do is make the buyer feel stupid for their expectations. Instead, you want to buyer to consider a fundamentally different approach to evaluating options like yours.

When a buyer has a pre-existing vision of a solution, they already recognize their problem, and they know what they need to solve it. Most often this buyer is reached the point of seeking shopping solutions. They're auditioning potential players to suit their desired solution.

Sellers, if inexperienced, will respond to their request thinking they've got this one in the bag. But that's rarely the case. Buyers use sellers as a means of making comparisons. Sellers, in this case, get in too late in terms of the buyer's path, and lose the business, or end up selling at a discount. This leads to commoditization.

The U-turn

However, the seller can create an advantage by re-establishing the buying criteria and biasing it to his products or services. Here are the steps to this flip:

1. Define your most unique and valuable attributes, capabilities, and assets that your business beholds.
2. Rank these 1-10, 10 being the highest value and unique qualities that inspire customers to create and maintain a relationship with you.
3. Ask your 10 best clients if these qualities are why they have a relationship with you to validate the data.
4. Put together 7-10 things to look for in hiring a company like yours. i.e., "The 10 Things to Look for In Selecting a World Class Business

458

Coach." Or "The Ten Things to Look for In Selecting a World Class Financial Advisor for your Business."

5. Insert your unique and valuable qualities into these as the criterion. You can use this as a required read up front, and/or use it later on in the helping process to prove and cost justify and reduce buyer's remorse after the transaction.

Figure 1.1 the 10 Things

6. During an initial call or conversation with your potential buyer, ask them how they see themselves using a (company like yours), what are they looking to accomplish?

7. Then ask some additional questions to add onto their existing vision of a solution. Use "when, who, and what" as the framework to wordsmith 5-6 of these yes/no control questions.

8. e.g., "When you distill your long terms goals down to short term ones with your team so that you can position your next steps, would it also help if you had a set of templates to distribute to make the process doable?" When asking it like this, the buyer can visualize themselves in a real situation with an alternative capability in hand. Putting them in the cockpit increases their urge to switch to new ground and rethink their needs.

9. Their answer will either be: yes, no, or what's that/tell me more/how that works?

10. The key word in the when, who, what questions is "also," meaning in addition to what you said you wanted to be able to do... would it also help if.... (yes or no?)

So instead of the buyer comparing apples to apples, they're now shifting the axis upon which their evaluation matrix is made. You're changing the rules of the game by awakening them to hidden needs that only you can provide. This gives you an advantage because you're moving them onto new ground to evaluate their wants and needs and compare other alternatives based upon it. Always assume you don't have enough information, to inspire yourself to pivot to this u-turn activity.

VERBAL JUJITSU

Buyers often bottom line you by asking for price and other information to feel safe. It's normal that they do this and will do it throughout your career, at the point of entry. However, you can create a bypass by having 4-5 karate kid comebacks that verbal jujitsu the buyer toward a conversation that develops their wants and needs before prescribing. Here are a few:

"I'm prepared to give you a quote, but also realize you may want to talk about what's really important to you, and what you're expecting, if you could paint me a picture of what you're thinking first, I can better suit you with the pricing question you're asking, ok?"

"I'm prepared to answer your request for information, but we have hundreds of examples, documents, and media to match the opportunities and preferences our customers approach us with, if you could help me clarify your expectations and preferences with five simple questions, I can help you save lots of time and money, even if you don't decide to do business together, fair enough? I'll need about 15 minutes. It'll be helpful, I promise, ok?"

"I appreciate your request for pricing; there are 3 reasons why other people in Orange County want to buy our insurance - would you like to know why?"

"The range is X to X, is that about what you're expecting?"

"Before going into the price, like a doctor, we make it a policy to diagnose before prescribing for your sake. Quoting, pricing, these are like auditions to us, which doesn't help us gather important information to determine if we can help or not. We're not aggressively looking for business, and will not insure you unless it's right for both of us. So, if we could slow down so I could get a clearer picture of why you're here, what you want, and what you expect, it'll enable me to be helpful on your investment, is that ok with you? I'll need about 15 minutes, and if we want to talk further, it's your choice, ok?"

Upon asking these questions and buying time to diagnose, have your Top 10 Things piece in hand to work from. Being professionally unconventional leaves a big mark.

PU Targets

So, who is your best prospect? The PU prospects? He or she is a go-getter in their organization, and you are the challenger who disrupts business as usual and is unafraid to upend old school thinking and operation norms.

Rather than thinking of solutions to pre-existing problems, the game is about how you PU prospect and clients could have greater influence on their organizations and the world around them. These mobilizers are change-makers, teachers, and skeptics. They like to test new ideas out then teach them. They are early adopters, and others come to them as a resource. PU prospects are not blockers; they are thought leaders.

Your strategy to influence them profoundly could be to focus on designing how they can navigate purchasing decisions, understanding how they know they need this or that, how to compare alternatives, and how to sell the "close" in their organization.

Building trust and gaining reach is key to success today. To be referable requires being strategic about your sphere of influence. You have three types of influencers who refer you: Nominators, Mobilizers, and Magnets.

Nominators are clients and associates who know your personal gift and look like a hero for making a favorable introduction to an ideal client. These relationships are significantly few, and if guided and motivated, they can be your best raving fans and bouncers. Bouncers are relationships that defend you against the competition and feel so strongly that your approach is the way to go.

Create a time and place every month for a PCRG: Private client resource group. Diversify this core group of 5 including yourself: Realtor, Title, Financial Planner, CPA, Estate planning attorney. You know which 4-5 industry professionals are involved in your clients' world. They depend on these helpers as a "brain-trust" to make great decisions. Bring this group together, create a time and place for dialogs, to cultivate your most prominent nominators, educate them on how to refer, who to refer, when to refer, what to say, etc. This PCRG could be one of the most valuable assets you have in your arsenal, a true annuity for lifetime business growth.

Magnets: These are individuals that have gigantic followings. Usually they have more than ten thousand followers on social media platforms, and if they share your approach and process, it will multiply into a buying frenzy. Cultivate five individual relationships who online are hugely sought after, have over 5k followers, 10k preferred, and your relationship with them is to help their followers gain value by teaming up--looking for ways to provide them an alternative revenue stream.

Mobilizers: These are individuals who run with you in common cause to a greater good. They may be co-creators in a social activist organization or membership group that share your vision and volunteer to support the cause. Cultivate five individuals who are your best evangelists, who love your community cause, you stand together, as social activists and teamsters---they want to see the changes you want in society, in the community, and they have the voluntary energy to turn old school thinking into new paradigms. They want to see changes in your close social domains, their backyard, city, region--all the above. Start a "nonprofit" together that you can all five be an important moving part.

Schedule two community dinners with education, enjoyment and social awareness. Make your guest list, and invoice your nominators, magnets, and mobilizers to meet and exchange information, and stories, and bond.

Here's a marketing tactical approach you might consider on these:

1. Mobilizers
Contact weekly
Monthly

What kind of difference can we make? Ask this question.
Circle of seven: Form a core group of social leaders who are linked to the same cause and create a runway for supporting each other. You might consider this a domain for emotional and transpersonal support.

2. Nominators
Start a PCRG
Action step: Get them meeting each other
- o Add 5-7 to the group as specialists
- o Begin lining up next steps for a time and place to convenient

o Create a power email introduction for each member of the group to refer at the right time and place, and to the right ideal prospect.

3. Magnets
• Get your 2-3 aligned with your blog post next on deck
• Schedule 15 minutes a day to follow them, comment and get a sense of their audience.

Your earnings are in proportion to your habits, support system, and your relationships. How much value you can create for them is in proportion to what opportunities come your way. To be referable you must do what you say, complete what you start, be punctual, and always be nice and courteous. These aren't to be taken for granted when you're successful, if you think you can out-last them with complacency. That's disastrous. That doesn't make your clients affair-proof, but great habits do. Learning to receive is first learning give without expecting a return. Consider what habits must align with creating a better future for you and others and focus on them! These habits are values-based, with the intention to serve anyway, no matter what the outcome.

CHAPTER 17

ORGANIZATION

There's a common concern or complaint that leaders tell me: "I need to get my act together and get organized." And then I ask them why. As they explain their reason, it appears their motivation is because they want to be more than they are. They have a false concept or story of not having it together, and perhaps setting the ideal of themselves as an organized person would convince them they're not what they're unwanted belief tells them.

So, what do they do? They take time management courses, bring great power to remove the old identity they don't want anymore, and voila! They're an organized person....and for a little, while it's triumphant, game set match won! People begin reacting and responding to them in noticing their new organization level.

Uh oh! What happened? After 3 months at it, the new actions start to fade away, backsliding to where things were before! When we attempt to live up to our ideals, we hide an unwanted belief and attempt to convince ourselves we're not that through our experiences. We can remove the constraints of being an unorganized person and still not create what we want! The point here is motivation. When our identity is the source of our motivation, who but a person needing to act organized is someone is not?

Any attempts to affirm ourselves to be different actually confirms the staying power of the unwanted belief that we're seeking to offset. Getting control in our lives is an externalization of feeling inferior inside. We aren't comfortable living in our own skin, as human beings. Our perfectionist beliefs persevere in forcing us to be something we're not.

And to inflame the pattern, we attempt to remove an unwanted quality in ourselves that, although we might reach a point of reaching this, problems removed also give rise to removing the proposed actions that made the problem go away. So, the problem symptoms typically find their way back on the scene. In this way, it seems like insanity that the more organized we attempt to be, the less organized we eventually become.

The clients then we introduced to another path for getting organized: "Getting organized in service to creating what you want." How organized does one need to be? Enough to create and keep what you want? Why is this different than the identity motif, or problem-solving motif? Because we act to generate rather than eliminate what we truly want. If you ask a person using the creative process how they use their time, they know what they want, have a keen sense of where they are in relationship to this, and their next step or action is a strategic choice they foster on behalf of the outcome.

There are four uses of time:
1. Reactive time. Following what comes at you. You enter from instant stuff that drops in like a parachute.

2. To do time. Following what things need to be knocked off a list of mounting tasks. You enter from what needs to get done to keep a sense of control.
3. Strategic time. Following the chosen actions that bridge a line of sight to goals and priorities desired. You enter with a pre-meditated plan.
4. Present time. Following the art, nature, and emerging moment by following where one's attention lands them here and now. You enter from emptiness.

Reactive time can work except your use of time may tend to place high urgency on unimportant things. Majoring in minor things is wasteful. "A waste is a terrible thing to mind." How do you outlaw or neutralize reactive time?

In our work with coaching clients, they learn that the only way to adjust their habitual tendency to give power to being busy with reactionary stuff is via their levels of awareness. One might ask, "Aware of what?" You can become aware of what matters most to you from the inside out. This implies that being overwhelmed isn't having too much coming at you, it's that everything has equal meaning. Therefore, not having any reflection or consideration of what is most important and not important to you makes everything equal. You have 24 hours in a day, and due to this limited dimension, the natural order of everything equal leads to demand overrunning supply. You will never get to it all because it is endless, infinite and unfinished by the mere fact you're moving into new moments in flux. You never know what is coming at you, so you might as well stop predicting the future and instead create one by starting from choice.

Orienting your life building process from choice implies that circumstances are no longer your orientation, but instead your values compose your decisions. When you find yourself saying "I don't have this or that," I don't have enough money" or "I don't have enough time" these are "I don't have enough." It's not a question of methodology; it's a question of commitment. Every time you say what you don't have enough of, it is a misstatement of a reality that you haven't made up your mind. When you say I don't have time, you probably struggle to say no. You don't want to do it, and you're so committed to be a good person, you need people around you to make refusals for you. Postponing your refusals is what lies beneath not having made up your mind and picking a direction, deciding about what matters. When you make up your mind on what matters, there's time for everything. There's a trade-off because as you prioritize what matters more, you set aside what doesn't matter. Then it's a matter of decisions.

This is a change in fundamental structure of operating. A fundamental choice to become the predominant creative force in your own life is different than the inclination to react and respond to life's conditions like a mouse in a maze. This doesn't suggest control over life, rather control over yourself and your own priorities. You take your cues from what matters to you, not what matters to someone else, what circumstances freak you out, what fears you attempt to avoid, what impression you might make on someone, etc. You aren't organizing your life by any of that, instead, what matters most to you as the primary organizing framework.

Staying aware is to know what matters, as you stay present to what is occurring, such that what matters is an ongoing conversation. You're disciplined to knowing what mattered before now as you understand things in the present that could bend the beam to what matters now. This could begin a new value, reinforce an existing one you're conserving, or stop what mattered before. You will change your mind, that is certain. Reflection is a way to reflect while in action. The more reflection and space made for what is going on, the better learning is available to make strategic adjustments via holding awareness of what matters most. Intention is not a onetime decision, it is prone to fall away, overhaul, and reinforce as experiences accumulate, and reflection offers integration with deeper potentials that are emergent.

Remember, you can consciously increase your quality of awareness to keep thoughts from ambushing your direct experience. You have the ability to open your heart and see beyond what your thoughts or stories are telling you about, not edited, and using sensing perceptions to be where someone is, other than your own voice. When you tune into their voice, you hear a certain quality of your voice because you're understanding, with compassion and empathy, the person behind the conversation.

And beyond resistance, fear, and shame is the capacity to sense what potential creative order is trending, emerging, and ready to integrate the emerging whole---a future standing in need of

470

leadership, goodness, wisdom, and concern that evolves by walking. The metaphor is you know the path by walking as if everything the future needs is given to you this moment. You can learn from the future as it emerges, instead of the past, in the form of awakening in the now.

The challenges, surprises, astonishments - all experiences become a source for integrating emergent properties that want to reach you, and to come into reality. Turning toward this requires turning away from what is certain. To look outside your own concepts is to see your own seeing. To treat another human being as a legitimate other is to conserve acceptance, vulnerability, and intimacy, to invoke service to another person. To meet life in its auto-poetic (continuous self-production) is to make valid the moment in which we are living it.

Your understanding guides your doing. Your understanding guides your intention from which you choose your creative acts.

What's the point of all that I'm doing? Great question.

For 10 days, write down everything you do and touch. When you touch a pen and sign something, when you type out a response in an email, when you are doing an activity, when you are in a meeting, ask yourself: Why am I doing this? Create an impact filter like a cooking strainer that you pour what you touch and go through. Something will slide through, but something will be kept behind. Simplicity begins by knowing what matters most and in order for you to liberate yourself you must depend on others and delegate your way of the work you're doing now to increase your strategic access.

EMAILS TERDS AND DREAMS

In my family, we call behavior that's negative or just downright pity party-ish "The TERD." Terds are the downers of the party, the naysayers of the new, the needy, the controlling, the time-bandits, and the ones who need the world to change for them to be in good status. Their mouth is shaped like an invert U sloping downward, not a normal one grinning ear to ear. We all have had TERDS in our life at one time or another. In fact, we both have them right now.

I can say this with certainty because you have a dream you're pursuing, and when you're acting toward it, TERD generation is inevitable. You will experience them as a byproduct of creating what you want. But I also know that you like to have an empty email inbox, don't you? You dream of having less stuff to do, less paperwork, less to-do's, all the emails, phone calls and stuff. You imagine the day when these mad dogs will stop barking in your ear drum.

Herein lies a conflict between two desires: clear the inbox or create the dream. One is pseudo work; the other is impact work. I sometimes get over 300 emails per day. I could start in the morning and work on email until 12 noon if I wanted to. Yet, my dreams are more important to me. Goal-centric behavior must get into my day, or I'm going in circles. What's the answer? Priority management. I have to be willing to pay the price to create my dream by declining the allurement of the vortex of stuff.

What muddies things up are two underlying concepts (beliefs): Accessibility equals success, and approval equals peace of mind. We become conditioned to be accessible with our time, and don't notice how we lower the drawbridge to intruders. And second, we avoid punting them because we don't want to confront someone or earn a bad opinion of us. You'd rather keep your TERDS quiet to have a short-term moment of jubilee than have a long-term dream come true. This is motivation out of scarcity and control, which conceal your ultimate freedom. You think response time is your silver bullet, but it's an illusion.

Your amazing personal brand - to come through and be reliable and credible - actually trumps your ability to create long term goals. Be honest. Deep down, this is a conflict between image and effectiveness, or pretense and success. Are you willing to take a serious look at letting go of these fears: isolation and confrontation? It's a big question to ask yourself? And what risks are you taking by NOT letting these go?

Being accessible is like being a doctor on call. You might as well drive an ambulance. Your life balance rests in the hands of the world. It's a choice you make to bet well-being on circumstances. It's up to you as to how you choose to orient your life. I suggest you choose to become the predominant creative force in your life. Your dream is more important than having an empty inbox.

Consider this for a moment: Don't answer emails first thing in the morning. Schedule two periods per day to answer emails on offense. This scare you? Walk into the fear; it's what you need to do. Answering emails when you decide to will help you process the meaning of each email properly instead of it getting out of control and interfering. If you're answering emails all the time, you're egging on your crowd to keep throwing dodgeballs at you. Immediate responses beget immediate response timing. I call this "Email on a Whim Syndrome" EWS. Scheduling it is an "Email Control System" ECS. Answer the emails when you schedule a time to do so, but furnish the reason why you're doing so. You want to give quality attention to people out of respect, not some sudden flurry of blurry answers that are unclear and incomplete. Short answer emails waste the time of others. And they feel misunderstood and unimportant anyway. Short emails attract TERDS.

Being overwhelmed is when too many things have equal meaning. Not every email will be as urgent or important as the others. And not every email will be handled the same way. As you answer your emails, apply the "4 D's model." Dump it, Do it, Delegate it, Delay it. The key is the email must go into one of these drawers.

- DUMP
- DO
- DELEGATE
- DELAY

Pileups and logjams in the inbox are a result of delayed decisions. You must put the email in one of these four "D's" when you process them. If you delegate it, CC yourself the email you're sending to the person to handle it and drag it over to a WAITING folder you've setup. This way you're able to keep a tab on what you've deployed to others and are hovering on either lightly or intensely.

474

STOP! I've just presented to you a field-tested method and game-plan for bypassing your accessibility urge and your need for approval, to have your dreams come true. Do you see a clear way forward here? Is your confidence up right now? Hold onto your hat; there's more…Let's look further into the approval piece.

Remember, there are two kinds of people in the world: GIVEN UPS and GROWN UPS. Grown-ups are those that hold steady to their most important dreams and aspirations, while GIVEN UPS give up. They're the compromisers of the world who outlaw others' dreams with judgment, fear, and cynicism. These enemies you will meet in pursuit of your dreams. Let go of your fear of isolation. You will never be alone. People come and go throughout your life; it is part of the natural order of your evolution and life journey.

Simple fact: TERDS WILL BE TERDS. You can't change them; you live with them and in spite of them, as you position yourself toward more dominant, exiting, and bigger horizons that matter to you. Like Freddy Krueger, you can't force out a TERD. Creating your dreams will outgrow TERDS, and eventually, they'll stop their stalking when they realize they have nothing to grab onto, only themselves. You've got bigger business to attend to than quiet your TERDS.

You might also realize that the primary TERD is you and has been as you're reading this. The TERD is your fear.

Create dreams for a living; it'll give your mind better instructions than something to avoid.

CHAPTER 18

PUTTING WOODEN STAKES IN VAMPIRES

You're probably so accessible that you're taking three more calls or emails than what you send out. Distractions like these are vampires sucking you dry and require you put a wooden stake in them. If that's the case, then your day is besieged by reactions, instead of getting control of your priorities and remaining goal-centric in your actions. 1 hour of 7 is actually productive, goal-centric time for executives each day. That's crazy!!

To remedy this, consider your intake process for help/service/sales requests. You may need a filter to categorize the request and insulate yourself from low priority non-urgent items that ambush your best use of time. "Access does not equal success." If people do business with you because you're fastest to respond, think again. You're consumed by that and aren't going to grow because you just too busy being busy to do what could make you a lot less busy! We insulate our clients with systems for this, so you can stay on purpose and grow a team of people around you free you up, batteries included.

Strategic Direction: Setup the emergency room triage model with an intake system for filtering and dispatching help requests. Just like a hospital, a nurse performs an initial assessment as a lens or filter for the emergency room, to determine who to call for help and how to help the patient. This way the patient wins, and the right doctor responds to the right issue efficiently.

To get started, you'll need use a single maintenance day (24-hour thematic work period) to work on your business and setup this system. Please schedule this day now and gather up your team to help you implement.

Step 1: Make a VIP list of the top 10 clients that you should drop everything and take their call when they need help. These accounts and individuals will affect your future the most and should be given urgency as well as vital importance in your response to them.

– Give this list to your support staff to keep handy when they're taking incoming calls.
– Anyone not on this list shouldn't be getting through the steel curtain.

Step 2: Make an Instructional Voicemail to free you up. Use your voicemail as a tool to gather the right data from a voicemail call.

Change your outgoing phone voice message to this:

"Thank you for calling. If you've heard this before, bypass this message by hitting the # key. Due to a high level of demand for our services, these messages are checked once daily, and calls will be returned within 48 hours, after 3pm weekdays or (between x and x on x days), to ensure the highest quality of service and attention to our clients. If this call is urgent, for faster response, please email urgent (company name) @ (yahoo; gmail) or xyzcompany.com. In your message, please give specific details as to the purpose of your call

477

and the best time to reach you. Most often, our world class account managers have the right attributes and expertise to suit your needs better than I do..." (Deflect here)

For processing, contact Sheri at (phone) ext. X
For customer service, contact Donna at (phone) ext. X
For underwriting contact Julie...
For X, contact Y.

*Note: Always try to centralize multiple message touch points into one format, such as email or fax. When put in writing, it slows the sender down to think about what they want, instead of voice. Voice messages tend to miss the detail levels to lessen the "tagging" that so often occurs by phone messages when contact isn't made." Fax or email slows down someone to consider in one shot what they need and why. It induces an easier interaction with less effort for both parties.

12. Delegate your assistant to retrieve all the urgent@xyzcompany.com emails and sort them for you. Only forward the ones on your VIP list.

2. Set up an auto response on your john@xyzcompany.com email that says: in the subject: Thank you for your email.

Due to a high level of demand for our services, we process emails once per day and ensure a response within 24 hours. We do this to ensure the highest quality of service to our clients and patrons. If your message is urgent, please email urgent@…... Or contact the person best at handling your needs: (then deflect)

For processing email Jennifer at (email address)
For customer service email Donna at (email address)

13. Set up an auto response on your urgent@xyzcompany.com…email that says: Thank you for your urgent email. We are now processing it and will respond by 5pm today. If after 5pm, tomorrow by 12 noon. We do this to provide the highest quality of service to our clients and patrons. Thank you for your continued teamwork!

Step 3: Organize your Intake Rotation. Break down three sections during the take for intake call/email activity – morning, mid-day, and afternoon-early evening. Determine who's going to be on deck dedicated to the intake protocols. Setup call forward on the phones of others who are not "active," so the designated person on-call is the reception area for service calls and active response-giving.

– Retrieve the call
– Ask the purpose of the call
– Advocate a next step
– Enter the note/message into a system where team-members can retrieve it (an email is most basic)
– Notify person needing to act, if not yourself
– Write clear instructions and expectations

Step 4: Schedule a "return call" block 1-2 periods daily for offense-centric return call activity. Make it a focused work habit to stay in the lanes of these return call times and exercise your self-control muscle outside these bounds—no fowls!!! Be strict about it! You're better to have a few calls go to voicemail and stay on purpose instead of being reactive and responsive and having zero traction on your priorities during the day you've structured your time and attention around.

Step 5: Setup a decision-making flow with 4 options in response to income service calls.

— Delete it. It's not worth the effort. Decide to negate it.
— Delegate it. Relay it to the appropriate team-mate with a unique ability and/or work description correlated with the call purpose.
— Delay it. Schedule a call back or next step and let the other party know when and how to settle their expectations.
— Do it. If you can handle it in two minutes, handle it. Putting it away later may take longer to rethink or remember what's involved, so consider the two-minute rule and handle it, especially if it's 1) what you're best at, and 2) something that gives you energy doing it.

SYSTEMIC DELEGATION

Delegation is one of the best remedies to offload a tiresome task. There are many forms of delegation that we often forget is in our repertoire such as

• Finding a friend

- Negating the task

- Hiring someone

- Outsourcing

- Trading or barter

- Adding it onto a current employee's role

- Automating it through a technology

These are all great as options. If you're concerned about the investment, consider making a more conscious effort of asking for assistance from friends or colleagues. Rather than assuming you're putting a burden on them, let go of you being the decision-maker of that and just ask. First, what you're asking for may give them energy. A colleague of mine once asked me to put together an article for him on hiring people. I love writing and volunteered right away when he asked. Had he withheld from asking I might have missed the opportunity to contribute and do what I love. Second, the other person may know someone who has a unique ability to help. Remember that to grow; you have to leave your security and comfort behind and multiply yourself in creative ways.

Delegation isn't a cost; it is giving you back the time and energy to create bigger and better results. But delegation (asking for and receiving help) is often far more complex of a process, especially when you're depending on someone for something that matters. The helping process is highly complex system, hence the name I've given it "systemic delegation." First, you define your needs and ask for help, and then the other has capacity to fulfill the request. The one needing help must define her needs well, and the other must be able to listen, despite the rigidity of their expertise, as to the best way to help. What can break down the process of giving and receiving are some deadly assumptions that play out and trump a successful end result.

Let's explore these assumptions and how they bring inadvertent consequences to following through. You might think you've delegated beautifully, you've furnished the context of the task, walked the person through the process, established a payoff and a deadline, and communicated super clearly. But....it starts off well and loses its run to the finish line. Here are some belief systems at play in the execution process that compete with the commitment to go all the way. The end result leads to "reverse delegation" where the task lands back on the person whose delegating.

#1: Giving instructions too much insults the other person. The way this belief is resolved may involve withholding key instructions to keep the other person's ego intact. Giving poor instructions like this can undermine the other by lacking clarity. Ambiguity leads to mistakes.

#2: Completing the task risks my value to the other person, I may look like a fool. The one completing the task is insecure about their capability and doesn't want to look stupid. To avoid judgment day, the resolve is not to complete what is asked. The person using stalling tactics to make things perfect, which often inspires dread, doubts, and resentment in the one who's delegating.

#3: If I clean up the final draft, it'll be done right. The leader delegating elects to be the final stop on the assemble line of completing the project. If the maid is coming tomorrow, the person leaves the dishes and house chores to be cleaned up. The leader as maid to clean up after the mess inspires the lazy behavior. Even though the leader should let the person sink or swim, the knowing the leader is the final touch, the consequences are taken away from the performance. Without facing any consequences, excellence has become unnecessary.

#4: I don't want to major in minor tasks. The leader delegating believes what they're delegating isn't going to make or break the company or their income, so the tasks are considered less important. This then trickles down to the one completing the task. If it's less important, why should there be a strong commitment to complete it?

#5: When I ask for feedback, it's not important. The leader delegating delays in his responsiveness to the process check sought by the one completing the task. This is construed as she must not really care much. When the leader delays her response time, it inspires the other person to work on other things that matter more, often losing sight of what does really matter, and leading to costly mistakes.

#6: When they dictate the deadline, I lose control. Often times the one fulfilling the task has competing work commitments. Deadlines given are seen as intruders that infringe upon other priorities. Not coming through on the task is a way of sending the message back

#7: The more I get it right, the less there will be to do later. Here's a control mechanism at play in the person's thinking who is given the task. They operate under the assumption that once it's finished what else is there to do? Why would one want to jeopardize their security?

Keeping things in limbo is a covert way of maintaining a dependency to keep the person feeling safe.

APPROACHING THE COGNITION PIECE

First, make a list of your own belief systems at play in your delegation process. Write down the transactions that took place in your most recent delegation process. Review blow-by-blow what motivated the trend. Write down the assumptions at play that positioned the way the end result occurred. Here are five suggestions to override poor thinking:

Consider any activity or task in your organization as marketing. Yes, marketing is the sum of every behavior in the business that become impactful customer experiences. No activity is minor. Even cleaning the bathroom is a marketing role.

Be mindful of your assumptions and keep an inventory in your journal as they arise. Ask your team to do the same and explore these during weekly tactical meetings. Acknowledge belief systems together and see how they play out in balancing or reinforcing patterns. Don't look directly at what the other person is doing wrong, always look at the system at play. The system is making a bigger contribution to the consequences than any single decision or individual.

Instead of reprimanding poor performance, use these as signs of where to look for thinking that enacts the performance of the system. Challenge each belief by asking if it is true, what could be possible if it wasn't and who you'd be, who they'd be if you didn't believe your assumptions at play. Remember that the driving force behind a belief or assumption is usually to prevent an unwanted situation from happening. Our mind's attempts to predict the future rather than create one gets in the way of our creative process to bring a design idea or task into fruition.

TO SEE IS TO CREATE

"Delegating" is defined as "developing someone else until they're ready to take the responsibility you expect and do it such that you're confident in their competency to get it done. Handing someone the authority who isn't ready and/or willing makes you cringe at delegating. In my coaching encounters I'm constantly discussing ways for leaders to get the most out of their people, so they feel ultra-confident, inspired and amazed by the way their team takes ownership and solves challenges.

One of the blind-spots in developing your team is how you look at employees in general. Are they family? Friends? Enemies? Hired hands? Each of these mental constructs gives rise to how you interact with them. If you see something you admire in others, the potential they can have can astound you. And that is what I'm suggesting: To see employees as lifelong allies and select and hire based on qualities and accomplishments that you admire.

Seeing the greatness in others is perhaps the best way to keep your team members from leaving your organization. Self-knowledge cannot come by itself, alone, on an island. We participate in the way others define themselves.

Back in the late 60's, a study was done by schools to see if teachers' perceptions and expectations of kids had an impact on their behavior. It was proven without variation that if a teacher sees the gifts in their children and expects them to use them with high hopes, the kids show up more readily to use it. Kids learned to trust themselves and trust the teacher when expectations were higher of them.

In fact, you might not register just how impactful your view of your teammates is until now. If your judgment is composed of how others are out to get you, or they have an agenda, be aware of your thinking. When you house your voice of judgment in what you construe to be true, you help make it true. This is because when you have reasons to think the other isn't trustworthy, the blind spot is that 1) the thought originated from you, not them, and 2) you withhold resources and hold back because of it.

Recently, a manager was stumped by people leaving his organization. The pattern was perpetuating a vicious cycle. The blind spot was that at first, the manager didn't see his own seeing. And yet, originally the manager had a negative assumption at play that went live. Taking an assumption live has four parts: The governing assumption, the strategy or emotion, the behavior or action, and the consequence or end result. What the manager was looking at was the behavior. He felt violated when the employee was interviewing with another company, so he cut the employee off clean, and fired him on the spot for being a "flirt."

When I mentioned to him that about 30% of his team were probably tipi-toers, he was even more nervous. According to his principles, people who leave are enemies. Like an affair, lack of loyalty was in violation of his principles. Of course, people leaving and jumping isn't on the wish list of most leaders, but people do quietly consider if something is better, not because they're bad people, but because it's human nature to be curious. Early on in his career, the leader erected a pre-emptive strike on the threat. He made a contract with his fear that he wouldn't ever be duped, cheated against, ever again. So, he made every attempt to be less vulnerable and held back resources, training, spending, and development to avoid the ending because it fell in on him. He held a view of definite all-or-nothing thinking and continued to prevent the situation.

What he couldn't see at first was that the problem started with him, not the other. His fear had led him to hold back employees from resources, such that they didn't feel important, recognized or developed. This made them seeking of leaders who believed in their goodness and looked to level up their potential. The leader in my coaching was actually helping the problem happen by trying to avoid it from happening in the first place. The fix became a backfire instead of dealing with the fundamental problem. People at the most basic fundamental level do great work when they are understood, feel important and valued, and therefore feel safe to be themselves. You have these three, you win. If they are capable and have the skills, these other aspects compose the will and ability needed for great work.

Perception is a generative process. If you see others as lifelong allies, your perception will shape an outcome. If you see others as enemies, your behavior will shape an outcome. You treat others as you see them, and how you treat them is who they become (Goethe). Mindfulness is being aware of the habituated thinking that categorizes others instead of seeing them with fresh eyes, such that you see the larger system in which your perception is enacting certain consequences that you probably don't want, nor anybody else.

CHAPTER 19

EASY IS HARD

We tend to overlook the simple changes to create what we want because they don't measure up to our standards of ourselves. When we get ambushed by our ideals of ourselves, our pride asks that we add extra steps to earn what we create. We trust the ideal instead of trust ourselves.

Small change we fail to register as progress because we won't acknowledge anything worthy enough until it is substantial. What we miss is the chance for momentum, a clearer picture of current reality, and a sense of confidence.

Things are so simple they are hard. A hug is simple, but hard to do for many individuals. Sitting then getting up and walking around is so easy it is hard. When we strengthen ourselves, we often expect difficulties commensurate with earning it, using it, and matching it. We overlook the small successes that give us powerful information on where to go next.

Sitting and breathing is so simple, and for this, it is hard. Chewing our food longer is simple, but hard. Our minds are full of chatter and decisions we have to make. What is simple is unpleasant. The initial reaction is to overlook or avoid being with it. We want victory sooner the lag time of doing simple things deliver it. So, we shoot past the simple and go for complicated things that will results in less suffering and faster gratification. Telling the truth is a simple action, but it's hard to do this when a fear of loss is envisioned.

When we are caught in the standard of difficulty and the level of complexity, we attempt to address these as problems to solve. But if we step back and look at this closely, this isn't creating; this is problem solving. Attempting to do what is easier or not is ameliorating pain. Yet in the creative process, what is hard or easy isn't relevant, instead whatever we must learn and go through toward the creation we want is the process. And that process may require more than we think or less as we move through it.

The point is we are deeply conditioned to overlook the simple because it doesn't qualify for who we're stuck in trying to be. The somebody we attempt to live up to seeks to deserve what we desire. To accomplish this, the process has to fit around it. The latency in moving upon what we want requires more effort. This effort isn't in service to what the outcome requires; it's what we require. I often think of how much extra work and effort is made that is over-exerted, unnecessary, and inefficient because of our identity.

Again, our conditioned thinking is full of clever concepts like our negative beliefs of ourselves. To offset these, an ideal is set to live up to it. Rather than staying true to simple actions the outcome requires, we make things difficult to earn our ideals. But when we rid ourselves of our ideals, we replace this effort with our values and create what is simple, hard, easy, whatever the creation we want requires coming to fruition.

It's ok to do simple things that are inclusive to your creative process. And it's ok to do complicated things, too. Some complicated things are easier, while some simple things are harder. Regardless, what is in service to our higher choice (what matters) is our compass. Not our ideals.

So, what compels action-taking? Your hierarchy of importance. An action required by the outcome is a secondary choice, while the outcome is a primary choice. First, you need to identify each. What is the desired state I want? What are the supporting elements or requirements in service to creating this outcome from where I actually am now? This is also so simple that it is hard because our human potential rules tell us to improve ourselves, and look at us, rather than focus on our creations. This makes lousy creators. When you're creating, the secondary choices are in service to the primary one. These secondary choices aren't motivated by the level of difficulty, state of mind, emotional position, nothing other than what is in service to the primary choice. Discipline, consistency, and execution become familiar when creating in this way. It is so simple that it is hard. And yet these fundamentals help us create subject matter precious to us.

CHAPTER 20

PULLING IT ALL TOGETHER

You are about to finish this book, and I want to pull it all together in a powerful poem of my own called "What to Remember when Walking." Please read it several times to set your internal compass on operating and listening from your places of your deepest sources of knowing. To reclaim your wholeness is to live with balanced intelligence, from which you access the finest quality of expression that you can occupy at any moment. This is the essence of leadership and the source from which you see better, sense better, and welcome the emerging future as your primary source of honing intention. And when you're mindful, unattached to the outcome, the past, and others' actions, you come home to the now, where the future is emerging, with InTen. You know the path by walking, being inter-wise. Every conversation is unexpected, astonishing, moving, challenging, inspiring to the point that everything at that edge can change you, as you see outside to inside the design of what's coming and going, what the future is needing this moment for you to meet. The Question: "What the fuck am I doing with what I take in?"

Here you go: *"I'm listening generatively from this place of my highest future possibilities standing in need of my best self and work—to be, create, relate, and earn, and show up as a whole person, with all I am in all I do for those I serve."*

"I stand at the living breathing conversational frontier of life, with my attention, intention, and connection, and use this information to make sense of a direction."

WHAT TO REMEMBER WHEN WALKING

I walk with palms extended out to each side
Lay yours on mine and I will help you
If you should take your palm off mine
I will not grasp for it is that time

If you feel my hand pull you forward
Trust that it is what you say is best for you not me
My listening is your listening
I am possessed by only this

Your coming and going is not of my doing or intending
It was in us all along until we remembered
Isolation is sweet tasting by itself
My palms are just a luxury

If you come again and lay your hands on mine
My palms remain open and available
But I will notice new things about you
The passing of time brought me to see what was hidden before

In time your palms may lift from mine again
Yet I am walking and walking through life

Each step unfolding another's gaze
Who will my palm be ready for next

If I see and if I take in what shines through
You will come to drink from its presence
To know me is to know this
To know you is to be seen

Lay your palms on mine forever
They are extended for whatever has called me

ONWARD

You wake up tomorrow morning... This is the good day to find your true love, or your spouse is expecting, or you're the lottery winner, or this is the black day that someone has left your life...

You have no idea or prediction how things will unfold or what life throws at you. Life always has a sharp edge to it, and you cannot create a life solely based on order. Can you hold this edge? Can you meet whatever comes?

We already possess the key to our own happiness no matter what happens to us; it is something you have to reclaim that is unintegrated and yet elemental. It is deep inside the complexity of your own experience---behind the possibility of your own grief and loss, like an underground current. And you can't access it by predicting and staying safe---it requires a more courageous way of living at the edge of mystery. And it is a conversational frontier of reality that you cannot afford to misstate to yourself, to retrieve the happiness you get to realize at the edge of everything.

Live your best life
Be a great soul
Make a great impact
Learn to receive

End.

STAY LONGER LISTEN DEEPER

For persons itching to change the world
without knowing how it can be done

Live your best life
Be a great soul
Make a great impact
Learn to receive

The journey begins now

A braided way of being, relating, creating, and earning
■■■

Namaste

I see the divinity in you because it is in me

Tashi Delek & Tat Tvam Asi

You are now re-entering the world made new, to proceed on through the pages of the book of your life…

<u>*Live it, learn it, name it, give it—Be Inter-wise!*</u>

InTen Practice Checklist

Ready to increase involvement and engagement? Every action, decision---every choice point can arise from a higher quality of being inter-wise. You have access to wiser care for all things if you relax your attention on what is not reduced to what you know. The key is bringing yourself to be more present at the current moment. The future will depend on how you live now.

Here are my top rituals for getting more present:

1. Intentional stillness of 30 minutes each morning

2. Taking three sacred pauses during the day to find a place of rest in the middle of things

3. Put the word "mindfully" after everything you do. Eat mindfully. Walk mindfully. Listen mindfully.

4. Do one thing at a time. Do not multi-task. Increase your concentration on choosing one thing to begin or progress and remain with it until finished.

5. Stop being busy. Make a list of every task and activity you do that goes under "busy", and stop doing it; instead, focus on the six most important things every day to focus your energy.

6. Spend free days in nature. Go places where the natural beauty and environment move you from fast to slow time.

7. Let go of worrying. Worrying does nothing for you except rob you of being present.

8. Get interested in what other people are doing and who they are.

9. Start journaling daily insights and thoughts that arise to bring outward mental content and give it a place to land

10. Stop answering emails and phone calls that make you always available. Carve time periods specifically to manage detail work.

11. Unhook yourself from the future. Setting an intention is knowing what matters to you and deciding to create it. But controlling the future is geared to avoid what you fear by prediction. Instead, focus on what you seek to create, but let go of forcing it, and instead honor your intention with unforced space. Bring your intention through time and learn it as you go along. What mattered before may matter more or less today.

12. Make a list of all the should's, would's, and ought to's and let them go. Let go of all the ideals and false standards you put on yourself of who you're supposed to be or not be.

13. Keep your mental constructs in check by staying in good company with them, write them down. Making space between

your awareness of them, and the concepts will make apparent more of what's going around you and what you have.

14. Know what does matter to you and focus on that. The most important thing is knowing the most important thing. When you stop doing it all and concentrate on doing what matters everything gets radically simple.

15. Stop comparing yourself to others or believing that you are not enough. It is important to distinguish what is different about you and others but do not attach this to your shame, or look to lower others as antidote to offsetting your hidden, unwanted belief.

16. Accept your humanness by letting yourself show up as a whole person—with all sides of you present—yes, all the good, bad, and ugly. You can stay tuned to what you like or don't like about you and know your best and worst qualities and be friends with your humanity. As you do this, you tend to increase legitimacy and acceptance with others because you aren't seeking ways to affect them to bury what you disown in yourself.

17. Embrace your vulnerability to let others change you, inspire you, move you, challenge you, because you are alive and witnessing the world such that it can reach you intimately.

18. Focus on what you seek to bring into being, let go of what you're trying to be. Don't lower or box in your true dreams, desires, and aspirations for fear and judgment. These are inner enemies. Let

your enemies be there, but shift your orientation to the creative---by organizing your life by the fundamental choice to become the predominant creative force in your life, who brings desired creations into the world.

19. Hold space for ambiguity. You can comprehend better by using time as an advocate to see what goes. Integrity is defined by how long you can tolerate ambiguity until you see what is true or clear. Holding unforced space can help your capacity to see and sense what is going on and connect with something wanting to mobilize through emergence.

20. Voice your noticeable shifts in internal currents, as you are relating to and with the environment around you. Don't wait, say what is real for you instantly.

21. Treat the wildcard of life like an invited guest. Consider meeting what life lands on your doorstep as unexpected perfection. Push against nothing, welcome everything.

22. Act on any communications that you're holding onto that need to be said. These probably need to move along with you and if you're holding back, be a vessel and let it move to where it belongs.

23. Treat pain, suffering, negativity and even betrayal as teachers. Seek the lessons in all of it and hold space for letting everything be what the future needs this moment. Trust it.

24. Meet grudges you hold with soft edges. Let these become like melting ice and thaw.

25. Let the world be where it is, in its conversation, and be where it is, not where you wished or expected it to be. When you meet the world this way, resources such as love, acceptance, compassion, and understanding become available dimensions that live in your higher quality of being. Remember that at the core, you are fundamentally conserving your quality of being as one who operates from love and a loving being out of which creations come, and the journey is legitimately a domain for learning and evolving. Love is the most intelligent quality in the universe. Love makes you honest.

26. Save 10-20% of whatever you earn and build your investment income to match the level of earnings your active income requires to pay your bills. Having money saved and investing gives you discretionary decisions over where you put your attention. When you are constantly running out of money you're never present because you're running by shortages.

27. Build a top supporting team around you to handle with uncommon skill any area or activity you need to accomplish in which you aren't unique at or valuable doing.

28. Choose to build your support network of friendships and cherished family relationship based on honest admiration. Choose the relationships that you admire most and build on your natural awe and admiration for what you see as gifts in them. Focus on bringing their gifts to the domain they belong.

29. Focus your career on what activity naturally fascinates you and motivates you most in life.

30. Use time off as your greatest source of innovation and for gathering new creative energy and perspectives; use them as design elements for what you place your gifts toward building.

31. Choose the path of mastery in all you do, such that you continuously hold a lab mentality on learning new levels and dimensions of your abilities to be relaxed at times when you need to take time away and renew your energy.

These 31 rituals compose a manner of living such that you make the most of the present moment. Select the five you prefer to integrate most and get to work on them.

For Claudia

Printed in Great Britain
by Amazon

18991803R00290